EU Electronic Commerce Law

Ruth Nielsen
Søren Sandfeld Jakobsen
Jan Trzaskowski
(editors)

EU Electronic Commerce Law

DJØF Publishing
2004

EU Electronic
Commerce Law
1. edition

Cover photo: Jan Trzaskowski
Print: Holbæk Amts Bogtrykkeri
Binding: Damm's Forlagsbogbinderi, Randers

Printed in Denmark 2004
ISBN 87-574-1107-7

DJØF Publishing
17, Lyngbyvej
P.O.B. 2702
DK 2100 Copenhagen

Phone: +45 39 13 55 00
Fax: +45 39 13 55 55
e-mail: forlag@djoef.dk
www.djoef-forlag.dk

Foreword

On 27-28 November 2003 Copenhagen Business School organised an international research conference on EU Electronic Commerce Law at Hotel Hvide Hus in Køge, Denmark. More than 40 legal researchers and lawyers from various private and public organisations around Europe participated and contributed in making the conference rewarding and unforgettable.

The conference focused on a number of topics which are of particular interest within the field of e-commerce law in EU these years, including marketing law, self-regulation, contract and information requirements, electronic signatures, jurisdisction and enforcement and Internet market places.

Besides traditional presentations on the various topics, the conference contained a number of "research workshops", where researchers were given the opportunity to present and discuss ongoing research projects relevant to the conference's overall subject.

This book contains contributions based on some of the presentations and workshops given at the conference. The articles are arranged in accordance with the conference programme, which is reprinted as an annex to this book.

With this book we wish to contribute to the understanding and discussion of this important area of the law.

Copenhagen, February 2004

Ruth Nielsen Søren Sandfeld Jakobsen Jan Trzaskowski

Table of contents

Megatrends in Electronic Commerce Law

by Ruth Nielsen

The need to adapt the provisions of international, regional and domestic legal instruments to the requirements of electronic commerce has been emerging for some 20 years both at the global, EU and national level.

The main EU legal approach to electronic commerce is to integrate it into the existing law on the internal market, eg the rules on free movement of goods, services and freedom of establishment, on competition and on consumers. Since the mid 1990's this body of law has been supplemented with a new legislative framework specifically targeting information society related problems such as e-business. This new legal framework is based on the old and well-established principles of internal market legislation such as the country of origin principle, mutual recognition, etc.

In the following I will first outline the international context and then move on to EU law.

1. International Context

1.1. UNCITRAL

UNCITRAL (the United Nations Commission on International Trade Law) has played a pioneering role in e-commerce law by issuing in 1985 a recommendation on the legal value of computer records and the adoption, in 1996, of a Model Law on Electronic Commerce with Guide to Enactment[1] and a Model law on Electronic Signatures in July 2001.[2]Art 6 provides:

> 1. Where the law requires a signature of a person, that requirement is met in relation to a data message if an electronic signature is used that is as reliable as was appropriate for the purpose for which the data message was generated or communicated, in the light of all the circumstances, including any relevant agreement.

---

1) Available at http://www.uncitral.org/english/texts/electcom/ml_ecomm.htm.

2) Available at http://www.uncitral.org/english/texts/electcom/ecommerceindex.htm.

The UNCITRAL is presently working on a draft convention on electronic contracting.[3]

The UNCITRAL provisions are based on the principle of functional equivalence, which means that when electronic communication is functionally equivalent with paper-based communication it should have the same legal effect. The UNCITRAL provisions have exerted considerable influence upon the United States and the way US regulation handles electronic commerce (or maybe it is the other way round, ie the US has influenced the UNCITRAL Model laws decisively).

1.2. WTO

In 1998, the WTO developed a Work Programme on Electronic Commerce.[4] At present, specific e-commerce issues are discussed at 'dedicated meetings' of the General Council, focusing on the question of how to classify electronic deliveries. The European Commission along with the EU Member States and many other WTO members promotes the view that electronic deliveries constitute services and thus come under the existing GATS regime.[5]

1.3. US and EU approach

In 1999 two uniform acts meant to bring legal certainty and clarity to the transactions that characterize the information-based economy in the US were adopted: the Uniform Computer Information Transactions Act (UCITA) and the Uniform Electronic Transactions Act (UETA). On June 30, 2000 President Clinton signed the Electronic Signatures in Global and National Commerce Act (popularly known as E-Sign) and most of its provisions went into effect on October 1, 2000.[6]

The core provisions of E-sign and UETA are substantially the same, with both drawing from the 1996 UNCITRAL Model Law on Electronic commerce. E-Sign and UETA both provide that neither a signature nor a writing may be denied legal effect solely because it is in electronic form, nor may a contract be denied legal effect solely because an electronic signature or record was used in

---

3) See further http://www.uncitral.org/english/workinggroups/wg_ec/, see also Katarina Kryczka, Principles of European Contract Law and Formation of Contracts in the Information Society in this volume.

4) Available at http://www.wto.org/english/tratop_e/ecom_e/ecom_e.htm.

5) See further COM(2003)702 p18.

6) See further Lynn Roseberry: Recent E-Commerce Legislation in the U.S. in Jens Fejø, Ruth Nielsen and Thomas Riis (eds): Legal Aspects of Electronic Commerce, Copenhagen 2001.

its formation. E-Sign, like UETA, also provides that an electronic record may be denied legal effect, validity or enforceability if it is not in a form capable of being retained and accurately reproduced by all persons who are entitled to retain it.

Christina Ramberg[7] has argued that what the EU wanted to achieve in the E-Commerce Directive[8] was accomplished more efficiently in the US by UETA, which, as mentioned, is greatly influenced by the UNCITRAL Model Law on Electronic Commerce and the principle of functional equivalence between paper-based writing and electronic communications. The principle of functional equivalency is, in her view, an exceptionally helpful tool in analysing problems related to e-commerce. Limiting the regulation of electronic commerce to analogies from paper-based writing and the functional equivalence of electronic and written forms of communications is, in my view, not generally in line with a civil law approach and has played a much more marginal role in EU law than in UNCITRAL and US law. The reference to paper-based communication is, however, used in Article 5(1) of the Signature Directive according to which a qualified electronic signature must be given the same effect as a handwritten signature.[9]

The E-commerce Directive allows Member States a considerable margin of discretion when implementing the Directive thereby leaving it to them to decide whether they will use the principle of functional equivalence or other techniques. In Germany the E-Commerce Directive has been implemented partly by amendments to the civil code *Bürgerliches Gesetzbuch*. A new legal form called *Textform* is created in addition to *Schriftform*. The new § 126 b BGB provides:

> Ist durch Gesetz Textform vorgeschrieben, so muss die Erklärung einem anderen gegenüber so abgegeben werden, dass sie in Schriftzeichen lesbar, die Person des Erklärenden angegeben und der Abschluss der Erklärung in geeigneter Weise erkennbar gemacht ist.

Electronic communications will often satisfy the requirements of § 126 b BGB and thus be Textform but only electronic communications with a qualified

---

7) See further Christina Ramberg: The E_Commerce Directive and formation of contract in a comparative perspective, European Law Review 2001 p 429, Christina Ramberg: European and U.S. Perspectives on Electronic Documents and Electronic Signatures, Tulane European and Civil Law Forum 1999 p 123 and Christina Ramberg: Contracting on the Internet _ Trends and Challenges for Law, in Law and Information Technology. Swedish views, SOU 2002:112.

8) 2000/31/EC.

9) Directive 1999/93/EC. See for a critical analysis of this use of paper-based communication as a reference point Jos Dumortier: The European Regulatory Framework for Electronic Signatures: A Critical Evaluation in this volume.

electronic signature will be considered Schriftform[10] under German law. The German concept *Textform* resembles the broad concept of writing in the UNCITRAL Model Law on Electronic Commerce and in the US E-Sign Act and UEATA whereas the German *Schriftform* is a narrower concept reserved for more qualified instances of Textform. There is no US equivalent to the European 'qualified electronic signature' established by the E-Signature Directive and implementing legislation.

2. Free Movement

The Treaty provisions on free movement of goods (art 28 EC), services (art 49 EC) and the freedom of establishment (art 43 EC) apply to electronic commerce.

The Gambelli case[11] concerned on-line gambling. A number of Italian agencies linked by the internet to an English bookmaker, established in Liverpool (UK) were accused of having collaborated in Italy with a bookmaker abroad in the activity of collecting bets which is normally reserved by Italian law to the State, thus infringing an Italian law which on pain of criminal penalties prohibited the pursuit by any person anywhere of the activities of collecting, taking, booking and forwarding offers of bets, in particular bets on sporting events.

The ECJ was asked whether there is incompatibility between Articles 43 et seq EC and Article 49 et seq EC regarding freedom of establishment and freedom to provide cross-border services, on the one hand, and on the other domestic legislation such as the provisions contained in Italian law. The first point to consider was whether legislation such as that at issue in the main proceedings constituted a restriction on the freedom of establishment. That question was answered in the affirmative. The second point considered was whether the Italian legislation constituted a restriction on the freedom to provide services. That question was also answered in the affirmative.

It was therefore necessary to consider whether the restrictions were acceptable as exceptional measures expressly provided for in Articles 45 and 46 EC EC, or justified, in accordance with the case-law of the Court, for reasons of

---

10) § 126 section 3 states: "(3) Die schriftliche Form kann durch die elektronische Form ersetzt werden, wenn sich nicht aus dem Gesetz ein anderes ergibt." The present § 126, section 1, which provides: '1) Ist durch Gesetz schriftliche Form vorgeschrieben, so muß die Urkunde von dem Aussteller eigenhändig durch Namensunterschrift oder mittels notariell beglaubigten Handzeichens unterzeichnet werden.' remains in force. The new § 126 a provides (emphasis added): "(1) Soll die gesetzlich vorgeschriebene schriftliche Form durch die elektronische Form ersetzt werden, so muss der Aussteller der Erklärung dieser seinen Namen hinzufügen und das elektronische Dokument mit einer *qualifizierten elektronischen Signatur nach dem Signaturgesetz versehen.*

11) Case C-243/01, Criminal proceedings against Piergiorgio Gambelli and Others [2003] ECR 00000 (nyr).

overriding general interest. The ECJ noted that it is settled case-law that the diminution or reduction of tax revenue is not one of the grounds listed in Article 46 EC and does not constitute a matter of overriding general interest which may be relied on to justify a restriction on the freedom of establishment or the freedom to provide services.[12] In order to be justified the restrictions on freedom of establishment and on freedom to provide services must satisfy the conditions laid down in the case-law of the Court.[13] According to this case law the restrictions must be justified by imperative requirements in the general interest, be suitable for achieving the objective which they pursue and not go beyond what is necessary in order to attain it. They must in any event be applied without discrimination. It is for the national court to decide whether in the main proceedings the restriction on the freedom of establishment and on the freedom to provide services instituted by Italian law satisfy those conditions. To that end, it will be for the national court to take account of a number of issues set out in paragraphs 67-75 of the judgment.

In conclusion the reply to the question referred was that national legislation which prohibits on pain of criminal penalties the pursuit of the activities of collecting, taking, booking and forwarding offers of bets, in particular bets on sporting events, without a licence or authorisation from the Member State concerned constitutes a restriction on the freedom of establishment and the freedom to provide services provided for in Articles 43 and 49 EC respectively. It is for the national court to determine whether such legislation, taking account of the detailed rules for its application, actually serves the aims which might justify it, and whether the restrictions it imposes are disproportionate in the light of those aims.

In DocMorris,[14] the ECJ ruled on an internet pharmacy. The claimant in the main proceedings was a German association whose aim is to protect and promote the economic and social interests of pharmacists. DocMorris, the first defendant in the main proceedings, was a limited company established in the Netherlands. As well as selling medicinal products by mail order, it carries on a standard pharmaceutical business via a traditional dispensary in the Netherlands, to which the public has access. Both that activity and its internet site are covered by a licence issued by the Netherlands authorities and are subject to control by the latter. Mr Waterval, the second defendant in the main action, a Netherlands national, is an authorised pharmacist in the Netherlands. Since 8 June 2000 DocMorris and Mr Waterval have been offering for sale, at the internet address

---

12) See, to that effect, Case C-264/96 ICI [1998] ECR I-4695, paragraph 28, and Case C-136/00 Danner [2002] ECR I-8147, paragraph 56).

13) See, inter alia, Case C-19/92 Kraus [1993] ECR I-1663, paragraph 32, and Case C-55/94 Gebhard [1995] ECR I-4165, paragraph 37.

14) C-322/01, Deutscher Apothekerverband eV v 0800 DocMorris NV [2003] ECR 000 (nyr).

0800 DocMorris, prescription and non-prescription medicines for human use, in languages including German, for end consumers in Germany. The defendants in the main action sell only authorised medicines, some of which have been authorised in Germany and others in the Netherlands. The following questions were referred to the ECJ for a preliminary ruling (emphasis added):

> 1. Are the principles of the free movement of goods under Article 28 EC et seq infringed by national legislation whereby medicinal products for human use the sale of which is restricted to pharmacies may not be imported commercially by way of mail order through authorised pharmacies in other Member States on the basis of individual orders placed by consumers over the *internet*?
>
> ....
>
> 2. Is it compatible with Articles 28 EC and 30 EC for a national prohibition on advertising medicines by mail order or medicines for human use available only on prescription or through pharmacies authorised in the State of origin but not the importing State to be interpreted so broadly that the *internet presentation* of a pharmacy of an EU Member State, which in addition to the mere presentation of its business describes individual medicines with their product name, prescription status, package size and price and at the same time offers the possibility of ordering those medicines by means of an on-line order form, is classified as prohibited advertising, with the result that cross-border orders of medicines by *internet*, including cross-border delivery of those orders, is at least made substantially more difficult?
>
> (a) Having regard to Article 1(3) of Directive 2000/31/EC ..., do Articles 28 EC and 30 EC require the *internet* presentation of a pharmacy of an EU Member State, as described above, or parts of that presentation, to be excluded from the definition of advertising to the general public for the purposes of Articles 1(3) and 3(1) of Directive 92/28/EEC ... in order to make it possible in practice as well to offer certain information society services?
>
> (b) Can any restriction of the definition of advertising required by Articles 28 EC and 30 EC be justified by the consideration that *on-line* order forms containing only the minimum information necessary for placing an order, and/or other parts of the internet site of a pharmacy of an EU Member State, are comparable with trade catalogues and/or price lists within the meaning of Article 1(4) of Directive 92/28/EEC?
>
> 3. If some aspects of the *internet* presentation of a pharmacy of an EU Member State infringe provisions concerning the advertising of medicines, is it to be inferred from Articles 28 EC and 30 EC that cross-border trade in medicines which takes place with the aid of such a presentation must be regarded as lawful despite the prohibited advertising, in order more effectively to implement the principle of the free cross-border movement of goods?

As appears there are references to the internet and on-line transaction several times in the questions referred to the ECJ. In its answers the Court likewise addressed the consequences of the internet expressly. It stated[15] that the emergence of the internet as a method of cross-border sales means that the scope

---

15) In paragraph 73-74.

and, by the same token, the effect of a prohibition against mail order sale must be looked at on a broader scale and that for pharmacies not established in Germany, the internet provides a more significant way to gain direct access to the German market than for pharmacies established in Germany. A prohibition which has a greater impact on pharmacies established outside German territory could impede access to the market for products from other Member States more than it impedes access for domestic products. It also noted[16] that internet buying may have certain advantages, such as the ability to place the order from home or the office, without the need to go out, and to have time to think about the questions to ask the pharmacists, and these advantages must be taken into account..

In conclusion, the ECJ ruled that a national prohibition on the sale by mail order of medicinal products is a measure having an effect equivalent to a quantitative restriction for the purposes of Article 28 EC. Article 30 EC may be relied on to justify such a prohibition in so far as the prohibition covers medicinal products subject to prescription. However, Article 30 EC cannot be relied on to justify an absolute prohibition on the sale by mail order of medicinal products which are not subject to prescription in the Member State concerned. Article 88(1) of Directive 2001/83/EC[17] precludes a national prohibition on advertising the sale by mail order of medicinal products which may be supplied only in pharmacies in the Member State concerned in so far as the prohibition covers medicinal products which are not subject to prescription.

3. Competition law

The ordinary competition law rules also apply to information services. There are express references to the internet in the Guidelines on Vertical Restraints.[18] Every distributor must be free to use the Internet to advertise or to sell products. A restriction on the use of the Internet by distributors can only be compatible with the Block Exemption Regulation to the extent that promotion on the Internet or sales over the Internet would lead to active selling into other distributors' exclusive territories or customer groups. In general, the use of the Internet is not considered a form of active sales into such territories or customer groups, since it is a reasonable way to reach every customer. The fact that it may have effects outside one's own territory or customer group results from the technology, ie the easy access from everywhere. If a customer visits the web site of a distributor and

---

16) In paragraph 113 and 114.

17) Directive 92/28/EEC which the national court referred to has been replace by Directive 2001/83/EC.

18) Commission Notice. Guidelines on Vertical Restraints (2000/C 291/01) paragraph 51.

contacts the distributor and if such contact leads to a sale, including delivery, then that is considered passive selling. The language used on the website or in the communication plays normally no role in that respect. Insofar as a web site is not specifically targeted at customers primarily inside the territory or customer group exclusively allocated to another distributor, for instance with the use of banners or links in pages of providers specifically available to these exclusively allocated customers, the website is not considered a form of active selling. However, unsolicited e-mails sent to individual customers or specific customer groups are considered active selling. The same considerations apply to selling by catalogue. Notwithstanding what has been said before, the supplier may require quality standards for the use of the Internet site to resell his goods, just as the supplier may require quality standards for a shop or for advertising and promotion in general. The latter may be relevant in particular for selective distribution. An outright ban on Internet or catalogue selling is only possible if there is an objective justification. In any case, the supplier cannot reserve to itself sales and/or advertising over the Internet.

4. New Legislative Framework at EU Level

At EU level problems relating to e-commerce have been addressed since the mid 1990's. The EU Commission issued a Communication[19] on electronic commerce in 1997 which set out the objective of creating a European coherent legal framework by the year 2000. The E-Signature Directive[20] was adopted in 1999, the E-Commerce Directive in 2000,[21] and the Infosoc Directive in 2001.[22] The most important consumer protection directives related to electronic commerce are the directive on protection of consumers in respect of distance contracts from 1997[23] and the directive on distance marketing of consumer financial services from 2002.[24]

---

19) A European Initiative on Electronic Commerce, COM(97) 157 final, 16.4.1997.

20) Directive 1999/93/EC of the European Parliament and of the Council of 13 December 1999 on a Community framework for electronic signatures.

21) Directive 2000/31/EC of the European Parliament and of the Council of 8 June 2000 on certain legal aspects of information society services, in particular electronic commerce, in the Internal Market ('Directive on electronic commerce').

22) 2001/29/EC.

23) 97/7/EC.

24) 2002/65/EC.

4.1. E-Signature Directive

Article 5 of the E-Signature Directive[25] provides that Member States shall ensure that a 'qualified' electronic signature, ie an advanced electronic signatures which is based on a qualified certificate and which is created by a secure signature creation device satisfies the legal requirements of a signature in relation to data in electronic form in the same manner as a handwritten signature satisfies those requirements in relation to paper-based data; and is admissible as evidence in legal proceedings. Member States shall ensure that an electronic signature is not denied legal effectiveness and admissibility as evidence in legal proceedings solely on the grounds that it is in electronic form, or not based upon a qualified certificate, or not based upon a qualified certificate issued by an accredited certification service provider, or not created by a secure signature-creation device.[26]

4.2. E-Commerce Directive

The E-Commerce Directive[27] aims at ensuring that Information Society services can move freely. It covers a wide variety of services provided online (so-called 'information society services') ranging from online newspapers and specialised news services (such as business or financial information), online selling of various products (books, computer hardware and software, pharmaceuticals, etc) to the online provision of financial services (online banking, online investment). The latter are of particular importance as they are particularly suitable for cross-border delivery. The Directive applies horizontally across all areas of law which touch on the provision of information society services, regardless of whether it is a matter of public, private, or criminal law. Furthermore, it applies equally both to business-to-business (B2B) and business-toconsumer (B2C) e-commerce.

The directive applies to Information Society services as already defined in the transparency directive,[28] ie any service normally provided for remuneration, at a distance, by electronic means and at the individual request of a recipient of the service. The key point of the definition is the term 'service', which refers to a service within the meaning of Article 50 EC, ie according to the interpretation by the ECJ a service which is normally provided for remuneration – but not

---

25) 1999/93/EC.

26) See for more detail Jos Dumortier's and Cecilia Magnusson's articles in this volume.

27) 2000/31/EC. See for an overview of the directive Pia Lindholm and Frithjof A. Maennel: DIRECTIVE ON ELECTRONIC COMMERCE (2000/31/EC) in Jens Fejø, Ruth Nielsen and Thomas Riis (eds): Legal Aspects of Electronic Commerce, Copenhagen 2001.

28) 98/34/EC as amended by 98/48/EC.

necessarily remunerated by the recipient of the service.[29]

By way of derogation certain services or areas are entirely excluded from the scope of application of the e-commerce directive, eg taxation, questions covered by the data protection directives[30] or certain gambling activities.

The core principle of the directive is the Internal market clause in Article 3. It obliges the country of establishment of the provider to ensure that the provider's activities comply with that Member State's legislation. Furthermore, it establishes that:

> Member States may not, for reasons falling within this Directive's coordinated field, restrict the freedom to provide information society services from another Member State.

This provision must be interpreted in the light of the definition of the coordinated field in Article 2(h), which covers all requirements in national legislation that could be applied to an Information Society service or a provider of an Information Society service (eg conditions on the establishment and access to the activity; legislation on content such as illicit content, defamation, language requirements; legislation on any type of commercial communications such as advertising, direct marketing, sales promotion; legislation on unfair competition, contract law; any legislation on consumer protection, etc) The coordinated field does not cover requirements applicable to goods as such or requirements applicable to the delivery of goods.

The effect of the internal market clause is that Member States cannot restrict information society services provided from another Member State (subject to the exemptions in Article 3(4) and in the annex). The directive thus follows the country of origin principle and the approach taken for example in the television without frontiers directive, in the data protection directive and the electronic signatures directive.

Article 9 of the directive requires Member States to ensure that their legislation allows contracts to be concluded by electronic means. Member States shall in particular ensure that the legal requirements applicable to the contractual process do not create obstacles to electronic contracts nor result in such contracts being deprived of legal effect and validity on account of their having been made by electronic means. Article 10 lays down information requirements. The specific requirements in the electronic commerce directive will apply in addition to other information requirements established by EU law.

Article 11 on the placement of the order stipulates that the service provider has to acknowledge the receipt of the recipient's order without undue delay.

---

29) Case C-20/92 Hubbard [1993] ECR I-3777 and Case C-109/92 Wirth [1993] ECR I-6447.

30) 95/46/EC and 2002/58/EC.

Acknowledgement of receipt is deemed to be received when the recipient of the service is able to access it.

Articles 12-14 establish limitations on the liability of internet interme diariesproviding services consisting of mere conduit, caching and hosting. The limitations on liability in the Directive apply to certain delimited activities carried out by internet intermediaries, rather than to categories of service providers or types of information. The limitations on liability provided for by the Directive are established in a horizontal manner, meaning that they cover liability, both civil and criminal, for all types of illegal activities initiated by third parties. The Directive does not affect the liability of the person who is at the source of the content nor does it affect the liability of intermediaries in cases which are not covered by the limitations defined in the Directive. Furthermore, the Directive does not affect the possibility of a national court or administrative authority to require a service provider to terminate or prevent an infringement. These questions are subject to the national law of the Member States.

Article 15 prevents Member States from imposing on internet intermediaries, with respect to activities covered by Articles 12-14, a general obligation to monitor the information which they transmit or store or a general obligation to actively seek out facts or circumstances indicating illegal activities. Article 15 does not prevent public authorities in the Member States from imposing a monitoring obligation in a specific, clearly defined individual case.

The Commission published a report on the application of the e-commerce Directive in November 2003.[31] Most Member States have implemented the e-commerce directive through horisontal legislation on e-commerce. In addition to the matters dealt with by Articles 12-14 of the e-commerce Directive, some Member States have decided to provide for limitations on the liability of providers of hyperlinks and search engines.[32] In the report on the application of the e-commerce Directive the Commission notes that the reports and studies on the effectiveness of blocking and filtering applications appear to indicate that there is not yet any technology which could not be circumvented and provide full effectiveness in blocking or filtering illegal and harmful information whilst at the same time avoiding blocking entirely legal information resulting in violations of freedom of speech.[33]

At the time when the e-commerce Directive was adopted, it was decided that notice and take down procedures should not be regulated in the Directive itself.

---

31) COM(2003)702. First Report on the application of Directive 2000/31/EC of the European Parliament and of the Council of 8 June 2000 on certain legal aspects of information society services, in particular electronic commerce, in the Internal Market (Directive on electronic commerce).

32) See further COM(2003)702 p13.

33) See further COM(2003)702 p18 note 73.

Instead Article 16 and Recital 40 expressly encourage self-regulation in this field. This approach has also been followed by the Member States in their national laws transposing the Directive. Out of those Member States which have transposed the Directive, only Finland has included a legal provision setting out a notice and take down procedure concerning copyright infringements only. All the other Member States have left this issue to self-regulation.

4.3. Intellectual Property Law

The information society has revitalized intellectual property law.[34] The interface between traditional legal subject areas such as contract law and intellectual property law may develop into new legal arrangements in the digital environment. The Infosoc Directive[35] aims at adapting and and supplementing the Community legal framework for the protection of copyright and related rights as far as is necessary for the smooth functioning of the internal market. Effective and easy accessible means of reproduction resulting from information technology poses a threat to right holders and make a traditional strategy for the administration of rights based on control with physical copies futile. Information technology enables the transformation of copyrightable goods into services, and digital rights management systems may be established to exercise the rights in these services. Article 6 of the Infosoc directive prohibits the circumvention of any effective technological measures.

The Infosoc Directive requires Member States to ensure that rightholders are in a position to apply for injunctions, under certain conditions, against intermediaries whose services are used by a third party to infringe a copyright or related right. The Commission has also presented a proposal on the enforcement of intellectual property rights, which, amongst other issues, provides for appropriate remedies with respect to internet-related infringements of intellectual property, including injunctive relief.[36]

4.4. Data Protection

Article 8 of the EU Charter on Fundamental Rights provides that everyone has the right to the protection of personal data concerning him or her. Such data must

---

34) See Thomas Riis' Intorduction in and Jon Bing: 'Lovely Rita Meter Maid ...' The Trade in Intellectual Property within a Digital Environment in Jens Fejø, Ruth Nielsen and Thomas Riis (eds): Legal Aspects of Electronic Commerce, Copenhagen 2001.

35) 2001/29/EC.

36) COM(2003) 46. Proposal for a Directive of the European Parliament and of the Council on measures and procedures to ensure the enforcement of intellectual property rights. Article 2 of the proposed Directive states that it shall not affect the e-commerce Directive.

be processed fairly for specified purposes and on the basis of the consent of the person concerned or some other legitimate basis laid down by law. Everyone has the right of access to data which has been collected concerning him or her, and the right to have it rectified. The Data Protection Directives[37] aim at striking a balance between the internal market requirements that personal data should be able to flow freely from one Member State to another in order to ensure the free movement of goods, persons, services and capital and the goal that the fundamental rights of individuals should be safeguarded. The main rule laid down in Article 6 of Directive 95/46 is that data can only be collected for *specific, explicit and legitimate* purposes and not further processed in a way incompatible with those purposes (the so-called *finalité* principle). Personal data must be adequate, relevant and not excessive in relation to the purposes for which they are collected and/or further processed. According to Article 7 Member States shall provide that personal data may be processed only if the data subject has unambiguously given his *consent*; or processing is necessary for the performance of a contract to which the data subject is party or ... processing is necessary for the purposes of legitimate interests pursued by the data controller except where such interests are overridden by the interests for *fundamental rights* and freedoms of the data subject (the so-called balance of interest test).

In a comparative perspective the EU has fairly stringent rules on data protection. In connection with e-business it is technically easy to collect and process personal data on a much wider scale than alllowed under the above directives.[38]

Protection Directives[39] aim at striking a balance between the internal market requirements that personal data should be able to flow freely from one Member State to another in order to ensure the free movement of goods, persons, services and capital and the goal that the fundamental rights of individuals should be safeguarded. The main rule laid down in Article 6 of Directive 95/46 is that data can only be collected for *specific, explicit and legitimate* purposes and not further processed in a way incompatible with those purposes (the so-called *finalité* principle). Personal data must be adequate, relevant and not excessive in relation to the purposes for which they are collected and/or further processed. According to Article 7 Member States shall provide that personal data may be processed only if the data subject has unambiguously given his *consent*; or processing is necessary for the performance of a contract to which the data subject is party or

37) 95/46/EC (data protection in general) and Directive 2002/58/EC on privacy and electronic communications.

38) See further Emily M. Weitzenböck: Electronic agents: Spies, lies and villains in the online world? in this volume.

39) 95/46/EC (data protection in general) and Directive 2002/58/EC on privacy and electronic communications.

... processing is necessary for the purposes of legitimate interests pursued by the data controller except where such interests are overridden by the interests for *fundamental rights* and freedoms of the data subject (the so-called balance of interest test).

In a comparative perspective the EU has fairly stringent rules on data protection. In connection with e-business it is technically easy to collect and process personal data on a much wider scale than alllowed under the above directives.[40]

5. What next?

In the report on the application of the e-commerce Directive[41] the Commission states that it is now necessary to collect information and gain experience on how the new legal framework works in practice. The analysis to date has not shown a need for an immediate revision of the e-commerce Directive. The same applies in other areas. No major EU legal reforms are in the pipe-line. The Commission and other EU actors are likely to focus on continuous monitoring, rising awareness, collecting information and international co-operation.

---

40) See further Emily M. Weitzenböck: Electronic agents: Spies, lies and villains in the online world? in this volume.

41) COM(2003)702. First Report on the application of Directive 2000/31/EC of the European Parliament and of the Council of 8 June 2000 on certain legal aspects of information society services, in particular electronic commerce, in the Internal Market (Directive on electronic commerce).

E-commerce on New Media:
- an overview of the EU regulatory regime

by Søren Sandfeld Jakobsen

Abstract

Media convergence – the coming together of IT, telecom and broadcast media - and the consequential emergence of new media and technologies is rapidly changing the notion of e-commerce. Previously, e-commerce was exclusively tied to the use of PCs and traditional telecommunications network. Today, however, the concept also comprises m-commerce (mobile commerce) and t-commerce (television commerce) and commerce on other so-called new media which combine the characteristics of traditional media. E-commerce on new media highlights the legal issues attached to traditional e-commerce on the Internet as well as creates a number of new legal issues.

Several regulatory initiatives have been taken from EU in recent years in order to meet the challenges imposed by media convergence and the emergence of e-commerce on new media. First, the new telecom regulatory framework represents a whole new approach to communications regulation; an approach seeking to reflect and adjust to the immediate consequences of convergence on telecom infrastructure and services. Hence, the framework treats all kinds of communication networks and services (telephony, data or broadcast) equally, thus no longer legally connecting specific services with specific kinds of technological infrastructure. Further, the framework seeks to take account of the accelerating developments in mobile and interactive broadcast communications – made possible through convergence.

Regulatory initiatives reflecting convergence – and its impact on e-commerce - have also been taken with respect to the Internet and the fact that the Internet as a way of transmitting information is rapidly being extended through development of new technologies these years. The regulatory initiatives as regards the Internet are both directly (through the e-commerce directive) and indirectly (through e.g. the infosoc directive).

Although broadcast regulation on EU level has so far only to a minor degree been influenced by convergence, the new EU telecom framework addresses a number of important issues linking communication infrastructure and broadcast content. Moreover, it is likely to believe that a greater impact on broadcast content regulation will be reflected in the coming revised Television Without

Frontiers directive.

Finally, it should be born in mind that also existing EU regulation, e.g. the distance selling directive, the electronic signatures directive and the directive on protection of personal data, will apply and play an important role for e-commerce in the converged media world of modern Information Society.

Regulatory actions will always lack behind the vast technological developments. The technological development will no doubt continue to disturb the regulatory pillars that the existent regulatory regime rests on. As such, a number of regulatory initiatives are presumably inevitably in order to create a regulatory EU-framework for e-commerce that takes account of convergence and the emergence of new media.

1. New Media and the Concept of Convergence

The expression "media convergence" (or simply convergence) is a concept often used to describe the coming together of IT, telecommunications and media technologies – and combinations thereof - taking place very rapidly these years.[1] Convergence creates a number of new networks, distribution platforms and services arising on the pillars of the traditional media: telephony, data communication and broadcast. The Internet – the worldwide network of data communication networks – is in itself an example of convergence, namely convergence between computing and telecommunication networks. As the information society develops, other converged media (often also called "new media") emerges. For example, different kinds of mobile technologies and terminals providing not only telephony services, but also high speed data communication and broadcast services, are growing fast these years. So is interactive television (iTV), a digital broadcast platform that provides not only traditional radio and TV, but also enhanced radio/TV (traditional programmes with different kinds of interactive elements added) as well as telephony, e-mail, Internet and other interactive services which could previously not be transmitted via traditional broadcast platforms.

For a systematic approach, the aspects of convergence are often categorised in 4 dimensions:[2]

1) *Network convergence*, meaning that different kinds of networks (e.g. the public switched telephone network (PSTN), the Internet, broadcast networks etc.) become capable of carrying multiple kinds of communication services, whether it be telephony, data, broadcast or

---

1) Walden and Angel: Telecommunications Law (2001), chapter 12.

2) KPMG: Public Policy Issues Arising from Telecommunications and Audiovisual Convergence (1996), 45.

combinations thereof.

2) *Terminal convergence*, i.e. convergence of traditional receiver terminals (fixed/mobile phones, radio/TV set, computers), making it possible to watch TV or listen to radio on the computer or cell phone, or the opposite: gaining access to the Internet via a TV set or a cell phone. Thus, the traditional distinctions between TV/radio, telephone and PC dissolve.
3) *Service convergence*, i.e. convergence of traditional services. Today, for example, due to increased bandwidth Internet websites very often form a combination of data, sound and video. Likewise, new mobile technologies make it possible to supplement traditional telephony conversation with live video of the persons engaged in the conversation (so-called video telephony). Or different kinds of interactive data services are added to the transmission of a traditional TV programme.
4) *Market convergence*, meaning the convergence of – formerly widely separated – communications market such as the IT/Internet, telecom and media markets. Many companies see the vast opportunities in vertical or horizontal market integration thereby gaining the benefits of the formerly separable markets suddenly becoming related due to convergence.

Why is convergence happening? Shortly speaking, it is a result of the propagation of *digital technology*. By using digital technology, communication can be stored and distributed in digital form – as data. Data is communication encoded into an electronic signal expressed by only two values, 0 or 1. Computer technology is based on digital technology. Thus, the Internet is born digital. Telephony and broadcast, however, are traditionally analogue communication forms, that is, information that – when converted into electrical signals – moves in wave forms that change constantly, analogue to the original input (the original input being the changing energy in sound or the changing light in a moving picture). The more energy the more information and the more fluctuations per second (frequencies) of the electronic wave. Telephone conversation operates at small frequencies, television at high frequencies.

As it appears, analogue and digital communication have fundamentally different characteristics. This is the reason why telephony, broadcast and IT/Internet previously were separable kinds of communication. What is happening now is that traditional analogue communication forms – telephony and broadcast – are becoming digital (or at least become able to handle digital signals) and adopt the core elements of computing network technologies, including operating systems, browsers and other basis computer software, transmission protocols etc.

Thus, the media are all being computerised. This applies to every element of the communication process: production, storage, distribution via networks and reception via terminals. The result is that all communication forms – voice, data and video – are adapting to the same basis formula. They become digital. When they all become digital, the presumption for convergence is present.[3] And convergence leads to emergence of new media and services.

2. The Implications for E-Commerce

In relation to e-commerce the implication of convergence is that e-commerce is no longer purely attached to computers connected to the Internet via cables, but is spread out to a variety of new media, mainly mobile media. Different kinds of mobile network technologies (WAP, GPRS, WI-FI, 3G) which opens for e-commerce on mobile platforms ("m-commerce") are emerging rapidly. Especially 3G, which opens for broadband services (including high speed Internet access) over mobile platforms and which is just being launched on a larger scale in Europe and the US, give rise to hopes of a new area in the telecom industry.

In addition to m-commerce via new mobile media, convergence also opens for "t-commerce", that is, electronic commerce via traditional television network and terminals. T-commerce becomes a possibility when broadcast network (e.g. the analogue terrestrial network) are digitized, a return path is established (from the receiver back to the sender) and the television set are either build digital or provided with a set top box.[4] In this case TV becomes interactive, and interactivity (along with digitization) is a prerequisite for t-commerce.[5]

Thus, convergence leads to emergence of new media for e-commerce transactions. Thereby not only highlighting legal issues known from "traditional" e-commerce, but also creating new legal questions emanating from convergence itself. Some of the new legal issues have been subject to regulation at EU level. These issues are described below.

3. EU Regulation

3.1. Telecom Regulation

EU took the initial regulatory step towards convergence when the Commission published a green paper on the subject in 1997, followed by two public hearings

3) See for a detailed description, inter alia Nellist and Gilbert: Understanding modern Telecommunications and the Information Superhighway (1999), chapter 10.

4) A set top box converts the digital signals into analogue (which is all that an analogue TV set can understand).

5) Gerbarg: The Economics, Technology and Content of Digital Television (1998).

in 1998 and 1999.[6] The green paper analysed the convergence phenonemom in relation to the existing telecom regulatory framework and proposed different kinds of regulatory approaches to meet the challenges of convergence. The paper launched the idea of replacing the existing vertical, i.e. sector specific, regulatory regime with a new regulatory regime taking a more horizontal and technology neutral approach covering all kinds of communications infrastructure and associated services.

In addition, the paper discussed the need for a more flexible administrative set-up where the role and competences of the national regulatory agencies (NRAs) were strengthened with the Commission undertaking a guiding role to ensure harmonisation, coherence and effective competition within the Community.

Based on the green paper and the public hearings the Commission in 1999 published a 1999-review of the telecom regulation.[7] The review laid out the principles for a new telecom regulatory framework which was adopted in 2002 via 5 directives (a framework directive and four specific directives covering licensing and authorisations, access and interconnection, universal service rights and consumers rights and telecom data protection) and a Council decision.[8] The framework should be implemented in the various EU member state's legislation no later than 25 July 2003.[9] The framework contains a number of important new regulatory principles taking account of convergence:

- Covering all communications infrastructure and related services (including IP based, mobile and broadcasting networks and services). In line with the previous regulation, content is not regulated. However, appropriate provisions for links between transmission and content are included.
- Setting forth an authorisations system based on the use of general authorisations to authorise all communications network and services (while the grant of specific rights of use are still permitted with respect to spectrum and numbering resources).
- Modifying the sector specific telecom competition principles to the general competition law in order to make a more coherent and flexible regulation of competition in the converging media markets.

---

6) Green Paper on Convergence of the Telecommunications, Media and Information Technology Sectors and the Implications for regulation, COM (1997) 623.

7) The 1999 Communications Review, COM (1999) 539.

8) Directives 2002/19/EC, 2002/20/EC, 2002/21/EC, 2002/22/EC, 2002/58/EC and Council Decision 2002/676. See for a detailed description Farr & Oakley: EU Communications Law (2002).

9) In defiance hereof several member states have at the time of writing not yet implemented the framework.

- Introducing a procedure at community level ensuring a harmonised and open approach to technological standards in the communications sector in order to avoid bottleneck barriers to market entry.
- Introducing procedures to modify, if necessary, the existing obligations for conditional access systems, universal services and consumer protection in the light of the technological and market development due to convergence.
- Updating existing telecom data protection rules to ensure that data protection rules in the converging communications sector are technologically neutral and robust.
- Strengthening the independence of NRA's and to improve transparency of their decision-making, however at the same time establishing an increased co-operation with the Commission and empowering the Commission to require NRA decision suspended if they are not justifiable according to the regulatory framework.

In relation to e-commerce the new regulatory framework means, inter alia, that a provider of communications network and services by which e-commerce is carried out, will be subject to the regulation *regardless* of the applied media. Thus, a provider of e.g. a mobile or broadcast communications network for e-commerce must comply with the regulatory framework, including provisions regarding interconnection, consumer protection, standardization and universal services.

3.2. Broadcast Regulation

As mentioned, the new telecom regulatory framework is an infrastructure regulation – not a content regulation. Broadcast regulation in the various member states is, however, primarily content regulation. The reason being that radio and TV are mass media through which the attitudes and values of a whole population can be influenced. And since radio and TV are carried over a scarce public good, radio frequencies, broadcast content (radio and TV programmes) has been regarded a cultural good that governments and legislators could and should exercise some kind of control over in the interest of democracy, freedom of speech and cultural diversity. Because EU has never been aimed at harmonizing the cultural differences between the member states, EU's powers regarding broadcast – and cultural policies as a whole – are very limited. Broadcast regulation, including the degree to which broadcasters and broadcast content should be regulated, has therefore mostly been a national issue.[10]

The EU has, however, adopted a number of directives etc. within the field of broadcast. The most important of these being the Television Without Frontiers

10) Garzaniti: Telecommunications, Broadcasting and the Internet, EC Competition Law and Regulation (2000), 75.

(TWF) Directive of 1989 (revised in 1997).[11] The TWF Directive aims at strenghtening the european television sector and ensuring the free movement of broadcast services within the EU, while at the same time protecting the consumers against harmful or illegal content from other member states. The directive includes provisions that restrain the use of advisertisements and sponsoring, protects minors against harmful and illegal content, prohibit discriminative content, recommend a minimum quote for European television productions and implement the country of origin principle, which establishes that the legislation in the member state where a certain broadcaster is located shall apply also where the broadcaster's programmes are broadcasted to other member states countries.

The TWF Directive does not contain provisions of direct relevance for the growing media convergence and e-commerce via new media, primarily since the scope of the Directive is narrowed to traditional *point-to-multipoint* broadcast. However, the Directive is currently under revision[12] and it is likely that a revised Directive will address some of the problems following from convergence in respect of e.g. interactive television and broadcast transmitted via other networks than traditional broadcast networks.

Further, Directive 95/47/EC on the use of standards for the transmission of television signals introduced the legal basis for establishing common standards within the EU for digital television whether by cable, satellite or terrestrial means. Such standards are regarded essential for creating effective free-market competition within the market for digital television.

As mentioned under 4.1. above, the new EU Telecom Framework covers only infrastructure issues and not content issues such as broadcast content. This does not mean that the Framework has no implications for the broadcast area.[13] As described, the traditional boundaries between infrastructure and content are subverted due to the increasing convergence. The Framework reflects this development and tries - where deemed necessary - to link infrastructure and content. First, the Framework applies to all communications network and services, including broadcast. Thus, the provisions in the Framework regarding authorisation to supply network and services as well as the provisions regarding allocation and assignment of radio spectrum are also of importance to providers of radio and TV broadcast.[14]

---

11) Directive 1989/552/EC (as amended by directive 1997/36/EC).

12) See for more details the Commission's website: www.europa.eu.int/comm/avpolicy/regul.

13) See the Commission working paper: The 2003 regulatory framework for electronic communications – Implications for broadcasting (14 June 2002).

14) See Directive 2002/21 (the Framework Directive) and Directive 2002/20 (the Authorisation Directive).

Second, the Framework also addresses the question of "must-carry" provisions. These provisions, which are contained in most member states' broadcast legislation, seek to ensure that certain radio and television broadcast channels and services are made universally available to users. Such political considerations are not always compatible with effective competition. Thus, the Framework aims at preventing an excessive use of must-carry rules by requiring that these obligations must be reasonable and transparent.[15] At present, the must-carry restrictions only apply to broadcast via traditional broadcast network, not broadcast via e.g. the Internet or 3G mobile networks. This may change as broadcast via such new media in a few years becomes a realistic alternative.[16]

Third, the Framework takes over the specific regulation of conditional access systems on the use of standards for the transmission of television signals. This regulation was previously a part of the broadcast regulatory regime.[17] Fourth, as convergence leads to appearance of new interactive television services, including e-commerce on television networks, it becomes necessary to ensure accessibility to facilities essential for the end-user's choice of services, such as accessibility to API's (application programme interface) and EPG's (electronic programme guide). The Framework provides the possibility for NRAs[18] to impose fair, reasonable and non-discriminatory obligations on operators in this respect.[19]

Thus, even though content regulation on broadcast networks still largely applies to traditional point-to-multipoint broadcast, the new telecoms framework also addresses issues related to new interactive broadcast media and services.

3.3. Internet Regulation

As mentioned, the Internet itself can be seen as a convergence between IT and telecom. This also reflects the regulation of the Internet. As regards the access to and *transmission* of data via the Internet, these issues – like other communications infrastructure issues - are regulated in the new EU telecom regulatory framework, re point 3.1. above. As regards content regulation, a broad consensus exists within the EU not to regulate content on the Internet (apart from general applicable rules set forth in, inter alia, criminal, copyright and consumer acts).

15) Directive 2002/22/EC (Universal Services) Article 31, cf. recital 43 to the Directive.

16) February 4, 2004 Pursuant to Article 31, Universal Services Directive, the article only applies to network that a substantial number of end users apply as their primary access to traditional broadcast services – at the moment only traditional broadcast network fulfil this requirement.

17) Cf. Directive 95/47/EC on the use of standards for the transmission of television signals.

18) The member states' National Regulatory Authorities.

19) Cf. Directive 2002/19/EC (Access Directive) Article 5.

While not regulating Internet infrastructure or content in itself, certain aspects related to the providers of commercial Internet content services have been regulated by the e-commerce directive.[20] These aspects include 1) the country of origin principle (stating that a provider of information society services is a starting point subject only to the law of the member state where the provider is established, regardless of whether it directs its e-business to other member states within the EU), 2) a number of information and contractual obligations imposed on providers, and 3) provisions regarding the liability of infrastructure providers and other intermediaries regarding the content carried through their network or infrastructure.

In terms of convergence and e-commerce on new media the e-commerce directive only has an indirect, but yet important impact. This is due to the fact that the directive applies to the broad concept of information society services. This concept must be construed as to comprise all kinds of commercial "online" services, i.e. services that require use of computers and are transported by means of an electronic network (and services which are not traditional broadcast or voice telephony). As convergence matures, online services are no longer just traditional data communication services sent between traditional computers by means of traditional data communication networks. Rather, online services include various wireless and mobile content services as well as digital broadcast services – since these services too are delivered by electronic networks by means of devices with similar characteristics as computers (the ability to store and process digital information). In a converged media environment it becomes meaningless to distinguish legally between information services provided via the traditional Internet networks, and information services that share the same characteristics but are provided via other networks and terminals.

Thus, the scope of the e-commerce directive is constantly broadened as convergence and e-commerce via new media grows. In this sense all content service providers, regardless of what technological platform they deploy, must be aware of that directive.

Besides the e-commerce Directive, the EU has also passed other directives which, although not directly aimed at the Internet, have significant impact on the Internet – and therefore also draw attention from a convergence angle. As examples the distant selling directive, the electronic signatures directive and the directive on protection of personal data should be mentioned.[21] In particular the distant selling directive and the directive on protection of personal data contain provisions of significant importance in relation to the formation of e-commerce contracts on all electronic communications network, primarily in the field of business-to-consumer e-commerce.

---

20) Directive 2000/31/EC.

21) Directive 97/7/EC, 99/93/EC and 95/46/EC respectively.

3.4. Copyright regulation – Directive 2001/29/EC

Copyright protected content plays an important role on e-commerce, both as a commodity to be traded and as elements of the websites etc. where e-commerce is exercised. In relation to the Internet and other new digital media it has been unclear as to whether copyright protected content on such new media was subject to copyright protection similar to content on traditional analogue media.

Pursuant to Directive 2001/29 (the Infosoc Directive) EU has now determined that copyright-protected works that are made available on demand on the Internet or other new media, e.g. mobile or digital broadcast media, are comprised in the author's copyright similar to analogue works.[22] This will no doubt have a significant impact on e-commerce on new media.

In addition, the Directive prohibits the circumvention of any effective technological measures to avoid the making of a copy and thus protect copyright protected content.[23] Since the 17 February 2004irective will apply not only to on demand content delivered from PC to PC, but also on other infrastructure platforms and terminals, the prohibition is likely to apply also on new media and thus has broad application.

---

22) Directive 2001/29/EC, Article 3.

23) Ibid, Article 6.

Will the Internet Turn into a Digital McWorld?[1]

The Possible Consequences of the
Expansion of the Copyright Monopoly on E-Commerce

by Robin Elizabeth Herr[2]

"The general rule of law is, that the noblest of human productions -- knowledge, truths ascertained, conceptions, and ideas -- become, after voluntary communication to others, free as the air to common use."
-US Supreme Court Justice Louis D. Brandeis[3]

The Problem

The Internet has wreaked havoc on copyright law. In the past, the law readily resolved challenges posed by technological innovation. But Internet technology allows unlimited copying and therefore potential infringement, even by the most unsophisticated user. The Internet is so easily accessed that today over 312 million people in Europe and the US alone are plugged into the Internet and could be infringing.[4]

For businesses, the financial repercussions are staggering. In A&M Records v. Napster, the US recording industry stated figures showing that

---

1) "Mc" means "basic, convenient, inexpensive and standardized." It refers to such diverse concepts as McGod and McMozart. *See* Quality Inns Int'l v. McDonald's Corp., 695 F. Supp. 198, 216 (D. Md. 1988).

2) In December 2000, Robin Herr graduated from Columbia University's School of Law (J.D.) and its Graduate School of Journalism (M.Sc.). She has taught an American law course at Copenhagen Business School and has practiced law in the United States.

3) Dissent, International News Service v. Associated Press, 248 U.S. 215, 250 (1918).

4) US Central Intelligence Agency, The World Factbook (2003), www.odci.gov/cia/publications/factbook/ (last visited 8 November 2003). Combined estimates of Internet access in the US and EU vary from 235.5 million to 368 million users. Sources include: Eurostat, Information Society Statistics (European Communities 2002); US Department of Commerce National Telecommunications and Information Administration, http://www.ntia.doc.gov/ntiahome (last visited 8 November 2003), and "New Media: We can provide for you," The Guardian, 9 September 2002.

Napster users illegally downloaded between 12 and 30 million songs daily.[5] Estimates of the number of US motion pictures illegally downloaded reach up to 500,000 full-length movies daily.[6] Software businesses are also being hurt. In Europe, 35% of business software is pirated. In the United States, the figure is 24%.[7]

Businesses are responding to the copying frenzy by expanding their copyright monopoly. Through the introduction of online license provisions, they are: 1) prohibiting copying that is normally allowed under traditional limitations to the copyright law; 2) protecting material that is non-copyrightable; and 3) creating perpetual copyrights.

Governments are supporting the increase. Within the US, private industry is taking the lead with the government playing a supportive role. In the controversial decision of ProCD, Inc. v. Zeidenberg, the 7th Circuit Court of Appeals validated a license provision that expanded the scope of copyright. 86 F.3d 1447 (7th Cir. 1996). Subsequent legal rulings have varied wildly.[8]

Within the EU, legislators are taking the lead by formulating directives to regulate the online economy. While they have placed a high level of protection on copyrights so that online business can flourish, they have also included provisions that potentially ensure the free flow of information. But

---

5) John Gibeaut, "Facing the Music," 86 A.B.A. J. at 37 (Oct. 2000), cited in Kimberly Kerry, "Comment: Music on the Internet: Is Technology Moving Faster Than Copyright Law?" 42 Santa Clara L. Rev. 967 (2002).

6) Cynthia L. Webb, "Sinking the Pirates of the Internet," Washingtonpost.com, 25 September 2003.

7) Piracy is defined as the amount of business software installed without a license. *See* International Planning and Research Corporation, Eighth Annual BSA Global Software Piracy Study: Trends in Software Piracy 1994-2002 (Business Software Alliance, June 2003), http://global.bsa.org/globalstudy/2003_GSPS.pdf (last visited 9 November 2003).

8) Policymakers are trying to solidify the erratic case law by proposing legislation that clearly legitimizes online licenses. All attempts have failed to date. The Uniform Computer Information Transactions Act was formulated in 1999 to resolve conflicting case law by clearly making clickwrap and shrinkwrap licenses enforceable. Applicable to software and digital content contracts, UCITA was severely criticized because it lacked clarity and would result in much litigation, it failed to protect the interests of licensees and it allowed licensors to expand the scope of their copyright. Its failure was made clear on 1 August 2003 when the National Conference of Commissioners on Uniform State Laws, which actually wrote the model law, withdrew its support.
As of May 2003, efforts have continued to revise Article 2 of the Uniform Commercial Code (UCC) which has been adopted in some form in 50 states. Strenuous critiques have arisen such as: 1) information, including digital information, appears to have been removed from the definition of a good resulting in a possible void in the law for online transactions; and 2) the revisions do not take a stand on delayed disclosure of standard form terms and, in fact, allow acceptance by a consumer of a delayed term, but not through express agreement as is the case under the current UCC 2-207.

the directives have clear weaknesses. In the Information Society Directive 2001/29/EC,[9] which includes the regulation of online copyrights, all but one of the copyright limitations is optional.[10]

Despite increased protection, companies continue to blame digital piracy for their fiscal woes.[11] An accurate accounting of the economic loss is impossible. Independent experts say a direct causal link between piracy and a drop in profits is far-fetched.[12] In fact, money can still be made. Apple computer's iTunes Music Store recently sold 10 million songs at US $.99 each in the first 4 months of operation.[13]

But the piracy hype is having an effect. The resulting loss in the flow of information to the public domain may be significant. Concrete consequences could include: 1) increased concentration and standardization of online industries and products; 2) less innovation and creativity among businesses; and 3) a decreased emphasis on meeting consumer needs.

Legislators have largely ignored these concerns. As online information becomes increasingly protected in favor of the copyright holder, deliberate efforts to ensure that the traditional copyright balance is maintained have become even more urgent.

In this article, I will attempt to describe how copyright holders are using online contracts to increase their copyright. My analysis will concentrate on US law because developments there show what can happen if there is no deliberate control. Ultimately, I hope to foster a debate for change.

---

9) Art. 5 of Directive 2001/29/EC of the European Parliament and of the Council of 22 May 2001 on the harmonization of certain aspects of copyrights and related rights in the information society.

10) Efforts to raise the stakes have intensified. In January 2003, the European Commission introduced a draft proposal to enhance intellectual property enforcement that includes double damages, penal sanctions for intentional infringement and third party liability regardless of knowledge. *See* Proposal for a Directive of the European Parliament and of the Council on Measures and Procedures to Ensure the Enforcement of Intellectual Property Rights: COM (2003), 46 Final, 30 January 2003, at http://europa.eu.int/eurlex/en/com/pdf/2003/com2003_0046en01.pdf (last visited 9 November 2003).

11) For example, Sony recently announced that it will cut 20,000 jobs as part of a plan to save US $3 billion in operating costs by 2006. *See* James Brooke, "Sony Plans To Eliminate 20,000 Jobs Over 3 Years," The New York Times, 29 October 2003, section w, p. 1.

12) Neil Strauss, "Record sales' woes go beyond file swapping; Legal tactics may alienate consumers," The International Herald Tribune, 10 September 2003, p. 11.

13) Amy Harmon, "Music; What Price Music?" The New York Times, 12 October 2003, Arts and Leisure, p. 1.

Welcome to the Digital McWorld

E-commerce comprises a relatively small, but expanding, portion of total sales ranging from .4% to 1.8% throughout most of the US and EU.[14] The amount is more significant in the United Kingdom and Scandinavia. In 2000, total sales in the business sector comprised 5.95% in the United Kingdom and 10% in Sweden.[15] Where the figures are lower, e-commerce is expanding. In the United States, e-commerce retail sales totaled 1.2% in the last four months of 2001. This marks a significant rise from .96% during the same period of the previous year.[16]

Online products range from tangible items such as music, video games and books, to information resources including news, travel reservations and online directories. Businesses use licenses to detail the rights and obligations of the parties. Standard provisions include those that prevent copying and further distribution, disclaim warranties, limit liabilities and remedies, and designate the legal forum for disputes.[17] In such mass market licenses, purchasers must accept terms on a take it or leave it basis.

Online licenses usually appear in two forms: clickwraps or browsewraps. A product with a clickwrap license cannot be used until the purchaser actively assents to the license terms, usually by clicking on an icon or by typing "I accept." Browsewrap licenses are more controversial. A browsewrap license, or a hyperlink to it, normally appears on a website owner's homepage. Although the user is advised not to proceed further if they do not agree to the license terms, nothing prevents the user from accessing the product without first reading the license.

Enthusiasts imagine e-commerce will be conducted on a pay-per-use, per-transaction, per-work basis. Purchasers would be offered the freedom to "negotiate" by picking and choosing license terms such as the number of copies made. Prices would depend on the type of user and the options picked. However, this digital future may be sugarcoated. Online licenses could provide a powerful tool of advanced control in the hands of private business.

---

14) Information Technology Outlook (OECD 2002), pp. 152-3.

15) Id.at 140, 153.

16) Id. at 144.

17) Since this paper is restricted to limitations that impact copyright, general contract law provisions will not be discussed.

The Copyright Balance

The traditional copyright regime of the United States strikes a delicate balance between granting authors incentives to create new works and ensuring a constant flow of free information to stimulate further creativity and the development of knowledge. The Supreme Court explains this rationale: "The limited scope of the copyright holder's statutory monopoly, like the limited copyright duration required by the Constitution, reflects a balance of competing claims upon the public interest: Creative work is to be encouraged and rewarded, but private motivation must ultimately serve the cause of promoting broad public availability of literature, music, and the other arts." Twentieth Century Music Corp. v. Aiken, 422 U.S. 151, 156 (1975).

The United States Constitution mandates the copyright balance by directing Congress: "To promote the ... useful Arts, by securing for limited Times to Authors ... the exclusive Right to their respective Writings." Art. I, §8, cl. 8. The Constitution thus limits the scope of copyright by decreeing that only authors receive protection and only for a limited duration.

Under the 1976 Copyright Act, Congress further refined the copyright monopoly. Protection is extended to authors who create original works, ranging from literature to computer programs, that are fixed in a tangible medium of expression. 17 U.S.C. §102(a). While copyright is provided for the expression of ideas, it does not extend to "any idea, procedure, process, system, method of operation, concept, principle, or discovery." Id., §102(b). As the Supreme Court explains, "Were an author able to prevent subsequent authors from using concepts, ideas, or facts contained in his or her work, the creative process would wither and scholars would be forced into unproductive replication of the research of their predecessors." Harper & Row, Publishers, Inc. v. Nation Enterprises, 471 U.S. 539, 582 (1985).

The statute grants copyright owners the following six exclusive rights: 1) to reproduce their work; 2) to prepare derivative works; 3) to distribute copies by sale, transfer, rental, lease, or lending; 4) to perform publicly; 5) to display the work publicly; and 6) to perform sound recordings publicly. If others want to reproduce, modify, distribute, perform, display or record a work, they must obtain authorization.[18] 17 U.S.C. §106.

Information flows into the public domain in a variety of ways. From the moment of inception, certain components of a work, such as ideas or facts, are not protected and automatically are part of the public domain. Under the first sale doctrine, the copyright holder loses the right to control a buyer of a physical copy of a copyrighted work from lending, reselling or disposing of

18) There are no general moral rights. However, §106(a) provides for the rights of paternity and integrity to creators of visual art. But these rights only last for the author's lifetime and there are many limitations, including for commercial use.

the item. Id., §109(a). Because the duration of most copyrights is the life of the author plus 70 years, all material eventually falls into the public domain. Id., §302(a).

Copyright limitations also allow for exploitation of a work without permission. The most important limitation is fair use. This doctrine authorizes appropriation of a copyrighted work for purposes such as criticism, comment, news reporting, teaching, scholarship or research. Id., §107. The statute mandates fair use to be determined on a case-by-case basis by balancing these factors: 1) the purpose and character of the use; 2) the nature of the copyrighted work; 3) the amount and substantiality of the portion used in relation to the copyrighted work as a whole; and 4) the effect of the use on the potential market for, or value of, the copyrighted work.

Important practices have been upheld under the fair use doctrine. Reverse engineering of a software program has been upheld "if such disassembly provides the only means of access to those elements of the code that are not protected by copyright and the copier has a legitimate reason for seeking such access." Sega Enterprises Ltd. v. Accolade, 977 F.2d 1510, 1518 (9th Cir. 1992)(reverse engineering to make games compatible with the Sega consul is fair use).

If a state law right impinges on federal copyright, preemption can strike down the state law right. Under the supremacy clause of the Constitution: "This Constitution, and the Laws of the United States which shall be made in Pursuance thereof … shall be the supreme Law of the Land." U.S. Const. Art.VI, cl. 2. Within the area of copyright, a state law right will be invalid if: 1) Congress expressly reserves a particular area of the law (express preemption); or 2) a conflict exists between state and federal law (conflict preemption).[19] Rights afforded by contract are governed by state law and can be preempted.

Section 301(a) of the copyright act expressly mandates preemption if the following two-pronged test is satisfied: 1) the work at issue falls within the "the subject matter of copyright;" and 2) the right asserted is "equivalent to any of the exclusive rights" of the copyright holder. 17 U.S.C. §301(a). The general subject matter of copyright is broader than what can be copyright protected. For example, facts fall under the general subject matter of copyright even though they are not copyrightable. If a work is part of the general subject matter of copyright, preemption will only occur if the state law right "is infringed by the mere act of reproduction, performance, distribution or display." Baltimore Orioles, Inc. v. Major League Baseball Players Asso., 805 F.2d 663, 677 (7th Cir. 1986).

---

19) A third type of preemption is when the court determines that congress intended to have exclusive authority over a particular area of the law (field preemption).

Many circuits require the 'extra element' that upholds a state right to be qualitatively different from rights afforded under copyright law. National Car Rental Sys., Inc. v. Computer Assocs. Int'l, Inc., 991 F.2d 426, 431 (8th Cir. 1993). While tortuous interference of contractual relations is often preempted, privacy right violations, trade secret infringements and deceptive trade practices such as false labeling, passing off and fraudulent representation, are generally not preempted because they contain elements that are different in kind from copyright. H.R. Rep. No. 94-1476 (1976).

A state law right that survives express preemption can still be invalid under conflict preemption. The Supreme Court has determined that "[w]hen state law touches upon the area of these federal statutes, it is 'familiar doctrine' that the federal policy 'may not be set at naught, or its benefits denied' by the state law. Sears, Roebuck & Co. v. Stiffel Co., 376 U.S. 225, 229 (1964). To determine conflict preemption, courts often compare the objectives and impact of the state law right with that of copyright to see if there is a clash. *See* Kewanee Oil Co. v. Bicron Corp., 416 U.S. 470 (1974).

The first decision to evaluate the intersection between contract and copyright was Vault Corp. v. Quaid Software Ltd. The 5th Circuit Court of Appeals employed both an express and a conflict preemption analysis to strike down a shrinkwrap license provision that prohibited reverse engineering. The state had passed a law that granted software producers the right to use specific terms in their licenses. The court found conflicts between the state law, upon which the license provision was based, and federal copyright. This included: 1) the state law allowed a perpetual bar on copying, while the federal act provided copyright for a limited duration; 2) the state law allowed a complete bar on copying, while the federal act provided limitations; and 3) the state law protected all works, while the copyright act only protected original works by authors. 847 F.2d 255 (5th Cir. 1988).

Since the Vault decision, courts have began to favor a contract law analysis and failed to correctly apply the preemption doctrine. This failure may have marked the beginning of the fall of the traditional copyright regime.

A Slow Demise

The demise of the traditional copyright balance began with disputes over shrinkwrap licenses that usually accompany off-the-shelf computer software programs. Typically, a sheet of license terms is wrapped in transparent plastic along with computer disks. Buyers allegedly signify acceptance by tearing open the plastic wrap and using the disks. Shrinkwrap licenses, or references to them, can also be printed on the outside of boxes or included in the product box or user manual.[20]

The question facing courts is whether a shrinkwrap license provision is part of the sales contract. The answer turns on when the contract was formed. Courts initially deemed shrinkwrap licenses invalid. In Step-Saver Data Systems Inc. v. Wyse Technology, a dispute arose over the faulty operating system of a computer hardware and software package. 939 F.2d 91 (3[d] Cir. 1991). The plaintiff asserted that the limitation on damages and warranty disclaimer contained in the shrinkwrap license was part of the contract.

The court disagreed. It stated that the parties' conduct had established a contract but that the nature of the terms was unclear. The court then applied Uniform Commercial Code (UCC) §2-207 which is used to discover contract terms in classic battle of the forms cases involving the sale of goods. According to the code, §2-207(1): "A definite and seasonable expression of acceptance or a written confirmation which is sent within a reasonable time operates as an acceptance even though it states terms additional to or different from those offered or agreed upon." In a contract between two merchants as in the case at bar, "(2) such terms become part of the contract unless: (b) they materially alter it." Since the shrinkwrap provisions materially altered the contract and the plaintiff did not expressly agree, the court invalidated the provisions.

Step-Saver was the first decision to strike down a shrinkwrap license under the UCC. In Arizona Retail Sys. v. Software Link, a federal district court applied a different UCC provision. It held that in the initial sale of computer software involving two merchants, receipt of an evaluation diskette through the mail was an offer and opening the envelope constituted acceptance.[21] 831 F. Supp. 759 (D. Ariz. 1993). In this particular instance, the court determined that the shrinkwrap license was part of the contract.

But in all subsequent sales, the contract was formed through agreement on price and quantity over the telephone and consequent shipping or an offer to ship. The shrinkwrap license appeared after the contract was formed and represented a proposal for a modification of the contract. Under UCC §2-209, the warranty disclaimer contained in the shrinkwrap license materially altered the contract and required express assent. Because plaintiff did not expressly agree to the additional term, the provision was held invalid.

A 7th circuit decision drastically changed the debate. ProCD, Inc. v. Zeidenberg was the first dispute since Vault that involved an expansion of the

---

20) *See* Mark A. Lemley, "Intellectual Property and Shrinkwrap licenses," 68 S. Cal. L. Rev. 1239, 1241 (July 1995).

21) The court also had to decide which law to apply. If the product was a service then state contract law applied. But if the product was a good, the UCC applied. Though the law is not clear on the issue, most courts apply the UCC even for software products.

copyright monopoly through contract. The defendant had purchased copies of plaintiff's software program which consisted of listings from 3,000 telephone directories and copyrighted software needed to access the data. A shrinkwrap license that accompanied the software restricted copying of the data to personal use and prohibited any distribution. The defendant took the telephone listings and made the raw data available to Internet users for a lower price. The plaintiff sued for copyright infringement and breach of the shrinkwrap license.

Contrary to the Vault decision, the court began by analyzing the contract. The district court agreed with the Step-Saver and Arizona Retail decisions and stated that regardless of whether the court applied an analysis under UCC §2-207 or §2-209, the defendant, not a merchant, was required to expressly assent to the terms of the shrinkwrap license regardless of whether the contract was materially altered or not. Since the defendant did not assent, the ProCD court held, "[m]ere reference to the terms at the time of initial contract formation does not present buyers an adequate opportunity to decide whether they are acceptable. They must be able to read and consider the terms in their entirety." ProCD, Inc. v. Zeidenberg, 908 F. Supp. 640, 654 (W.D.Wis. 1996).

Even if the shrinkwrap license was valid, the district court preempted plaintiff's breach of contract claim. Employing the two-pronged test under §301 of the Copyright Act, the court found that: 1) the data, though not copyright protected, did fall under the subject matter of copyright; and 2) the rights asserted were equivalent to the exclusive rights of reproduction and distribution. In making its decision, the court opined, "It is ironic that after plaintiff has attained the benefits of copyright law, it wants to prevent others from receiving that same protection. Unfortunately for plaintiff, the rules of the game have not changed. Just as plaintiff had public access to the telephone listings, so do defendants. Plaintiff cannot use a standard form contract to make an end run around copyright law." Id. at 659.

The 7th Circuit Court of Appeals reversed. ProCD, Inc. v. Zeidenberg, 86 F. 3d 1447 (7th Cir. 1996). It pointed out that reference to license terms on the product box at the time of contract formation was indeed sufficient. The court further stated: "Notice on the outside, terms on the inside, and a right to return the software for a refund if the terms are unacceptable ... may be a means of doing business valuable to buyers and sellers alike." Id. at 1451.

The court employed the flexible provision of UCC §2-204(1) on general contract formation to argue that the shrinkwrap license was part of the contract. According to §2-204(1), "A contract for sale of goods may be made in any manner sufficient to show agreement, including conduct by both parties which recognizes the existence of such a contract." The court interpreted the provision to mean: "A vendor, as master of the offer, may invite acceptance by conduct, and may propose limitations on the kind of conduct that constitutes acceptance. ... ProCD proposed a contract that a buyer would accept by *using* the software after having an opportunity to read the license at leisure." ProCD, Inc., 85 F. 3d at 1452.

Turning to the question of preemption, the court agreed that the work fell under the subject matter of copyright. However, it held that contract rights are not equivalent to rights under copyright. Although not specifically spelling out the distinction, the court implied, through the use of prior case law and examples, that the element of promise made a contract qualitatively different. It concluded, "A copyright is a right against the world. Contracts, by contrast, generally affect only their parties; strangers may do as they please."[22]

Online License Validity

The ProCD decision smoothed the way for the enforcement of online licenses. From the beginning, clickwrap licenses were deemed clearly valid. Because the purchaser affirmatively clicks or writes "I agree" to the terms before the product is received, mutual assent is not controversial. Barnett v. Network Solutions, Inc., 38 S.W.3d 200, 203-04 (Tex. Ct. App. 2001)(parties agree there is a contract); Moore v. Microsoft Corp., 741 N.Y.S.2d 91 (N.Y. App. Div. 2002)(license valid because it was prominently displayed on screen and user was required to click "I agree" before software could be installed). I. Lan Sys., Inc. v. Netscout Serv. Level Corp., 183 F. Supp. 2d 328 (D. Mass. 2002)(clickwrap valid under either UCC 2-204 or 2-207).

The binding nature of a clickwrap license has also been held undeniable. Barnett, 38 S.W.3d 200, 203-04 (user bound to clickwrap license because one has obligation to read what one signs and absent fraud is not excused from the consequences).

Browsewrap licenses are more problematic. The issues are whether there is sufficient notice and mutual assent. Although court decisions vary, a certain

---

22) The ProCD decision is not the last word. Within the federal court system, only the 7th circuit recognizes shrinkwrap licenses. *See also* Hill v. Gateway, 105 F.3d 1147 (7th Cir. 1997)(shrinkwrap license enclosed with computer upheld). Some state courts have also validated shrinkwrap licenses. *See* Brower v. Gateway 2000, 676 N.Y.S.2d 569 (N.Y. App. Div. 1998)(shrinkwrap delivered with computer valid); M.A. Mortenson Co. v. Timberline Software Corp.,93 Wa. App. 819 (Wash. Ct. App. 1999)(shrinkwrap license terms of software program part of the contract); Rinaldi v. Iomega Corp., No. 98C-09-064 RRC, 1999 Del. Super. LEXIS 563 (Del. Super. Ct. Sept. 3, 1999)(shrinkwrap included with zip drive valid).
Shrinkwrap licenses remain invalid in the 5th and 3rd circuits. *See* Vault Corp., 847 F.2d 255; Step-Saver, 939 F.2d 91. Although not at the court of appeal level, a 9th circuit district court has also denied the validity of a shrinkwrap license. *See* Arizona Retail, 831 F. Supp. 759. A district court in the 10th circuit recently followed suit. Klocek v. Gateway, Inc., 104 F. Supp. 2d 1332 (D. Kan. 2000)(shrinkwrap enclosed with computer invalid because: 1) UCC 2-207 applies; 2) vendor is not typically master of the offer; and 3) purchaser must expressly accept terms).

pattern based on the ProCD analysis may be emerging in some jurisdictions. For these courts, sufficient notice on a website's initial homepage serves to incorporate license terms imbedded further into the website, just like the reference outside the box in ProCD. If the notice clearly indicates that using the site binds the consumer and the consumer uses the site, then mutual assent is found. *See* Pollstar v. Gigmania, Ltd., 170 F. Supp. 2d 974, 981-82 (E.D. Cal. 2000)(motion to dismiss denied because under 7th circuit case law the license may be arguably valid and enforceable. But the court is concerned that notice appears in small, gray text on a gray background on a linked webpage); Register.com, Inc. v. Verio, Inc., 126 F. Supp. 2d 238 (S.D.N.Y. 2000)(because of the warning: "by submitting to this query, you agree to abide by these terms" there is no question that the user manifested assent); *But see* Specht v. Netscape Communs. Corp.,150 F. Supp. 2d 585 (S.D.N.Y. 2001) aff'd 306 F.3d 17 (2d Cir. 2002)(notice insufficient and downloading the software does not manifest user's assent).

The clearest example of an emerging rule can be found by tracking the progress of Ticketmaster v. Tickets.Com. The defendant copied and deeplinked public domain information from other websites, including from Ticketmaster. Ticketmaster's homepage contained a browsewrap restricting its information to personal use. Notice was placed at the bottom of Ticketmaster's homepage in such a way that without an unusually large computer screen, the user had to scroll down to see it. The district court refused to honor the license because: "Many customers instead are likely to proceed to the event page of interest rather than reading the 'small print.' It cannot be said that merely putting the terms and conditions in this fashion necessarily creates a contract with any one using the web site." No. CV 99-7654 HLH (BQRx), 2000 U.S. Dist. LEXIS 4553, 8 (C.D. Cal. 27 March 2000).

Three years later, Ticketmaster changed its notice by prominently placing a warning on its homepage. Although the court stated that clickwrap licenses provide more legal certainty, it refused to grant summary judgment against a breach of contract claim based on the browsewrap license. Referring to ProCD, the court stated, "a contract can be formed by proceeding into the interior web pages after knowledge (or, in some cases, presumptive knowledge) of the conditions accepted when doing so." Ticketmaster v. Tickets.Com, No. CV99-7654-HLH(VBKx), 2003 U.S. Dist. LEXIS 6483, 10 (C.D. Cal. 6 March 2003).

While the 9th Circuit seems to be leaning towards validation of browsewrap licenses, the 2nd Circuit has refused to validate them. Specht v. Netscape Communs. Corp., 150 F. Supp. 2d 585 (S.D.N.Y. 2001) aff'd 306 F.3d 17 (2d Cir. 2002)(notice insufficient and downloading the software does not manifest user's assent). The district court in this case said, "The case law on software licensing has not eroded the importance of assent in contract formation. Mutual assent is the bedrock of any agreement to which the law will give force. Defendants' position, if accepted, would so expand the definition of assent as to render it meaningless."

Copyright Unbalanced

ProCD is the public domain guardian's nightmare. In one stroke, the decision effectively eliminated the only mechanism that preserves the copyright balance: the preemption doctrine. Other courts have followed suit by refusing to preempt mass market license provisions that expand copyright. *See* Lipsher v. LRP Publs., Inc., 266 F.3d 1305 (8th Cir. 2001)(subscription agreement restricting public domain jury verdicts not preempted because agreement affects only the parties); Information Handling Servs. v. LRP Publs., Inc., No. 00-1859, 2000 U.S. Dist. LEXIS 14531 (E.D. Pa. Sept. 20, 2000)(shrinkwrap license provision prohibiting copying of public domain administrative decisions not preempted); Bowers v. Baystate Techs., 320 F.3d 1317 (Fed. Cir. 2003)(shrinkwrap license prohibiting reverse engineering not preempted because mutual assent and consideration renders the contract claim qualitatively different).

Just as in Vault and ProCD, the license provisions in all three cases: 1) protected data that is expressly non-copyrightable; 2) prohibited all copying; and 3) created a perpetual copyright. Each plaintiff alleged that the state contract right was infringed by an act of reproduction, performance, distribution or display and nothing more. Baltimore Orioles, 805 F.2d 663, 677. But following the ProCD logic that contracts are different, the 8th Circuit Courts of Appeals, the Federal Circuit, and the 3rd Circuit District Court did not preempt the mass market license.

Though other courts have followed its precedent, the ProCD decision has been severely criticized. The court's opinion that contracts are different is based on three cases that are not on point because each contract in question did actually have an extra element and therefore would not have been preempted. *See* Taquino v. Teledyne Monarch Rubber, 893 F.2d 1488, 1496 (5th Cir. 1990)(prohibition against using sale materials for competing business in exclusive dealer agreement not preempted); Acorn Structures v. Swantz, 846 F.2d 923, 926 (4th Cir. 1988)(implicit promise to pay for architectural plans or building materials not preempted); National Car Rental Sys., Inc. v. Computer Assocs. Int'l, Inc., 991 F.2d 426, 433 (8th Cir. 1993)(prohibition using software program for third parties for payment not preempted).

Moreover, the concrete examples the court mentions, such as if the preemption doctrine applied the promise to return a rented videotape would not survive scrutiny and neither would trade secret infringement, are similarly incorrect and unpersuasive.[23]

An equally faulty contract analysis compounds the problem. The court acts as if the contract in question is the product of an individual negotiation between two equal parties. But it is a mass market license in which the buyer must either accept the terms or return the product. In fact, returning an item could prove difficult or downright impossible. Stores often refuse to accept returns once a package has been opened. Although the court says that the shrinkwrap's restrictions are applied against an individual party, its mass market nature makes it effectively apply against the world. In such a context, one would expect even more protection than that given in the cases of Step-Saver and Arizona Retail which involved licenses between merchants.

Instead, the ProCD court further weakened the buyer's power by making the vendor the master of the offer. In most consumer purchases, however, price lists and catalogues are invitations to sell, not offers. The buyer, by ordering the product, is considered the offeror. The seller, by shipping or offering to ship, is deemed the offeree. But this fact did not stop the court which concluded: "Wisconsin [the state in question] would not let the buyer pick and choose among terms. Terms of use are no less a part of 'the product' than are the size of the database and the speed with which the software compiles listings. Competition among vendors, not judicial revision of a package's contents, is how consumers are protected in a market economy." ProCD, Inc., 85 F. 3d at 1453.

It is not clear that competition among vendors always protects consumers. It may protect the copyright balance even less. Even in the best of circumstances, it is unlikely that individual consumers will challenge license provisions that expand copyright. To the individual, the stakes do not seem high and the erosion of copyright is barely apparent. Thus, when it comes to works that fall under the subject matter of copyright, the need for a coordinated effort to preserve the copyright balance may be even more critical.

The Economics of Copyrighted Works

The rationale behind the ProCD decision is primarily economic. The court explained that the package of 3,000 telephone directories cost US $10 million to create. To sell its product, the plaintiff decided to price discriminate by

---

23) The court also failed to analyze the case under the doctrine of conflict preemption. As the Supreme Court has stated, "The most fundamental axiom of copyright law is that "no author may copyright his ideas or the facts he narrates." Feist Publications v. Rural Telephone Service, Co., 499 U.S. 340, 344-5 (1991). Clearly any license that prohibits the copying of facts touches on an area of copyright law and conflicts with congress' decision to make facts automatically part of the public domain.

charging a lower price to individual consumers than to businesses. The court asserted that in order to charge that lower price, the plaintiff needed to control arbitrage. Rather than provide an inferior product with, for example, data that was older, the plaintiff introduced a license to restrict the data to private use and to prohibit its distribution. Without the license, the court argued that a higher price would have to be charged to recoup investment costs. Consumers would lose as a result.

The court thought the issue should be resolved through market mechanisms. But should copyrighted works and public domain material be treated just like any other commodity? Advocates of private ordering believe that vesting the copyright owner with full control over their work increases the value of information. When information has a higher value, there will be greater production and improved distribution of better quality information. Ultimately, consumers will benefit.[24]

But public goods may require different treatment. Works under the subject matter of copyright clearly possess features of a public good. One characteristic is that no matter how many people exploit the good, it will not be exhausted. Due to its inexhaustibility, the cost of such a product could reach zero. Incentives to encourage private production must thus be created. Even if companies are motivated to make a public good, subsequent free riding could discourage further production.

By granting a limited monopoly, the traditional copyright regime provides an incentive to create copyrighted works. It also curbs free riding. But the copyright monopoly is limited so that works can ultimately flow into the public domain. This flow of free information becomes even more critical in the context of copyrighted works because they form the basic building blocks of creativity and the development of knowledge.

The ProCD court argues that price discrimination benefits the consumer because it promotes greater product availability to more people at a lower price. Its economic forecast may be short-term. A license provision against reverse engineering, such as that upheld by Bowers v. Baystate Techs., highlights some of the problems. 320 F.3d 1317 (Fed. Cir. 2003). Reverse engineering is considered fair use. The rationale behind this policy is that other companies need to reverse engineer in order to create compatible products. Since reverse engineering is difficult, the original maker is given a short respite from any potential competition on the production of compatible goods.

But if the Bower decision becomes industry standard, there may be a decrease in innovation and creativity. Smaller, more creative companies with less money may refrain from reverse engineering because the potential

---

24) Joel R. Reidenberg, "Lex Informatica: The Formulation of Information Policy Rules Through Technology," 76 Tex. L. Rev. 553 (February 1998).

liability costs could be deadly. Bigger companies, who have the ability to negotiate for source code, create new products from scratch or soften the threat of potential liability, may have more chances of surviving. This could result in a concentration of bigger companies whose products become more standardized and are less reflective of true consumer needs.

The prohibitions against using public domain data may result in a similar decrease in creativity, increase in standardization and less concern about meeting consumer needs. The ProCD case provides a good illustration. In the wake of the decision, the court mentioned that a company could still start from scratch and spend US $10 million to create a similar database. However, the cost may be prohibitive. If such license provisions continue to be valid, there will be fewer companies that can enter into the market to produce the product. Once again the ultimate result could be an increase in bigger companies whose products are more standardized and display less concern for consumer needs.

The Future

The ease of digital copying has created a panic among copyright holders and a consequent need to better protect works that are the subject matter of copyright. However, the ProCD case highlights a number of problems in the US law. In the short-term, upholding contract licenses that expand copyright may seem like a good answer. As license provisions chip away at the traditional copyright balance, the long-term effects may be damaging.

Legislative control, such as in the EU, may seem like a more viable solution. For example, in the EU, a contract restriction against reverse engineering is void. In addition, a term of protection of 15 years is extended to the contents of databases in which there has been a substantial investment in obtaining, verifying or presenting the information.[25] But, the *sui generis* right is severely criticized because, among other things, it provides for a copyright of unlimited duration since any substantial change in a database creates the possibility of 15 additional years of protection.

Rather than offering piece-meal solutions that may or may not be viable, it may be wise to evaluate the need to preserve the copyright balance in the digital environment as a whole. Many questions will have to be answered, including whether copyrighted works should be treated as public goods or ordinary commodities, who should control the copyright monopoly and how such regulation should occur. With a deliberate and coordinated effort, the potential remains strong to create a truly dynamic Internet environment which reinforces innovation and variety and which meets consumer needs.

---

25) Art. 10 of Directive 96/9/EC of the European Parliament and of the Council of 11 March 1996 on the legal protection of databases.

Information Obligations in EC E-Commerce Law

by Geraint Howells and Annette Nordhausen

1. Introduction

Information obligations are become an ever more important issue in EC E-Commerce Law. All the Directives dealing with this area include such obligations. Whenever such Directives apply and so long as the contract is not explicitly exempted the supplier has to provide the consumer with prescribed information.[1] The general Roman law principle *Emptor curiosus esse debet* (the contracting parties should be concerned enough to make sure they have all important information before concluding the contract),[2] though originally found in all continental European jurisdictions is not being preserved any more in the recent European law developments.[3] The reasons for this are various. One is the development and integration of consumer protection in the Treaty. Others result from technical developments, which make it generally more difficult to understand products and their possible impact. Distance and electronic marketing give rise to their own rationales for information provision given that the consumer is dealing with a remote trader, whom he may know little about and at least needs to have contact details of the trader and information about the product or services being supplied.

A chronological view shows that information obligations in the relevant Directives become more and more detailed and more and more demanding.

---

1) A. R. Lodder / M. B. Voulon, "Intelligent agents and the information requirements of the Directives on distance selling and e-commerce" I.R.L.C.T. 2002, 277; A. Rose, *Distance Selling and the Internet*, Paisner I.P.B. 1997, 12; R. Lawson, "E-Commerce and distance selling", C.S.R. 2002, 94; J. Hornle, "Germany – distance selling – information requirements and withdrawal right" E.B.L. 2002, 14; J. Newton, "Distance selling: keeping the customer in the know" E.B.L. 2001, 16.

2) Möllers, JZ 2002, 121, 129.

3) Fleischer, ZEuP 2000, 772; S. Grundmann, "Privatautonomie im Binnenmarkt", JZ 2000, 1133; generally on information duties in EU law: S. Kind, *Die Grenzen des Verbraucherschutzes durch Information – aufgezeigt am Teilzeitwohnrechtegesetz*, (Berlin, 1997); N. Reich, "Verbraucherpolitik und Verbraucherschutz im Vertrag von Amsterdam", VuR 1999, 3, 5ff; P. Rott, "Informationspflichten in Fernabsatzverträgen als Paradigma für die Sprachenproblematik im Vertragsrecht" ZvglRWiss 98 (1999), 382; P. Mankowski, "Fernabsatzrecht: Information über das Widerrufsrecht und Widerrufsbelehrung bei Internetauftritten" CR 2001, 767.

This is not only due to the regulation of increasingly complicated products and services (such as financial services), but also because of a desire to learn from practical experience with the earlier directives. This is perfectly understandable from the legislator's point of view, but nevertheless the question arises if this is appropriate to achieve its main aim of improving consumer protection and enhancing the internal market for consumers. This paper will describe the existing EC legislation on information obligations and examine the extent to which it is suitable.

Four main issues are relevant for answering this question.

First, what information should be given? Only the right – relevant – information given to the consumer can be of use for the consumer.

Second, how much information should be given? Consumers can only deal with a limited amount of information at a time and an information overload may have contrary effects to those intended. If a consumer is confronted with too much information he might not take any of the information given into account. In this case the information would not serve any of the aims of information obligations. Indeed, too much information can sometimes simply lull consumers into a false sense of confidence that the product is well regulated.

Third, when should the information be provided? The way consumers will take information into account will vary depending on the time the information is given. If all information is given before the consumer can enter into a contract, much of this information will not be relevant for the consumer at the time he is confronted with and the most likely reaction is to ignore it. If all information is provided after the contract is concluded (or even completed), the consumer will generally feel bound to the contract and not be particularly interested the information given to him at that time. Therefore, the information needs of consumers need to be divided into sub-categories, depending on the time the information is required.

Fourth, what is the appropriate style and means for the information to be provided? Especially with the use of different means of distance communication the style and the means used to communicate the information is important. The effect information has on the recipient is determined by the way the information is presented. This includes the technical means used. Generally, style and means of information obligations have to correspond with the style and means of the contract.

A fundamental overarching question however remains as to the aims of information obligations in general – why are we providing information? The EC legislator seems to intend information to fulfil the dual functions of both acting as an instrument to change behaviour by enabling the consumer to make an informed choice and also serving as a record of the agreement.

Finally, if information can fulfil all aims and change behaviour, the question arises whether information can replace regulation and give businesses and consumers more freedom when contracting. If the consumer can make informed choices it might not be necessary to protect him by regulation.

2. Relevant EC Directives

Before all these questions can be examined the existing legal regulation will be described. So far, three directives regulate information obligations in EC E-Commerce Law. The first directive, the Directive 1997/7/EC on protection of consumers in respect of distance contracts ("distance selling") has a rather broad approach and regulates all distance contracts regardless of the technical means used. Directive 2000/31 on electronic commerce ("e-commerce") regulates specifically the use of electronic communication and does – in contrast to the Distance Selling Directive – not only govern business to consumer transactions, but also business to business transactions.[4] The third directive in chronological order is Directive 2002/65 on distance marketing of consumer financial services ("financial services"). This directive governs only business to consumer contracts and is a specific regulation for the distance marketing of a group of products, namely, financial services. Financial services had been exempted from the general Distance Selling Directive for a number of reasons, and been left for regulation in a specific directive. After a long legislative process the directive includes very elaborated information obligations, which can only partly be explained by the specific nature of financial services. Contrary to both of the other directives, this directive tries to follow the maximum harmonisation (full harmonisation) approach, which guarantees a high level of harmonisation but leaves hardly any scope for the Member States in implementing the directive into their national law. However, as regards information obligations it had to accept that pending further harmonisation member states could maintain or introduce more stringent rules on prior information so long as the provisions were in conformity with Community law[5].

3. Types of information

All three relevant directives distinguish as to the form of the required information. The Distance Selling and Financial Services Directive require

---

4) Albeit in a less mandatory way, as most of the provisions are generally applicable but allow an opt-out agreement between business parties.

5) Art. 4(2).

pre-contractual and contractual information and this distinction not only affects the form, but also the time the information has to be given. Pre-contractual information includes all information a consumer needs before making an informed decision and obviously has to be provided before the conclusion of a contract. Contractual information can be supplied later and shall give information in a more detailed form, providing information needed after the contract has been concluded as well as acting as a record.

In addition to these categories the E-Commerce Directive requires "General Information". This is geared to the specific medium and ensures that information that may be needed even before a pre-contractual stage is available to the user – this is a provision which is generally applicable to all contracts, not only consumer contracts. General information obligations also have to be provided before any steps to enter into a contract are undertaken. This information can therefore be classed as pre-contractual, but unlike the pre-contractual obligations in the Distance Selling and Financial Services Directives, does not necessarily relate to a contract and is more concerned with the identity of the service provider. The E-Commerce Directive also regulates other specific information obligation for commercial communications.

4. General Information

General Information is required by article 5 of the E-Commerce Directive. This information has to be given regardless of whether the customer is actually ordering or considering whether to conclude a contract or not. This shall give the user (not only the consumer) essential information at a very early stage. The general information obligations include the name of the service provider and their geographic address. This explicitly excludes PO Box addresses. The user shall have the opportunity to see with whom he is dealing or find out more about the service provider. In addition, details about means for rapid contact and communication, including an e-mail address, must be provided. This shall ensure that the user can communicate with the service provider directly and effectively. The requirement to provide an e-mail address causes the service provider to incur no additional costs and it ensures that the user can communicate with the provider through the same medium he has chosen for offering his products or services. The service provider also has to inform about any details of trade registry entries, professional details and VAT details. Any indication of price should be clear and unambiguous and state whether tax and delivery costs are included.

5. Commercial Communications

According to article 6 of the E-Commerce Directive all commercial communications have to be clearly identifiable as such and the person on whose behalf the commercial communications are made has to be identified. Special requirements exist for promotional offers, competitions and games. These have to be clearly identifiable and the conditions have to be easily accessible and clearly and unambiguously presented.

Unsolicited commercial communications are generally permitted by this Directive, but the Member States have to ensure that opt-out registers exist and are respected. All unsolicited commercial communications have to be clearly identifiable as soon as the user receives them. For the most common unsolicited communications – e-mail Spam – this means that the identification as Spam must be obvious in the heading. The user can then decide if he wants to download the message or could also introduce a Spam-filter and avoid unsolicited commercial communications completely. In practice this quite often causes problems, as some desired e-mails get blocked or deleted whereas other Spam still reaches the user's mailbox. The Privacy in Electronic Commerce Directive[6] has now imposed a requirement of prior consent for e-mail commercial communications.

6. Pre-contractual Information

A. Distance Selling Directive

Article 4 of the Distance Selling Directive requires this information to be given "in good time prior to the conclusion of any distance contract". The latest possible point of time for providing this information is just before the last step necessary for the binding conclusion of the contract, depending on the national laws.

The information required is the following:

1. *The identity of the supplier (and additionally the address if prior payment is required):*
   This is particular important for contracts concluded over the Internet. Unfortunately the address is only required if prior payment is required and not in all cases. For contracts concluded over the Internet usually payment by credit card is offered (or required). Even if the supplier

---

6) Directive 2002/58/EC, OJ 2002 L201/37, art.13.

promises to charge the amount only after delivery, this should be considered as prior payment as it is completely at the discretion of the supplier.

2. *The main characteristics of the goods or services:*
   This requirement is fairly obvious and will in most Member States be essential for the contract (*essentialia negotii*), but this information has also to be given prior to the conclusion of the contract.
3. *The price of the goods or services including all taxes:*
   The price is also an essential issue for the consumer and needs to be as detailed as possible. As the price has to be mentioned including all taxes, the taxes have to be added to the price of the goods or services and cannot be noted separately or as a percentage rate. If a supplier is contracting with consumers as well as businesses he may show the taxes separately.
4. *Delivery costs, where appropriate:*
   Delivery costs are another crucial issue in distance contracts and depending on the goods or services (and their origin) may be a high percentage of cost of the goods or even higher.
5. *The arrangement for payment, delivery or performance:*
   Payment and delivery arrangements are also important at the pre-contractual stage. In an extreme case an arrangement for delivery could be that the consumer has to collect the goods at the supplier's premises – and the consumer ought to be informed about this before he enters into a contract.
6. *The existence of a right of withdrawal, except in the cases referred to in Article 6 (3):*
   The right of withdrawal is one of the main issues of the Directive and the consumer has to be informed about the existence prior to the conclusion of the contract. The information about the existence does not include the information about the details of the right and also not the information that a right of withdrawal does not exist for the particular contract. The cases referred to in Article 6 (3) are cases in which the consumer may not exercise the right of withdrawal, unless the parties have agreed otherwise, and cover situations like goods made to the consumer's specification, products dependant on fluctuations in the financial market or where performance of a service contract has begun with the consumer's consent.
7. *The cost of using the means of distance communication, where it is calculated other than at the basic rate:*
   The normal communication costs (i.e. telephone) are foreseeable for the consumer and beyond the supplier's knowledge and control, whereas concerning other costs (i.e. special phone numbers or costs for using databases which will be charged through the telephone companies) the

consumer needs information to enable him to decide if he wants to enter in the contract in question.

8. *Where appropriate, the minimum duration of the contract in the case of contracts for the supply of products or services to be performed permanently or recurrently:*
   This ensures that the consumer is informed about the fact that the contract runs over a longer period as well as the length of that period. Where other provisions exist (i.e. for standard contract terms) and the minimum length is generally restricted, these provisions remain in force. The notice period does not necessarily have to be mentioned at the pre-contractual stage.

All information has – according to article 4 (2) – to be given in a clear and comprehensible manner, appropriate according to the means of distance communication used. This means that the information can – and shall – be given differently on a website, for instance, as compared to during a telephone conversation. The language in which these information have to be given is not specified and therefore it must not necessarily be the first language of the consumer, but the information must also be given with due regard to the principles of good faith in commercial transactions[7]. Information given in a language other than the first language of the consumer (or his country of residence), the language of the origin of the supplier, a commonly understood language or the language of the advertisement or the contract will be against these principles[8].

B. Directive on Financial Services

Like the Distance Selling Directive, the Directive on Financial Services requires certain information to be provided to the consumer *in good time before the conclusion of the contract.* Compared to the general Distance Selling Directive a lot more information has to be provided and all the information has to be given in good time before the conclusion of the contract and in a way appropriate to the means of distance communication used. Article 5 (1) also requires in the case of financial services that this information be given in writing or on another durable medium before the consumer is bound by any contract or offer. This obligation to provide it in writing or a

---

7) P. Mankowski, "Verbraucherschutzrechtliche Widerrufsbelehrung und Sprachrisiko," VuR 2001, 359.

8) N. Reich / A. Nordhausen, *Verbraucher und Recht im elektronischen Geschäftsverkehr*, Nos. 37ff, 112ff; P. Mankowski, "Verbraucherschutzrechtliche Widerrufsbelehrung und Sprachrisiko", VuR 2001, 359.

durable medium is, due to the complexity of financial services, considerably earlier than for the general Distance Selling Directive. The wording "before the consumer is bound by any distance contract or offer" seems to imply that the information has to be communicated before the consumer can make an offer and it could be argued that this communication of the information is a necessary pre-requisite for the conclusion of a contract. This argumentation would be very much in favour of the consumer, but it would make redundant Article 11 of the Directive, which requires the Member States to provide appropriate sanctions for the event of non-compliance with provisions pursuant to the Directive. One sanction suggested in Article 11 is the right for the consumer to cancel the contract at any time. As this is only one possible option for sanctions, it does not exclude the possibility for the Member States to include the information duties as one of the essential requirements for a contract (essentialia negotii), but neither is it required. In certain cases it might also be disadvantageous for the consumer and therefore incompatible with the aim of the Directive. The interest of the consumer might be to adhere to the contract although the information obligations have not been properly fulfilled if he is generally satisfied with the conditions of the contract or may even have made a profit.

At any time during the contractual relationship the consumer shall be entitled to receive, at his request, the contractual terms and conditions on paper[9]. Indeed, the consumer should be given a choice of the means of distance communication used, unless it is incompatible with the contract or the nature of the financial service.

Article 3 requires the consumer to be provided with information in a clear and comprehensible manner in any way appropriate to the means of distance communication used, concerning the supplier, the financial service, the distance contract and redress. The commercial purpose of the contract must always be made clear and all communication must follow the principles of good faith in commercial transactions and the principles governing the protection of persons unable to give consent, such as minors.

The consumer has to be provided with detailed information by the means of distance communication used and this should be confirmed on paper or another durable medium. The information required includes information about the supplier, the financial service itself, the distance contract and redress mechanisms. The specific information required shall be described in detail below.

(i) Information about the Supplier

The information to be given about the supplier includes:

---

9) Art. 5 (3).

1. The identity and the main business of the supplier, the geographical address at which the supplier is established and any other geographical address relevant for the customer's relations with the supplier. For the geographical address a post box address alone will not be sufficient, although the supplier can of course use a post box address for the correspondence.
2. The identity of any representative of the supplier established in the consumer's Member State of residence and the relevant geographical addresses. This shall ensure that the consumer can contact local subsidiaries whenever they exist and allows the consumer to do so in the language of his state of residence and at low costs.
3. If the supplier is registered in a trade or similar public register the registration number and the public register. This is required in most Member States for offline transactions as well and may provide the consumer with more relevant information about the service provider if the consumer wishes to obtain these information.
4. If the activity is subject to an authorisation scheme, the particulars of the relevant supervisory authority.

(ii) Information about the Financial Service

The information about the financial service itself requires:

1. A description of its main characteristics.
2. The total price to be paid by the consumer. This must include all fees, charges and expenses as well as all taxes, including the taxes paid via the supplier. If it is not possible to name the exact amount, the basis for the calculation of the price has to be indicated to enable the consumer to verify the price.
3. If special risks are involved in specific features or instruments, or if the price is dependent on fluctuations in the financial markets outside the supplier's control, these risks have to be mentioned expressly.
4. A notice of the possibility that other taxes or costs may exist that are not paid via the supplier or imposed by him.
5. Any limitations of the period for which the information is valid.
6. The arrangements for payment and for performance.
7. If any specific additional cost is charged for using the means of distance communication, these costs have to be specified.

(iii) Information about the Distance Contract

The information to be given about the distance contract concerns:

1. The existence or absence of a right of withdrawal according to Article 6 of the Directive. If such right exists, its duration and the conditions for exercising it, including the information on the amount, which the consumer may be required to pay for services provided before withdrawal. The conditions for this payment are specified in Article 7 (1). Information has also to be given in appropriate cases about the non-exercise of the right of withdrawal. In contrast to the general Distance Selling Directive the consumer has to be informed not only about the existence of a right of withdrawal, but also if for that particular contract a right of withdrawal does not exist. This ensures that the consumer cannot be misled by any general information he might have about a right of withdrawal and assume that he will benefit from it, whereas it is excluded for the specific contract.
2. If the financial services to be performed permanently or recurrently, the minimum duration of the distance contract has to be specified.
3. If the parties have any rights to terminate the contract early or unilaterally by virtue of the terms of the distance contract, the terms and conditions, including any penalties imposed by the contract have to be notified. This covers the right of termination for the parties, the consumers as well as the suppliers.
4. Practical instructions for the exercise of the right of withdrawal, including the address to which the notification of a withdrawal should be sent.
5. The Member State or States whose laws are a basis for the establishment of relations with the consumer prior to the conclusion of the distance contract.
6. The law applicable to the distance contract and/or the competent court.
7. The language or languages, in which the contractual terms and conditions, and the pre contractual information are supplied. Furthermore the language or languages in which the supplier undertakes to communicate during the duration of the distance contract should be specified. The latter needs the agreement of the consumer.

(iv) Information about Redress

The information about redress includes the following:

1. Whether or not there is an out-of-court complaint and redress mechanism for the consumer, as well as the methods for accessing to it.
2. The existence of guarantee funds or other compensation arrangements other those required by the EU-law for deposit guarantee schemes and investor compensation schemes.

For all means of distance communication, other than telephony communication, the full information requirements have to be fulfilled before the consumer is bound by an offer. Article 3 (3) regulates the special information duties for telephony communications. The use of the telephone is regulated specially as fulfilment of the information requirements over the telephone are especially difficult. Reading out all information requirements to the consumer would – especially with the amount of information required for financial services – be completely meaningless to the consumer and would probably in practice exclude telephony communications completely. During telephony communications the supplier has to provide the consumer with the following information:

1. The supplier has to make his identity and the commercial purpose of the call explicitly clear at the beginning of any conversation with the consumer. The consumer has to agree to the use of the telephone for the communication. This provision allows the use of telephony communications generally, including the so called cold-calling but ensures that the consumer is informed about the commercial purpose and the identity of the supplier and has to consent to any further communication by phone. As the Directive follows the maximum harmonisation the Member States have, in contrast to the general Distance Selling Directive, no possibility to prohibit cold-calling for the marketing of financial services, other than the prohibitions on unsolicited communications found in Article 10 and other EC Directives.
2. Only if the consumer consents to the communication generally and the use of the telephone explicitly does specified information have to be given on:
    a. The identity of the person calling and his link with the supplier.
    b. The main characteristics of the financial service.
    c. The total price to be paid by the consumer, including all taxes paid via the supplier. When the calculation of the exact price is not possible the basis for the calculation of the price has to be given to enable the consumer to verify it.
    d. Notice of the possibility that other taxes and/or costs may exist which are not paid via the supplier.
    e. The existence or absence of a right of withdrawal. If a right of withdrawal exists the consumer also has to be informed about its duration and the conditions to exercise it, including the information on any payment for services, which have already been provided before the withdrawal.
3. Furthermore, the supplier has to inform the consumer about other information, its nature and that it is available on request.

4. In any case the supplier has to provide the full information according to Article 5 on paper or another durable medium either in good time before the consumer is bound by any contract or offer or, if the contract has – on the consumer's request – been concluded before these requirements could possibly be fulfilled, immediately after the conclusion of the contract.

Article 4(1) of the Directive also requires additional information to be provided where this is required by other EU-law provisions require prior information additional to the information requirements of the Directive. Article 4 (2) allows the Member States to maintain or introduce more stringent provisions on prior information requirements as long as these requirements are in conformity the Community law.[10] The Member States have to communicate any provisions requiring additional information to the Commission and the Commission shall communicate this information to suppliers and consumers to enable them to comply with these requirements. This provision is an exemption from the general maximum harmonisation approach of the Directive, but the exemption is restricted only to more stringent information requirements and only pending further harmonisation. This stresses the maximum harmonisation approach underpins the philosophy of the Financial Services Directive and has to be read in conjunction with Article 20, which requires a review following the implementation of the directive and a report to be presented before April 2006. This review and the report shall examine the impact of the directive and in particular the effect of the information requirements and the right of withdrawal.

C. E-Commerce Directive

In addition to the general information obligations in article 5, the E-Commerce Directive has pre-contractual information requirements in article 10. The obligations arising from article 10 of the E-Commerce Directive are generally applicable for business-to-consumer as well as business-to-business transactions, although in business-to-business transactions the parties can agree to exclude all or certain information obligations. In business-to-consumer transactions an exemption exists for e-mail or equivalent individual communication. The case of individual communication between the business and the consumer viewed as equivalent to individual negotiations in the offline

10) I.e. for German law see the comprehensive analysis: S. Abegglen, *Die Aufklärungspflichten in Dienstleistungsbeziehungen, insbesondere im Bankgeschäft*, (Bern, 1995); regarding Standard Contract Terms: P. Derleder / A. Pallas, "Vertragsschluss und AGB-Einbeziehung im kreditwirtschaftlichen Distanzgeschäft" ZIP 1999,1285.

world. The consumer will either have some knowledge about the business or be more likely to inquire.

Information must be provided on:

1. The different technical steps to conclude a contract.
   This requirement is not only an information obligation, but also of a completely new nature. In contrast to the offline environment this requires the supplier to explain not only the technical steps, but their legal implications as they relate to the process of contract formation. Although the consumer will generally be more familiar with the mechanisms of the conclusion of contracts in the offline environment, this is not true for all consumers and is certainly not usually the position in international consumer contracts where an equivalent requirement does not exist.
2. Whether the concluded contract is filed and accessible for the consumer.
3. Technical means for identification and correction of input errors.
4. The languages offered for the conclusion of a contract.
5. Relevant codes of practice and their electronic accessibility.
6. Contract terms and general conditions have to be available and storable. This will also include allowing the consumer to print the terms and conditions.

7. Contractual Information

Article 5 of the Distance Selling Directive requires that a written confirmation of the information has to be provided to the consumer.[11] In all cases save the right of withdrawal this is not restricted to writing, but can either be given in writing or on another durable medium available and accessible to the consumer. This includes other forms than old-fashioned writing on paper, and would certainly cover floppy or compact discs. The wording of the Directive "the consumer must receive" should be interpreted as it being the supplier's duty to ensure that the consumer receives the information. One would therefore think that it would not be sufficient if the supplier merely allows or ask the consumer to download the information from the website and save it on his computer or sends an e-mail that must be saved. The Distance Selling Directive does not define durable medium, but the Financial Services Directive's definition does indeed imply that the onus can be placed on the consumer, it states:

---

11) E. Madden, "A safe distance?", G.L.S.I. 2002, 14 (Gazette of the Law Society for Ireland).

"'durable medium' means any instrument which enables the consumer to store information addressed personally to him in a way accessible for future reference for a period of time adequate for the purposes of the information and which allows the unchanged reproduction of the information stored."

Recital 20 makes it clear that durable medium includes floppy discs, CDs, DVDs and the hard drive of the consumer's computer, but it goes on to say that it does not include Internet websites (unless they fulfil the criteria contained in the definition of durable medium). Ironically, as we discuss below, some definitions of writing are so broad as to include representation on a web-site. Of course the fact the consumer must receive this information means that the trader will be at risk, unless he puts in place measures to ensure proof of receipt of the information, such as checking a box on a web-site conforming information has been read.

The time for the written confirmation is the time of delivery at the latest. Again, the language is not regulated but following the general rules it should be the language of the language of the negotiations[12].

The information to be provided are the pre-contractual information required in article 4 (1) (a) to (f) and in addition:

1. The conditions and procedures for exercising the right of withdrawal, including possible exemptions
2. The geographical address of the place of business of the supplier to which the consumer may address any complaints
3. Information on after-sales services and existing guarantees
4. The notice period for contracts for unspecified duration or a duration exceeding one year.

Excluded are services supplied on only one occasion which are performed through a means of distance communication and invoiced by the operator of the communication means, but the consumer must still be able to obtain the geographical address of the place of business to which he can address any complaints. This information shall enable the consumer to exercise the right of withdrawal without further investigation.

The Financial Services Directive requires all pre-contractual information to be provided as contractual information on paper or another durable medium available and accessible to the consumer in good time before the consumer is bound by any distance contract or offer (article 5). The E-Commerce Directive does not specifically require written confirmation but as all E-Commerce contracts are distance contracts the requirements arising from the Distance Selling Directive apply for E-Commerce contracts as well.

---

12) N. Reich / A. Nordhausen, *Verbraucher und Recht im elektronischen Geschäftsverkehr*, Nos. 37ff, 112ff.

8. Analysis

So how do EC E-commerce information obligations fare when judged against the questions we posed at the start of this essay? It will be remembered these concerned the nature and quantity of the information, when it was given and the style and means by which it was communicated. Of course these questions overlap and also relate to the more fundamental question of why the information is being supplied. The general thrust of our argument is that to impact on the consumer's decision-making process the policy with regard to the amount of information should be that "less is more".[13] This leads us to conclude that priority should be given to flagging up key information in a prominent manner. This does not mean that we oppose additional information being made available. Indeed we think detailed information providing an accurate record is important to help the parties organise their ongoing relationship and assist when disputes arise. It is a question of when that information can most effectively be provided, or perhaps more accurately the prominence that should be given to key information.

Psychologists suggest that the average person can only digest around seven chunks of information.[14] Certainly the Financial Services Directive requires far more than that to be provided and the overlay of E-Commerce and distance selling directives simply adds to the burden. That said, all the information required to be given can be viewed as useful and indeed the information requirements in the Financial Services Directive do directly address many of the special issues raised by cross-border sales. It is also desirable that the majority of the information is provided before the consumer is bound, for although there will often be the legal right to cancel the contract there are psychological barriers to exercising that right.[15] What is probably be needed is to decide what information is key to the consumer's decision to contract for those goods or services, with that trader at that price on those conditions and group these together and present them in a prominent manner. The US Truth in Lending Act uses the so-called Schumer 'honesty' box to bring together key information. Interestingly, in the UK it is currently, being

---

13) B. Wendlandt, "EC Directives on Time-Sharing and for self-employed commercial agents – Apples, Oranges and the Core of the Information Overload Problem" in *Information Rights and Obligations: A Challenge for Party Autonomy and Transactional Fairness, G.Howells, A Janssen and R. Schulze (eds) (Ashgate, forthcoming)* quoting a German thesis by Kind (see footnote 3).

14) G. Miller, "The Magical Number Seven, Plus or Minus Two: Some Limits on Our Capacity for Processing Information" (1956) 63 *The Psychological Review* 81.

15) *P. Rekaiti* and *R. Van den Bergh*, "Cooling-Off Periods in the Consumer Laws of the EC Member States. A Comparative Law and Economics Approach." (2000) JCP 371.

recognised that our extensive information obligations in consumer credit are not providing effective assistance to consumers. There have been calls for summary boxes, both in relation to credit cards[16] and credit contracts generally.[17] We are not yet in a position to prescribe what the core terms should be, but we can detect that EC E-Commerce information obligations have fallen into the trap of believing the consumer is better protected simply by increasing the list of information that has to be provided. This list has grown with little discrimination between the relative importance of the information being provided. This extensive list of information should indeed probably be given at some point to the consumer. It should also probably be available for the consumer to peruse. In this respect the internet has the advantage of making a lot information potentially available to consumers at little cost or inconvenience and in a non-intrusive manner by using links on websites. Nevertheless, at the early stages of contracting the focus should be on identifying key information and prominently drawing these to the consumer's attention.

One important contribution of EU law to consumer protection has been to underline the transparency principle whereby information must be provided in both a clear and comprehensible manner.[18] This is central to the Unfair Terms in Consumer Contracts Directive[19] and is supported by the Directives discussed above, i.e. the Distance Selling Directive requires information to be provided in a "clear and comprehensible manner". What is more at issue is the method by which the information has to be communicated. In particular, to what extent can the requirements that information should be provided in writing or another durable medium be satisfied by electronic communications or web-sites?

We noted above that whilst the Distance Selling Directive gives the option for most information to be given either in writing or another durable medium, it insists that the right of withdrawal must be given in writing only. This might suggest that writing is a more demanding standard than durable medium and might be thought to require the writing be on paper. This is not, however, the mainstream view in the UK. The Interpretation Act 1978 states:

16) Treasury Select Committee, *Transparency of Credit Card Charges*, HC 124 (2003-4), Ch. 2.

17) White Paper, *Fair, Clear and Competitive*, Cm 6040 (DTI, 2003).

18) H.W. Micklitz, "Principles of Social Justice in European Private Law" (2000) 19 *Yearbook of European Law* 167.

19) Directive 93/13/EEC: OJ 1993 L 95/29.

"Writing includes typing, printing, lithography and other forms of representing or reproducing words in a visible form, and expressions referring to writing are construed accordingly"[20]

In its Advice *Electronic Commerce: Formal Requirements in Commercial Transactions,*[21] the Law Commission believes that e-mail and websites satisfy the test for writing as they are another form of representing or reproducing words in a visible form. They rejected the alternative view that the digital information was not itself visible until a coding convention had been applied to it.[22] Since the writing requirement derives from EC legislation, it is entirely possible that European law might be more demanding. However, when Commission officials speak about the requirement, their views seem as liberal as those of the Law Commission. However, analysis of the Directives might not entirely support this view and in particular the stress on their being a written notice of the right of withdrawal needs to be explained. As currently interpreted even communication via a website might be written communication, although it is probably not a durable medium. The definition of durable medium would seem to include situations where the consumer has to download material himself. Presumably as the information is delivered to the consumer's address and he only has to open it is viewed like getting letters out of the letterbox and opening them. However, it might be questioned whether this is an appropriate analogy. E-mail addresses are less likely to be checked than letterboxes and there is nothing tangible for the consumer to be reminded of the agreement. Although the definition of durable medium might exclude websites, as we have noted these might paradoxically be treated as written sources of information.

The important issue in the e-commerce context is the extent to which it should be possible to fulfil the information obligations entirely electronically using e-mail and websites. In the pre-contractual phase the rules are fairly liberal allowing any means appropriate to the means of distance communication used. If goods are being delivered or services rendered off-line, there seems little hardship in requiring the contractual information to be provided in tangible form. The information can simply be included when the goods are delivered or service carried out. Where goods or services are provided entirely on-line there must equally be reasons to permit information to be provided on-line. However, it is important to note that some information in some contexts is so vital that it needs to be delivered the old-fashioned way

20) Sched. 1.

21) (2001).

22) See C. Reed, *Digital Information Law – Electronic Documents and Requirements of Form*, (Centre for Commercial Law Studies, 1996).

by letter. The UK government, whilst proposing a very flexible regime to facilitate the selling of consumer credit over the internet, will still require cancellation and default notices to be sent by traditional, rather than electronic, means.[23] It recognises the consequences of failing to read these documents can be severe for consumers and it is much more difficult to overlook or destroy postal communications. Although well motivated in terms of consumer protection, this might be thought to be contrary to the E-Commerce Directive's aim of enabling electronic contracting and not covered by a specific exemption. It is perhaps an indication that the Directive was rushed through with inadequate consideration of its implications.[24]

9. Conclusions

Information is a central strategy in protecting consumers in e-commerce. Well- intentioned legislators have compiled a long series of information obligations to the extent that the consumer will often feel bombarded with a surfeit of information. Reflecting on the practical needs of consumers should lead one to question whether consumers can fully take on board all the information available to them. Whilst consumers should have access to this information, they also need key information prominently displayed so that it is at the forefront of their mind when deciding whether to contract. Also further attention needs to be paid to when electronic means of communicating the information can safely be relied upon and when traditional postal communications might continue to serve a useful purpose.

Finally, we note that the internet is a fledgling retail sector. If it is to flourish – and particularly if small businesses are to compete with brand names – consumers need to have confidence that it is well regulated and their interests are secure when purchasing from the internet. The internet will always be a difficult medium to regulate given its global dimension and lack of apparent physical presence. Information obligations form part of a package of consumer protection measures needed to promote confidence in the internet as a shopping medium. However, they are only a part of the picture. Consumers also need substantive right with regards to matters such as privacy, payment protection and performance. They need confidence that regulators have the right powers and resources and are able to co-operate across borders

---

23) *Establishing a Transparent Market*, (DTI, 2003) at 27. See also, *Consultation Document on Enabling and Facilitating the Conclusion of Credit and Hire Agreements Electronically Under the Consumer Credit Act 1974,* (DTI, 2002).

24) R. Brownsword and G. Howells, "Europe's E-Commerce Directive - A Too Hasty Rush to Judgment?" (2000/1) 11 *Journal of Law and Information Science* 77.

to protect their interests. Redress mechanisms need to be easily accessible. Information is only one pillar of this regulatory edifice, but a central one. Certainly anyone shopping on the internet would be well advised to be an active information seeker.[25]

25) See T. Wilhelmsson, "Consumer Images in East and West", in H-W. Micklitz, *Rechtseinheit oder Rechtsvielfalt in Europa? Rolle und Funktion des Verbraucherrechts in der EG und den MOE-Staaten*, (Nomos, 1996).

The European Regulatory Framework for Electronic Signatures:

A Critical Evaluation

by Jos Dumortier[1]

Introduction

On 8 October 1997 the European Commission adopted a Communication "Ensuring security and trust in electronic communication: Towards a European framework for digital signatures and encryption".[2]

One of the conclusions of this Communication was formulated as follows:

> "In order to stimulate electronic commerce and the competitiveness of the European industry as well as to abolish free circulation obstacles and to facilitate the use of digital signatures across national borders, a common framework at Community level is urgently needed and should be put in place at the latest by the year 2000."

In the meeting of the Council of 1 December 1997 the plan of the European Commission was favourably accepted. Following the request of the Council, the European Commission issued two documents: 1) a proposal for a directive on a Community framework for electronic signatures, and 2) a mandate to the European standardization bodies to analyse the needs for standardization activities in relation to electronic signatures·

Two years later, December 1999, the Directive 1999/93/EC "on a Community framework for electronic signatures" was officially adopted and published in the Official Journal in January 2000. [3]

---

1) This contribution is based on the study performed for the European Commission by J. Dumortier, S. Kelm, H. Nilsson, G. Skouma and P. Van Eecke, The Legal and Market Aspects of Electronic Signatures in Europe, available at http://europa.eu.int/information_society/eeurope/2005/all_about/security/electronic_sig_report.pdf

2) COM(97)503 "Ensuring Security And Trust In Electronic Communication: Towards a European framework for Digital Signatures and encryption; The text can be found at http://www.swiss.ai.mit.edu/6805/articles/crypto/eu-october-8-97.html , http://www.datenschutz-berlin.de/sonstige/dokument/com97.htm or http://www.cyber-rights.org/documents/97503.htm .

3) Directive 1999/93/EC of the European Parliament and of the Council of 13 December 1999 on a Community Framework for electronic signatures, JOCE L13/12, 19 January

About at the same moment the European standardization bodies launched the European Electronic Signature Standardization Initiative (EESSI).[4] EESSI started its work in the autumn of 1999 and published a set of deliverables in the form of ETSI Technical Specifications and CEN Workshop Agreements related to electronic signatures. Together with the Directive, the EESSI standardization documents constitute the regulatory framework for electronic signatures in Europe.

In this paper we first present the main provisions of the European Directive on electronic signatures, to continue with an overview of the transposition of the Directive in the EU Member States. We conclude with a critical evaluation of the European regulatory framework for electronic signatures.

1. Overview of the European Directive

According to Article 1 the purpose of the Directive is 1) to facilitate the use of electronic signatures and to contribute to their legal recognition and 2) to establish a legal framework for electronic signatures and certain certification-services in order to ensure the proper functioning of the internal market. The Directive has, in other words, a dual objective.

The term "electronic signature" has been given an extremely wide sense: "data in electronic form which are attached to or logically associated with other electronic data and which serve as a method of authentication". Recital (8) justifies this approach, stating that "rapid technological development and the global character of the Internet necessitate an approach which is open to various technologies and services capable of authenticating data electronically". The same recital makes it also clear that the term "electronic signature" relates to "data authentication" and does not cover methods and technologies for "entity authentication". For example, entering a PIN-code to get access to an electronic bank account will not fall within the scope of the "electronic signature" definition. Entering the same code in order to confirm a financial transaction, on the contrary, is an example of data authentication and is therefore considered as an electronic signature.

Notwithstanding the very wide definition it has to be kept in mind that the notion of "signature" as it is used in the Directive, refers to a legal and not to a technical concept. The objective of the definition is to cover not only all current and future technologies that can be used for electronic signatures, but also to include all possible meanings of the term "signature" in the law of the Member States. It is well known that the term "signature" has not the same

---

2000.

4) For an overview of the activities of EESSI, look at http://www.ict.etsi.org/eessi_home.htm

legal meaning in every Member State of the Union. For example, a printed name or even a company stamp on a document, will be considered as a valid legal signature in the U.K. whereas the notion of "signature" in France, Belgium or Germany – until recently at least – only included handwritten signatures. One could say that the "electronic signature" definition adopted in the Directive is the greatest common denominator of all "signature" concepts that are used in the laws of the Member States.

A "signatory" is defined as "a person who holds a signature-creation device and acts either on his own behalf or on behalf of the natural or legal person or entity he represents". The European Parliament suggested to specify that a signatory could only be a "natural" person but this amendment was not integrated in the final text. The probable reason for this is that in some Member States, such as the United Kingdom, a document is not only considered to be "signed" if it contains a handwritten signature by a natural person but also when it bears a company's seal, a stamp or simply a name, as long as the authentication is sufficiently clear.5 Following current technical standards, however, only a natural person can be the holder of a "qualified" digital certificate.

A signature-creation device is defined in Art. 2.5 as: "configured software or hardware used to implement the signature-creation data". A common example of a signature-creation device is a *smart card* but there are many other possible devices such as a *smart pen*, a mobile phone, a PDA or a computer hard disk. The signatory is the person who holds this device and who acts in order to generate a signature. The signature can be either on behalf of the signatory himself or on behalf of a natural or legal person or entity he represents.

Signature-creation data are "'unique data, such as codes or private cryptographic keys, which are used by the signatory to create an electronic signature". The term "signature-creation data" consequently refers to the private key, whereas "signature-verification data" – defined as "data, such as codes or public cryptographic keys, which are used for the purpose of verifying an electronic signature" – is used as a technology-neutral synonym for the public key. The software or hardware used to verify the public key is called "signature-verification device".

Signature-creation devices and signature-verification devices are both part of the more general category of "electronic signature products". These are defined in Art. 2.12 as "hardware or software, or relevant components thereof, which are intended to be used by a certification service provider for the provision of electronic-signature services or are intended to be used for the creation or verification of electronic signatures".

Article 2.9 defines a "certificate" as "an electronic attestation which links

---

5) Chris Reed, "What is a signature?", JILT 3000/3, available at http://elj.warwick.ac.uk/jilt/00-3/reed.html.

signature-verification data to a person and confirms the identity of that person". A "qualified certificate" is "a certificate which meets the requirements laid down in Annex I and is provided by a certification service provider who fulfils the requirements laid down in Annex II of the Directive. Annex I lists ten requirements for qualified certificates.

The Directive contains a very broad definition of the concept of "certification service provider": "an entity or a legal or natural person who issues certificates or provides other services related to electronic signatures".6 Recital (9) justifies this by stating that "electronic signatures will be used in a large variety of circumstances and applications, resulting in a wide range of new services and products related to or using electronic signatures; the definition of such products and services should not be limited to the issuance and management of certificates, but should also encompass any other service and product using, or ancillary to, electronic signatures, such as registration services, time stamping services, directory services, computing services or consultancy services related to electronic signatures."

The main provision concerning certification services – in its widest sense – is Article 4.1 of the Directive. It provides that each Member State shall apply the national provisions which it adopts pursuant to the Directive to certification service providers established on its territory and to the services which they provide. Member States may not restrict the provision of certification-services originating in another Member State in the fields covered by this Directive.

Following Article 3.7 Member States may make the use of electronic signatures in the public sector subject to possible additional requirements. Such requirements shall be objective, transparent, proportionate and non-discriminatory and shall relate only to the specific characteristics of the application concerned. Such requirements may not constitute an obstacle to cross-border services for citizens.

Article 3.1 prohibits Member States to make the provision of certification services subject to prior authorisation. Recital 10 specifies that "the internal market enables certification service providers to develop their cross-border activities with a view to increasing their competitiveness, and thus to offer consumers and businesses new opportunities to exchange information and trade electronically in a secure way, regardless of frontiers. In order to stimulate the Community-wide provision of certification services over open networks, certification service providers should be free to provide their services without prior authorisation. Prior authorisation means not only any permission whereby the certification service provider concerned has to obtain a decision by national authorities before being allowed to provide its certification services, but also any other measures having the same effect."

---

6) The German electronic signature law, on the contrary, defines a certification service provider as a provider of "qualified" certification services (§ 2,8 of the law). See A. Rossnagel, "Auf dem Weg zu neuen Signaturregelungen", MMR 8/2000, p. 452.

At the same time the Directive requires the EU-Member States to make sure that the provisions of the European directive are adhered to by the certification service providers.7 As a result, Member States have to ensure that certification service providers that operate on their territory offer their services in compliance with the EC-directive, but may not exercise supervision by requiring prior authorization. Thus, national legislators have to find a way to exercise supervision without setting up a system of mandatory examination prior to the commencement of services.

Article 3.2 states that, without prejudice to the prohibition formulated in Art. 3.1, "Member States may introduce or maintain voluntary accreditation schemes aiming at enhanced levels of certification service provision. Art. 2.13 defines voluntary accreditation as "any permission, setting out rights and obligations specific to the provision of certification services, to be granted upon request by the certification service provider concerned, by the public or private body charged with the elaboration of, and supervision of compliance with, such rights and obligations, where the certification service provider is not entitled to exercise the rights stemming from the permission until it has received the decision by the body".

Further, according to Article 3.2 of the Directive, "all conditions related to such schemes must be objective, transparent, proportionate and non-discriminatory. Member States may not limit the number of accredited certification service providers for reasons which fall within the scope of this Directive." recital 11 explains that "voluntary accreditation schemes aiming at an enhanced level of service-provision may offer certification service providers the appropriate framework for developing further their services towards the levels of trust, security and quality demanded by the evolving market; such schemes should encourage the development of best practice among certification service providers; certification service providers should be left free to adhere to and benefit from such accreditation schemes.".

Article 3.3 provides that national law has to establish appropriate systems to allow *supervision* of CAs established on its territory and issuing *qualified certificates to the public*. National law thus has to establish supervisory bodies, which see to it that CAs issuing qualified certificates comply with the requirements laid down in Annex I, II and III. It is one of the most problematic provisions of the Directive, because at the same time it is prohibited to make the provision of certification services subject to prior authorisation. The prohibition does not only extend to authorisations given by national bodies prior to the actual provision of certification services by a provider, but also includes all measures with a similar effect.

Article 4.2 of the Directive urges the Member States to ensure that electronic signature products complying with the Directive are permitted to circulate freely in the internal market. recital (5) specifies, "the interoperability

---

7) See recital (13)

of electronic signature products should be promoted. In accordance with Article 14 of the Treaty, the internal market comprises an area without internal frontiers in which the free movement of goods is ensured. Essential requirements specific to electronic-signature products must be met in order to ensure free movement within the internal market and to build trust in electronic signatures, without prejudice to the regulation regarding dual-use goods".8

Article 3.5 provides that the Commission may, in accordance with the procedure laid down in Article 9, establish and publish reference numbers of generally recognised standards for electronic signature products in the Official Journal of the European Communities. Member States shall presume that there is compliance with the requirements laid down in Annex II, point (f), and Annex III when an electronic signature product meets those standards.
According to Annex III to the Directive, secure signature-creation devices must, by appropriate technical and procedural means, ensure at the least that:

(a) the signature-creation-data used for signature generation can practically occur only once, and that their secrecy is reasonably assured;
(b) the signature-creation-data used for signature generation cannot, with reasonable assurance, be derived and the signature is protected against forgery using currently available technology;
(c) the signature-creation-data used for signature generation can be reliably protected by the legitimate signatory against the use of others.

Annex III further requires that secure signature-creation devices must not alter the data to be signed or prevent such data from being presented to the signatory prior to the signature process. These requirements for secure signature-creation devices ensure the functionality of advanced electronic signatures. They do not cover the entire system environment in which such devices operate. There are no formal requirements in the Directive regarding the signature creation process and environment. However, a CEN Workshop Agreement (CWA 14170) supports the objectives of the Directive by specifying "voluntary" security requirements for the signature creation systems which create advanced electronic signatures with the help of secure signature-creation devices and qualified certificates by means of 1) a model of a "signature-creation environment" and a functional model of "signature-creation systems", 2) overall requirements that apply across all of the functions identified in the functional model, and 3) security requirements for

---

8) Council Regulation (EC)No 3381/94 of 19 December 1994 setting up a Community regime for the control of exports of dual-use goods and Council Decision 94/ 942/CFSP of 19 December 1994 on the joint action adopted by the Council concerning the control of exports of dual-use goods.

each of the functions identified in the signature-creation system, excluding the secure signature-creation device. The CWA thus gives guidance to implementers to ensure that application and computer system environments incorporating signature creation are implemented in a way and provide functionality necessary for signature creation that is of sufficient quality to minimize chance of dispute.

Article 5 is without any doubt the most controversial provision of the Directive. It states in its first paragraph that "Member States shall ensure that advanced electronic signatures which are based on a qualified certificate and which are created by a secure-signature-creation device: (a) satisfy the legal requirements of a signature in relation to data in electronic form in the same manner as a hand-written signature satisfies those requirements in relation to paper-based data; and (b) are admissible as evidence in legal proceedings.
Following Article 5.2 Member States shall ensure that an electronic signature is not denied legal effectiveness and admissibility as evidence in legal proceedings solely on the grounds that it is:

- in electronic form, or
- not based upon a qualified certificate, or
- not based upon a qualified certificate issued by an accredited certification service provider, or
- not created by a secure signature-creation device.

Recital (20) explains: "advanced electronic signatures which are based on a qualified certificate and which are created by a secure-signature-creation device can be regarded as legally equivalent to hand-written signatures only if the requirements for hand-written signatures are fulfilled". Recital (21) further specifies that "in order to contribute to the general acceptance of electronic authentication methods it has to be ensured that electronic signatures can be used as evidence in legal proceedings in all Member States" and "the legal recognition of electronic signatures should be based upon objective criteria and not be linked to authorisation of the certification service provider involved".

In the same recital one can also read: "national law governs the legal spheres in which electronic documents and electronic signatures may be used" and "this Directive is without prejudice to the power of a national court to make a ruling regarding conformity with the requirements of this Directive and does not affect national rules regarding the unfettered judicial recital of evidence".

Article 5.1 thus deals with "advanced electronic signatures which are based on a qualified certificate and which are created by a secure-signature-creation device". They are commonly called "qualified electronic signatures". The Directive attributes to this category of electronic signatures, in relation to electronic data, the same status as hand-written signatures have in relation to paper documents.

In its Article 6, the Electronic Signature Directive contains liability provisions for issuers of qualified certificates. Providers of qualified certificates are liable for certain information contained in the certificate and the accuracy of revocation lists.

Articles 7 and 8 of the Directive deal with the status of certificates issued by providers established outside the EU and with data protection issues. The remaining provisions concern mainly procedural issues. One of these provisions, in Article 12, announces a "review" of the Directive. Two years after its implementation the Commission has to carry out a review of the Directive so as, inter alia, to ensure that the advance of technology or changes in the legal environment have not created barriers to achieving the aims stated in the Directive. "It will examine the implications of associated technical areas and submit a report to the European Parliament and the Council on this subject. The report will in particular include an assessment, on the basis of experience gained, of aspects of harmonization. The report shall be accompanied, where appropriate, by legislative proposals."

2. The transposition of the Directive in the Member States

In order to prepare the review of the Directive, the European Commission ordered a study on the legal and practical issues concerning the implementation of EU Directive 1999/93 and on the practical usage of electronic signatures and related services on the European market. This study has been published in October 2003.[9] In the following pages, we present the main findings of the study.

The Member States had to transpose the Electronic Signature Directive before 19 July 2001. The study reports that most of the EU Member States have, more or less faithfully, transposed the Directive into national legislation. In addition, many of the non-EU countries surveyed have based their own electronic signatures and delivery of signature related services legislation on that of the EU Directive. From a technical point of view the Directive has even influenced international standardization initiatives, such as the IETF standardization work on qualified certificates. It is clear that the Directive has influenced legal and technical activities outside of the European Union boundaries.

Although the broad lines of the Directive have been respected by the Member States when transposing the Directive, a number of issues have nevertheless been identified as problematic. These problems can mainly be attributed to a misinterpretation of the Directive's wording, which in turn leads to divergences in national laws and/or divergences in the practical application of the rules.

The good news is that for the moment, none of the Member States

9) J. Dumortier, S. Kelm, H. Nilsson, G. Skouma and P. Van Eecke, The Legal and Market Aspects of Electronic Signatures in Europe, http://europa.eu.int/information_society/eeurope/2005/all_about/security/electronic_sig_report.pdf.

surveyed submit the provision of certification services by providers established in another Member State to prior authorization, thus formally respecting Article 3.1 on market access. It is, indeed, perfectly possible for a certification service provider established in one Member State to provide certification services in another Member States, without having to ask the prior permission of a national authority. This was not possible everywhere in Europe before the Directive was issued and transposed.

On the other hand, various Member States have established supervision schemes that are very close to prior authorization, and are possibly infringing Article 3.1 provisions. Given that certification service providers have been established in all but a few of the countries surveyed and given that the majority of supervision schemes are still in the very early stages of development, it is impossible to compare yet the practical implications of the supervision systems. Nevertheless, it has become obvious that there are very important divergences between the various supervision schemes in the Member States. Although the effect of these divergences remains limited, since most of the certification service providers still operate exclusively in their home country, the divergences will begin to show a negative impact once European or non-European providers start to launch more cross-border certification services across the EU.

Also, the Directive's rules on voluntary accreditation seem to be misunderstood by national governments. Many European countries wrongfully consider voluntary accreditation schemes as a means of controlling whether or not a certification service provider operates in compliance with the provisions of the Directive. Another alarming observation is that the voluntary accreditation schemes, in many European countries, are in practice, not really voluntary. A typical example being that many national e-government programmes only accept accredited certification service providers to participate in the programme, and thus indirectly oblige a certification service provider to get an accreditation. This evolution is certainly not in line with the Directive's vision.

Concerning the so-called "public sector exception" of Article 3.7, which allows Member States to make use of electronic signatures in the public sector subject to possible additional requirements, we have seen divergences in both the interpretation and implementation of this provision. It seems clear that in many countries the use of electronic signatures in the public sector is subject to additional (security) requirements. Communicating electronically with public authorities is in many European countries possible only through the use of signatures based on qualified certificates issued by an accredited certification service provider. Member States need to be reminded that applying additional conditions can only be justified by objective reasons and should only relate to the specific characteristics of the application concerned. Also, Member States need to ensure that basic competition rules are not being infringed by their initiatives.

As to the conformity assessment of secure signature-creation devices many countries seem quite reluctant to designate their own designated bodies for secure signature-creation device assessment. This may be due to the very high secure signature-creation device security requirements and the lack of active vendors in most countries. Another reason is the very large resources needed for operating an assessment body. The process of assessing a product is usually extremely expensive as well as time-consuming. Two further reasons why vendors are sometimes reluctant to have their products assessed is that an assessment is usually only valid for a fairly short amount of time (the product needs to be re-assessed), and a conformity assessment "freezes" a product so that it cannot be changed (e.g., in order to apply a security patch) without making invalid the assessment.

The non-discrimination principle of electronic signatures, as regulated by Article 5.2 of the Directive, has been taken over by most of the national legislators. However, the transposition of Article 5.2 has not always been explicitly done and in those countries with an explicit transposition the scope of Article 5.2 has not always been covered in its entirety. It is not yet clear whether this rather vague transposition in some countries will have a practical impact on the legal use of electronic signatures. Thus, how electronic signatures will be treated in future national legislation and case law requires close monitoring.

As to the legal effect of qualified electronic signatures (the ones regulated by Article 5.1 of the Directive), there has been a general tendency in the majority of European countries to explicitly recognise the equivalence between a handwritten signature and a specific "type" of signature by imposing the same or slightly different conditions than the ones stipulated in Article 5.1. It is, however, important to know that the Directive obliges Member States only to make sure that a qualified electronic signature is legally speaking treated in the same way as a handwitten signature, but that it does not regulate the legal use and consequences of a handwritten signature itself, and thus not the legal consequences of the qualified electronic signature either. The legal use and consequences (which transactions need a signature, which evidential value is given to a signature, etc) remains a nationally regulated matter.

Qualified electronic signatures need to be in compliance with the requirements as stated by the first three Annexes of the Directive. It is, therefore, important that the Annexes are correctly transposed into national legislation. The implementation of Annex I is very similar in most of those countries surveyed. For the implementation of Annex II, implementation levels are sometimes quite varying, meaning that the establishment and running of a certification service provider will differ considerably. Any organization wishing to establish a certification service provider business in several countries must therefore adapt itself to different requirements and procedures. Product vendors will also have difficulties building products for this very fragmented market. In addition, several countries put additional detailed and unnecessary requirements on the certification service provider, thus creating barriers for the establishment of a certification service provider. For the implementation of Annex III, there is also evidence of fragmentation. The requirements for secure signature-creation devices are, for example, much higher in Austria and Poland than in some other European countries. As far as Annex IV is concerned, Article 3.6 is very clear. The list contains only recommendations, which have to be taken into account by the Member States and the European Commission when they work together in order to promote the development and the use of signature-verification devices. They can certainly not be changed into obligatory requirements at a national level, as some Member States have done.

An important question, which needs to be posed, is what the use of electronic signatures in Europe really is? There is currently no natural market demand for qualified certificates and related services. The largest application area in Europe for electronic signatures is generally linked to e-banking applications in a closed user environment, and thus outside the scope of the Directive. Within the scope of the Directive, very few applications are in use today and they are almost completely limited to e-government.

Technology evolves rapidly and in the near future many electronic signature technical solutions will be based on new technological developments, such as new secure PC environments, mobile signatures and signature servers. Consequently, supervision bodies, designated bodies and others involved in the regulation of qualified electronic signatures should look at these technologies with an open mind and not restrict security assessments to what is known and available today.

The lack of interoperability, both at national and cross-border level, is a big obstacle for market acceptance and the proliferation of electronic signatures. It has resulted in many isolated "islands" of electronic signature applications, where certificates from only one CA can be used for one application. In a few cases only can certificates from multiple CAs be used for multiple applications. Much more should therefore have been done earlier at a European level to promote interoperability.

The EESSI (European Electronic Signature Standardisation Initiative) programme has developed some standards that are Directive compliant. However, the delay in developing the standards and having their references published in the Official Journal, has led to a situation whereby several countries have either developed their own technical interpretations of the Directive, (leading to varying requirements in different countries), or else have waited for standards to be developed, leading to a vacuum for product and service vendors on the market.

3. Evaluation of the European regulatory framework

The EU Directive has led to the adoption of national regulatory frameworks for electronic signatures in a large number of European countries, not only in the EU but also beyond its borders. The divergences between these regulatory frameworks are however noteworthy and the resulting picture is very complex. The main aim of the Directive has been to create a Community framework for the use of electronic signatures, allowing for the free cross-border flow of products and service provisions, together with a basic legal recognition of electronic signatures throughout the EU. This objective has clearly not completely been reached. Some of the Directive's provisions seem to have been misunderstood and the Member States, while transposing the Directive into national law, have sometimes failed to focus on the European dimension of the new regulatory framework. We are therefore under the impression that there is a primary need for a consistent, clear and workable re-interpretation of the Directive's provisions.

The European Directive had three main objectives: 1) stimulating the internal market, 2) promoting legal acceptance of electronic signatures and 3) creating a favourable climate in this area for business and consumers. For each of these three objectives it is worthwhile to examine in how far they have been reached.

3.1. Stimulating the internal market

As far as the internal market is concerned, recital (10) is illustrative of the vision forming the core of the Directive's provisions:

> "*The internal market enables certification-service-providers to develop their cross-border activities with a view to increase their competitiveness, and thus to offer consumers and business new opportunities to exchange information and trade electronically in a secure way, regardless of frontiers (...)*"

The recital refers explicitly to the provision of cross-border certification services. This is not surprising given that when the Directive was agreed, certain Member States had already introduced legislation submitting the provision of certification services to prior authorization by national authorities.[10]

Prohibiting a Member State from establishing or maintaining licensing schemes or other similar barriers for service providers in this area is therefore directly linked to the internal market objectives of the Directive. If every

---

10) § 15 of the former German Signaturgesetz of 01 Aug. 1997 stated: "Digital signatures capable of being verified by a public signature key in another Member State of the European Union or in another State party to the Agreement on the European Economic Area shall be deemed equivalent to digital signatures under this Act *insofar as they show the same level of security*"; Article 8 of the Italian Presidential Decree n. 513 of 10 Nov. 1997 was formulated as follows: "The certification process referred to in Article 1 may also be carried out by a certifying authority, whose license or authorization was issued, *subject to equivalent requirements*, by another Member State of the European Union or the European Economic Area".

Member State were to submit the provision of certification services to a prior authorization by authorities of that Member State, it would evidently be impossible - or at least very cumbersome - for a service provider to develop European-wide certification services.

None of the Member States[11] submits the provision of certification services by providers established in another Member State, to any form of prior authorization. Theoretically, it is perfectly possible for a certification service provider established in one Member State to provide certification services in another Member State, without having to ask the permission of the national authorities of these other Member States. This was not possible everywhere in Europe prior to the Directive being issued and transposed. It has often been over looked that this is one very positive outcome stemming directly from the Directive. One of the most important internal market objectives of the Directive has, in this respect, been achieved.

On the other hand various Member States have established supervision schemes that are very close to prior authorization. Article 3.1 is however very clear. Making the provision of certification services – qualified, accredited, or other – subject to prior authorization or taking other measures that have the same effect, are strictly prohibited by the Directive.

Fortunately the supervision of certification services by the Member States' authorities only affects providers established on their own national territory. One could have expected that Member States would keep the supervision regime for the providers established on their own territory as limited and as flexible as possible in order not to affect negatively the competitive position of their "own" service providers in comparison with providers established elsewhere.

However, bar a few exceptions the Member States and the other countries covered by this study have followed a completely different strategy. We have seen in our overview how some of the national supervision schemes sometimes put heavy burdens on the local certification service providers before these can begin to provide qualified services. Apparently Member States are still convinced that most of the qualified certificates issued to the public on their own territory will be provided by certification service providers established on that territory. Another reason could be that some Member States use the supervision schemes to raise the security level of the certification service providers established on their territory in order to improve their quality and hence their competitiveness on the European and international market. Last but not least Article 3.3 of the Directive explicitly requires the establishment of an appropriate system allowing for the

---

11) The situation is different for the accession and the candidate countries. But, for example, Section 17.2 of the Slovakian Electronic Signature Act of March 2002 (see: http://www.e-podpis.sk/laws_en.html) is formulated as follows: "On the day of Slovakia's entry into the European Union, any certificate, issued by a to whose principal place of business is in a Member State of the Community, whose validity is verifiable in Slovakia, shall be an equivalent of a certificate issued in Slovakia".

supervision of certification service providers. recital (13) makes clear that the objective of supervision is to control whether or not an established certification service provider issuing qualified certificates to the public, provides this service in compliance with the requirements of the Directive. The requirements are listed in Annex II. Member States have, very understandably, thought that supervising the compliance with these complex technical requirements necessarily includes a close and detailed control of the certification service providers and the way they operate.

The majority of the supervision schemes are still at a very early stage of development. It is therefore impossible to compare the practical implications of supervision systems. Nevertheless, it remains obvious that very important divergences between the supervision schemes in the Member States exist. Conditions on how to enter the market for qualified certification services vary considerably from Member State to Member State. For the time being the effect of these divergences remains limited because most of the certification service providers continue to operate exclusively from their home country. This is expected to change once European or non-European providers begin to launch more cross-border certification services in the EU.

Article 3.2 of the Directive stipulates that Member States can maintain or even introduce voluntary accreditation schemes aiming at enhanced levels of certification-service provision. The European legislator has estimated, very rightly, that voluntary accreditation schemes could be beneficial for the development of the market. It can give certification service providers operating in Europe the possibility of demonstrating their level of security and trustworthiness. Accreditation schemes could certify the adequacy of the security level of a particular certification service for being used in particular contexts or applications. For instance, specialized accreditation schemes could certify the adequacy of particular certification service for the health care sector.

When new solutions are discovered and introduced into the market, accreditation schemes can help providers gain user trust. The accreditation schemes should mainly be created or maintained for the benefit of the providers themselves. They should encourage the development of best practices and remain up-to-date with state-of-the-art technology in the sector. They are a form of common quality control, organized at the level of a particular sector. Of course, setting up such accreditation schemes requires considerable resources, mainly in terms of expertise.

Consequently the aim of the Directive has never been to have a national accreditation scheme in every Member State. It is also fully incorrect to consider voluntary accreditation schemes as a means to control whether or not a certification service provider operates in compliance with the provisions of the Directive. Our study has shown that, unfortunately, many European countries are merging the supervision of certification service providers which issue qualified certificates to the public with the voluntary accreditation. We have also seen that in the majority of European countries accreditation is, in practice, not really voluntary, for example because it is a necessary condition to participate in the national e-government programmes.

Such a development is certainly not in line with the Directive's vision. The provision concerning voluntary accreditation schemes was intended mainly to prevent Member States from misinterpreting the prohibition of prior authorization. This prohibition should not be understood as incompatible with existing or future voluntary accreditation schemes. On the contrary, the Directive encourages the creation of such schemes, as long as the conditions related to those schemes are objective, transparent, proportionate and non-discriminatory. Moreover, as is stated in recital (12): "Member States should not prohibit certification-service-providers from operating outside voluntary accreditation schemes; it should be ensured that such accreditation schemes do not reduce competition for certification services".

It is worth noting that the Directive does not contain requirements for electronic-signature products as such. The requirements of Annex III are only applicable to secure signature-creation devices or, in other words, for devices to be used for the creation of qualified electronic signatures. One of the objectives being that secure signature-creation devices have to be easily recognized by the users. When using a secure signature-creation device, users should feel confident that the security of this device is legally recognized, not only in their own country but also in the other Member States. If a user creates an advanced electronic signature based upon a qualified certificate and using a device labelled as an secure signature-creation device, he should be certain that this signature will be considered as the legal equivalent of a handwritten signature everywhere in the European Union. It is our understanding that, from the perspective of the Directive, either the producer, under his own responsibility, may put the secure signature-creation device-label on the device, or the label can be the result of a conformity assessment by a designated body. In the latter case, the designated body should fulfil the criteria of independence and professionalism determined by the European Commission.

In order to avoid divergences in the conformity determination of signature-creation devices by designated bodies or to guide the manufacturers wishing to introduce secure signature-creation devices in the market, the Directive has explicitly emphasized the need to have legally recognized standards. It is for this reason that Article 3.5 gave the European Commission the possibility to establish and publish reference numbers of generally recognized standards. Manufacturers of signature-creation devices can be certain that their devices will be considered as secure signature-creation devices by all the EU Member States, assuming that their products "meet those standards".

Of course this whole construction had to be put in practice very swiftly. Therefore the European Commission published already in November 2000 its Decision 2000/709/EC on the minimum criteria to be taken into account for the designation of the conformity assessment bodies. Designated bodies were very rapidly operational in Germany and in Austria. Of course it was never the intention of the European legislator to have conformity assessment bodies in every Member State.

Many countries appeared to be quite reluctant to designate their own designated bodies for secure signature-creation device assessment. This may be due to the very high secure signature-creation device security requirements and the subsequent lack of active vendors in most countries. Another reason being the very large resources needed for operating an assessment body. Therefore all countries seem either explicitly or implicitly – but very rightly - to accept assessments made by bodies based in other Member States.

The level of competence and running cost of the assessment laboratories are such that not every country will be able to afford such services at a national level. This would not be a real constraint if a network of laboratories would provide these services at European level based on mutual recognition of methodology and criteria. Furthermore, such a network could include international laboratories as well, with all agreeing on a mutual recognition protocol.

Currently the main problem in this area appears to be the lengthy and costly character of the conformity assessment procedures. Even for an experienced secure signature-creation device vendor the process of having a relevant product evaluated and assessed by designated bodies might take up to one year. The most time-consuming tasks include the vendors' preparation of documents describing the product to be assessed in great detail. Thereafter, the assessment body has to both evaluate those documents as well as test the product against the documentation as provided by the vendor. It is likely that this process requires multiple changes before the vendor can fix any problems that might have been found during the evaluation. Since all these tasks involve a large amount of time at both the vendor level and the assessment body level, the overall process becomes costly.[12] The process itself may be only slightly reduced by using previously assessed components, e.g., crypto processors.

Article 3.7 of the Directive contains the so-called "public sector exception". Member States may make the use of electronic signatures in the public sector subject to possible additional requirements. However these requirements should be objective, transparent, proportionate and non-discriminatory and relate only to the specific characteristics of the application concerned.

There are divergences in both interpretation and implementation of this provision. It seems clear that in many countries the use of electronic signatures in the public sector is subject to additional (security) requirements. Communicating electronically with public authorities is in many European countries only possible when using signatures based on qualified certificates issued by an accredited certification service provider.

---

12) As an example we were provided with a cost range from 50.000€ to 200.000€ for a single assessment.

The Directive does not strictly forbid this if the requirement is justified by objective reasons and relates only to the specific characteristics of the application concerned. Moreover a measure introducing such a requirement should be proportionate, transparent and non-discriminatory. Consequently, it would be prohibited, for example, to issue legislation imposing the use of qualified electronic signatures for *all* electronic relations between citizens and the government. Such a rule is in contradiction with Article 5.2 of the Directive because it denies the legal effectiveness of electronic signatures solely on the grounds that these are not qualified.

Even imposing the use of qualified electronic signatures for a single e-government application, for example, introducing electronic communication for a tax declaration, without justifying objectively the necessity of such a measure, is clearly in contradiction with the Directive.

When introducing the use of electronic signatures for public sector applications, Member States should also be aware of other rules. For example, imposing the obligation to obtain an accreditation for certification service providers as a condition to participate in e-government programmes, is also in contradiction with recital (11) of the Directive because the consequence of such a measure would be that the certification service providers are no longer free to adhere to an accreditation scheme. The measure would also reduce in a disproportional way the competition for certification services.

Member States should also be careful not to intervene directly in the market for certification services if this contradicts the EU's competition rules. For example, a government is perfectly allowed to set up a public key infrastructure in order to support the use of electronic signatures for its own e-government applications. Setting up a public key infrastructure, whether or not in a partnership with one or more private companies, in order to support the use of electronic signatures outside the public sector would however not be admissible. Such an initiative, even if the private partner has been chosen in compliance with European and national public procurement rules, clearly reduces competition in the market for certification services and can constitute a barrier for the internal market in this area.

3.2. Promoting legal acceptance of electronic signatures

For the European legislator, it was clear that "national law lays down different requirements for the legal validity of handwritten signatures". The objective was clearly not to harmonize the requirements for the legal validity of electronic signatures but instead to establish in every Member State an equivalency between the legal status of handwritten signatures in the paper-based environment and the legal status of electronic signatures in the electronic environment. In other words, the European legislator tried to determine a type of electronic signature, which should consequently be considered by every Member State as the equivalent of a handwritten signature. The type of electronic signature being chosen by the European legislator is the so-called qualified electronic signature, described in Article 5.1 of the Directive: an Advanced Electronic Signature based on a qualified certificate and created by a secure signature-creation device. The Member States were required to attribute to this type of electronic signature the same legal status as the one attributed by their national law to the handwritten signature.

It should be very clear that, as a consequence of this choice, the legal status of qualified electronic signatures has not been harmonized between the Member States. The legal requirements for handwritten signatures differ from Member State to Member State. Qualified electronic signatures have the same status as handwritten signatures. Therefore the legal requirements for qualified electronic signatures remain also different in each of the Member States. This principle is expressed at the end of recital (20)[13] and it is very important for understanding many of the discussions about the transposition of Article 5.1 in the Member States.

Further, it should be made clear that European legislation has opted for a solution in which the legal regime for qualified electronic signatures "follows" the national legal regime for handwritten signatures. If a Member State has, for example, very strict rules for the legal validity of a handwritten signature on a certain type of contract, this Member State will then adopt the same strict rules to qualified electronic signatures for this same type of contract. If another Member State has very flexible rules for handwritten signatures for that type of contract, the rules for the use of qualified electronic signatures on that same type of contract will also be very flexible. The legal regime for handwritten signatures is, in other words, the *reference point*, the principle being to award qualified electronic signatures in the electronic environment the same legal status as handwritten signatures in a paper-based context.

During the transposition of the Directive, some Member States, such as the UK, discovered that their legal system has no legal provisions for handwritten signatures. In the absence of national legislation for the use of handwritten signatures, it follows that there can be no legal status for the use of qualified electronic signatures either. Even more - if a legal system does not legally recognise the concept of a "handwritten signature", it is impossible to adopt provisions introducing a legal equivalency between a handwritten signature and something else. It is difficult to use something as a reference point if this "something" does not exist.

A further consequence of the approach adopted by EU law has been to make the legal status of the qualified electronic signature dependent on the legal status of handwritten signatures. Implicitly this approach is based on the presumption that there is – but not necessarily always will be – a choice

---

13) "(...); Advanced Electronic Signatures which are based on a qualified certificate and which are created by a secure signature-creation device can be regarded as legally equivalent to handwritten signatures only if the requirements for handwritten signatures -e fulfilled;"

between two alternatives. In other words either to sign by hand or to sign electronically. Nevertheless more and more, specific rules are being addressed to the electronic environment, with the paper-based context no longer being referred to. It is not hard to imagine that, ten or twenty years from now, many applications will only use communications in an electronic form and that the rules applicable to those applications will no longer refer to handwritten signatures. In other words, the handwritten signature will, bit by bit, loose its value as a reference point. It is therefore doubtful whether the concept of the qualified electronic signature as an "electronic equivalent" to the handwritten signature will survive over a long period of time. Nevertheless, for the time being, and for most of the Member States' legal systems, the linkage of the qualified electronic signature to a handwritten signature can perhaps be useful. Whether or not this will actually be the case, largely depends on how clear the concept of a" qualified electronic signature" actually is. It does not make much sense to require a Member State to award electronic signatures the same legal status as a handwritten signature on condition that it is a "qualified electronic signature", especially if this concept is not uniformly understood across the EU. A Belgian citizen, for example, wishing to make an electronic commercial transaction with a Greek company by using qualified electronic signature should be certain that his/her signature will have, under Greek law, the same legal status as a handwritten signature. What I, as a Belgian, consider a "qualified electronic signature" should be equally recognised as such by Greek authorities. The whole system adopted by European legislation is only useful on condition that there is one common European concept of "qualified electronic signature".

The most delicate problem of the European electronic signatures Directive is precisely the difficulty of defining exactly what a "qualified electronic signature" means. Of course, Article 5.1 contains a definition. For example, a "qualified" certificate is necessary and must make mention of the certificate itself. Supervisory bodies, instruments and/or procedures ensure that certification service providers are forbidden from making untruthful claims regarding their qualified status . Secure signature-creation devices can be submitted to conformity assessment bodies which in turn can receive a conformity label. In the foregoing chapters we have amply demonstrated the difficulties that have to be solved before qualified certificates and secure signature-creation devices will be widely distributed in Europe. However these problems are not the result of the Directive's text rather to the way in which the text has been interpreted and subsequently transposed by some of the Member States.

One should also not forget that a qualified electronic signature must fulfil the four requirements of the Advanced Electronic Signature as well. Is the signature uniquely linked to the signatory? Is it capable of identifying the signatory, even if the name of the signatory is "Jean Dupont"? Has the signature been created using means that the signatory can maintain under its sole control? Is it linked to the data to which it relates in such a manner that any subsequent change of the data is detectable?

It has often been stated that the Directive only focuses on the security of the signature-creation device and of the certificate, in order to determine whether or not an electronic signature fulfils the requirements of Art. 5.1. This is not entirely correct. One could say that a qualified electronic signature has to fulfil **six** requirements: the four requirements of the Advanced Electronic Signature and the two additional requirements that are expressly mentioned in Art. 5.1 itself. It is true that the four requirements of the Advanced Electronic Signature have not been given more provisions in the Annexes, unlike the approach adopted for qualified certificates and secure signature-creation devices. However, from a legal point of view, the absence of further provisions is not totally relevant. The lack of greater provisions on how to fill in the criteria of the Advanced Electronic Signature is in the first place a practical problem, which can be solved by further standardization.

The rule of Article 5.1 – "if it is a qualified electronic signature, deal with it as if it would be a handwritten signature" - is simple, but only on condition that everyone can easily discern one qualified electronic signature from another. Ideally a qualified electronic signature should be as easy to recognize as a handwritten signature.

In order to guarantee this as much as possible, European legislation chooses not only to list in detail the requirements to be fulfilled by certificates, certification service providers and signature-creation devices but also to make sure that a qualified certificate can be recognized easily: 1) does the certificate contain the mention "qualified" or not? and 2) did the signature-creation device receive a conformity declaration by a designated body?

It is evident that these very simple means of control can hide a world of differences. The requirements that need to be fulfilled in order to qualify as a certification service provider or to obtain a conformity declaration for a secure signature-creation device can vary considerably from one country to another. It should be clear, however, that these divergences are deliberately not taken into account by the European legislator. If a certification service provider operates as a "qualified" certification service provider in one Member State, under the supervision of the authorities of that Member State, he has to be a recognised certification service provider in every other Member State. If a signature-creation device is confirmed to be a secure signature-creation device by a designated conformity assessment body in one Member State or if it meets the standard referenced by the European Commission in the Official Journal, every other Member State will have to accept this device as an secure signature-creation device.

Notwithstanding these very simple principles, it is interesting to note how the requirement for qualified certificates, qualified certification Service Providers and Secure Signature-Creation Devices, listed in Annex I to III of the Directive, have been transposed by the European countries surveyed for this study. Even if divergences in the implementation of these Annexes might not have important legal consequences, the fact remains that a more or less uniform implementation of these technical requirements is necessary to guarantee that a qualified electronic signature created in one country, remains technically verifiable in another country. This is the whole problem of interoperability. To realize the vision of the European legislator – a "European" qualified electronic signature that can be used for cross-border electronic communications in the Union and beyond – the "qualified electronic signature" should be something more or less identical throughout the EU. One additional problem, evidently, is the language barrier. Certificates contain text and refer to other documents such as practice statements or policies, and these texts are all written in one or another language. For a user in Ireland, it might not be evident to read and understand the messages accompanying certificates that have been issued in Greece, or vice versa. Standardizing the most important fields and messages as much as possible or to use one common language for these purposes appear to be the only way to solve this problem.

Regarding Annex II, implementation does sometimes vary meaning that the effort needed to establish and run a certification service provider will differ considerably amongst the countries. Any organization that wants to establish a certification service provider business in several countries must therefore adapt to different requirements and procedures. Product vendors will also have difficulties building products for this very fragmented market. In addition, several countries put additional detailed and unnecessary requirements on the certification service provider, thus creating barriers for the establishment of certification service provider. The Commission should therefore point out any unnecessary and excessive requirements for certification service providers, which might be perceived as market obstacles.

For the implementation of Annex III, there is also a fragmented situation. The requirements for secure signature-creation devices are for example much higher in Austria and Poland than in some other European countries.

As far as Annex IV is concerned, Article 3.6 is very clear. The list contains only recommendations that have to be taken into account by the Member States and the European Commission when they work together in order to promote the development and the use of signature-verification devices. And although more guidelines on the security and the functionality of such devices would benfit the users, the recommendation as of Annex IV can certainly not be changed into obligatory requirements at the national level, as some Member States have done.

One of the most fundamental principles of Directive 1999/93/EC is outlined in recital (21): "the legal recognition of electronic signatures should be based upon objective criteria and not be linked to authorization of the certification-service-provider involved". Consequently, Article 5.2 of the Directive stipulates that an electronic signature should not be denied legal effectiveness and admissibility as evidence in legal proceedings solely on the grounds that it is, for instance, not based upon a qualified certificate or not created by a secure-signature-creation device. All kinds of electronic signatures should be taken into consideration and their legal effectiveness should only depend on an objective examination of the given signature.

Unfortunately the principle as laid down in Article 5.2 did not receive very much attention. It has also become clear that there is some confusion in the Member States as to how Article 5.2 should be interpreted. What is actually meant by "not to deny legal effectiveness of an electronic signature solely on the grounds that it is not based upon a qualified certificate or not created by a secure signature-creation device"? Is it forbidden for the Member States to introduce legislation in which they require a qualified electronic signature for certain types of documents? By issuing such a provision, don't they deny legal effectiveness of electronic signatures that are not qualified in the sense of Article 5.1?

Article 5.1 of the Directive states that Member States have to ensure that "qualified electronic signatures" satisfies the legal requirements of a signature in relation to data in electronic form in the same manner as a handwritten signature satisfies those requirements in relation to paper-based data. Therefore Member States can, for example, issue legislation stipulating that a qualified electronic signature on an electronic document will have the same legal effect as a handwritten signature on a paper document. The denial of the legal effectiveness of other electronic signatures in such a provision is, in other words, not solely based on the grounds that they are not "qualified" but on the ground that the electronic document needs an electronic signature that is the equivalent of the handwritten signature on the paper document.

This is exactly what we have called "taking the paper-based environment as the reference point". What Article 5.2 prohibits, is to attribute to the "qualified" or "accredited" electronic signature a legal value beyond this equivalency. The Member States should, in other words, never introduce legislation requiring the use of "qualified electronic signatures" except in a context where there is a need to have an electronic substitute for a handwritten signature. As an example, legislation referring to "qualified electronic signatures" in a context where paper-based procedures have completely disappeared would be in contradiction with Article 5.2.

The objective of Art. 5.1 has certainly never been to introduce, neither now nor in the future, a more or less unique European standardized secure electronic signature that can be used for various legal transactions. That would be a very dangerous strategy, of a sort constantly avoided by legislators. In order to remain stable and to avoid constant changes and updates, laws formulate only rules but rarely describe *how* people have to implement the rules. The "how" is the object of standards, which have, by definition a voluntary character. As long as people comply with the rule, they are free to decide how they do this. Sometimes legislation refers explicitly to standards, but only insofar that this is strictly necessary and the reference to a particular standard is mostly interpreted in a restrictive manner.

These elementary principles should be borne in mind when interpreting Art. 5.1 of the Directive and having regard to these principles, the reference to the (standardized) "qualified electronic signature", should not be extended.

Meeting the requirements of a "qualified" electronic signature only results in a presumption of equivalency with the handwritten signature. Art. 5.2 explicitly forbids to go beyond this restriction and to use the "qualified" electronic signature-concept for other purposes.

It should also be made clear that Article 5.2 does not deal uniquely with the legal admissibility of electronic signatures as evidence in legal proceedings. The provision is not only meant to guide judges in the Member States but also legislators. Article 5.2 mentions also the denial of legal effectiveness.

One could call Article 5.2 for this reason a "long-term" provision. European legislation has not sought to use the concept of "qualified electronic signature" beyond the context of Article 5.1. As soon as it is no longer necessary to search an "automatic" electronic substitute for the handwritten signature, the concept should be abandoned. Every kind of electronic signature should, from that moment onwards, be judged only with regard to its objective adequacy in the specific context.

3.3. Creating a favourable climate

Besides the internal market objectives and the promotion of a European-wide legal acceptance of electronic signatures, the European Directive also seeks to create a favourable electronic communications and e-commerce climate in the EU. This objective has often been misunderstood. The European Directive has frequently been criticized because it was not able to generate a large-scale use of (PKI-based) electronic signatures in Europe.

It has become quite apparent that the introduction of a Community legal framework for electronic signatures could never lead to a massive introduction of PKI. This has never been the intention of European legislation. The Directive certainly aims to promote the use of electronic signatures and also to encourage secure electronic commerce - but only by removing some of the possible legal obstacles.

From the Directive's perspective, its primary objective was to protect the Internal Market in order to create a geographically larger market for European product vendors and service providers. In the second place it promotes the general legal acceptance of electronic signatures, thus removing legal obstacles for cross-border electronic transactions in Europe. It is clear that the Directive's objectives have not entirely been realised. The Directive has resulted in a whole series of national regulatory frameworks which have not lead to a European-wide environment for the use of electronic signatures. In previous paragraphs we have seen what can be done in order to remedy this situation.

It has never been the Directive's intention to facilitate the launching of PKI for electronic signatures in Europe. Whether or not there is a demand for this kind of option is not dependant on a comprehensive legal framework. Nevertheless it may be worth examining what can be done to stimulate the use of electronic signatures and secure electronic communications in general. In our view specific efforts are needed in the area of standardization. Moreover, initiatives can be taken in order to increase general trust in electronic signatures by, for example, taking the user more into account.

Regarding the security standards related to the qualified electronic signatures of the Directive, currently only one set of standards exists. These have been developed by EESSI and based on PKI technology, since the requirements of Article 5.1 presume certificate-based solutions. This may hinder other technologies from being used for qualified electronic signatures, and prejudices the use of PKI for other electronic signatures. Although the present standards are mostly technology neutral (within the framework of PKI), they still favour the use of smart cards.

The development of a common specification for algorithms and parameters used for electronic signatures should have been done much earlier at a European level, for example through EESSI. The present lack of commonly recognised specifications will lead to interoperability problems and lack of cross-border acceptance. The current situation being that several national specifications are more often than not published in a national language only. This can potentially act as a market barrier.

The lack of interoperability, both at a national and cross-border level, is a big obstacle for market acceptance and proliferation of electronic signatures. It has resulted in many isolated "islands" of electronic signature applications, where certificates from only one CA can be used for one application. In a few cases only can certificates from multiple CAs be used for multiple applications. Much more should therefore have been done earlier at a European level to promote interoperability.

The development, promotion and use of interoperability standards must now be done at a European level. If done only at the level of the nation state the result will be varying standards, which in turn hinders cross-border use whilst at the same time putting different requirements to product vendors from every national market, thus diminishing the probability that vendors will adopt their products to the standards. We can only hope for interoperability in standard products if European-wide requirements can be put to the vendors.

Our final reflections in the framework of this study focus on the user. In our view it is absolutely necessary to put more emphasis on the user's perspective in all discussions regarding the European electronic signatures regulatory framework. The absence of this perspective has been a more or less constant theme not only in the legal discussion but also in the standardization activities around the Directive. Business and/or technical considerations prevailed strongly in every debate in this area. This has resulted in a set of legal and technical solutions that are often far removed from the daily needs of the common user.

As far as standardization is concerned, it is probably useful to systematically *scan* the existing standardization documents from a user's perspective. With regard to qualified electronic signatures the aim of the standardization activities should be to develop the specifications of a solution that gives the user the possibility to use electronic signatures on a European-wide scale. Such a solution has to take into account *all* aspects of electronic signatures, not only covering the whole signature chain but also taking account of typical users' concerns such as ease of use, language obstacles, cost considerations, etc.

With regard to the legal framework it may become necessary to take a more practical approach. The Directive focuses very strongly on one business model, which took centre stage from 1998 to 2000 but which has since been replaced by a much more heterogeneous and complex market. As a result of this, the current regulatory framework includes detailed rules for issuers of certificates but fails to consider other types of certification providers. Services like time-stamping, revocation, repository, and archival can be offered by third parties which are contracted by the authority issuing certificates. And yet regulatory needs relating to other categories of trust service providers are at least as important as those relating to the certification service providers. There is, for example, a clear need for regulation dealing with archival service providers, or with registered mail services. From a users' point of view it is difficult to understand why such services remain completely unregulated, while complex regulatory frameworks have been well established for those issuing certificates. We therefore recommend that further studies be carried out dealing with other categories of trust services.

Last but not least it is necessary to combine electronic authentication with personal data protection. The current European regulatory framework is very much focused on the use of identity certificates. In recent years, attention has shifted towards better privacy protection in the online environment. Research has been focused on the possibility of combining electronic authentication with the needs for anonymity or the use of multiple virtual identities. The efforts of the European Union to promote advanced personal data protection for its citizens should not be contradicted by its regulatory framework for electronic authentication. Further research is needed into the possibility of combining anonymity and pseudonymity with the provisions of the electronic signatures Directive.

Managing electronic signatures

by Cecilia Magnusson Sjöberg

1. Implementation

There is a continuously developing *legal framework* directed towards acceptance of electronic signatures equal to handwritten ones. The EC Signature Directive (1999/93/EC)[1] is of course an important contribution, at least in theory. The Directive elaborates on legal effects related to different security levels of electronic signatures, certificates etc. Current reports show, however, that comparatively few so called qualified signatures have been issued.[2] Furthermore, *legal uncertainties* remain in spite of this EU initiative e.g. within the taxation area. A key issues is whether or not an electronically signed e-invoice must be associated with a specific individual or merely a legal person. From a practical point of view, *managing electronic signatures* is a critical factor in the context of e-commerce as well as in communications with public agencies.

This analysis of electronic signatures will place an emphasis on *practical issues from a legal point of view*. The title "Managing electronic signatures" indicates the importance of a legal approach not only addressing rules and regulations but also challenges in the context of *implementation*.

Regardless of electronic signatures being a feature of the modern information society there is every reason to revisit the notion of legal system management.[3] Historically, legal system management addresses core components in legally well-founded automatic decision making,[4] information retrieval,[5] and

---

1) Directive 1999/93/EC of the European Parliament and of the Council of 13 December 1999 on a Community framework for electronic signatures.

2) See further The Legal and Market Aspects of Electronic Signatures, Jos Dumortier et.al. Study for the European Commission – DG Information Society (Leuven 2003).

3) See Seipel, Peter, Computing Law (Stockholm 1977).

4) See e.g. Magnusson Sjöberg, Cecilia, Rättsautomation: Särskilt om statsförvaltningens datorisering (Stockholm 1992) and Schartum, Dag Wiese, Rettssikkerhet og systemutvikling i offentlig forvaltning (Oslo1993).

5) Including advanced legal information retrieval based on probabalistic methods.

electronic document management.[6] The use of information technology (IT) for the above mentioned purposes can be related to the legal domain either directly, e.g. an application for knowledge management in a business law firm, or indirectly, e.g. an electronic market place where actions taken have legal implications. More precisely, legal system management takes into consideration system development approach, system design and system management. Let us now reflect upon electronic signatures in the same way.

2. System development approach

Evidently, the choice of system development approach for an implementation of electronic signatures is *application area dependent.* Implementing electronic signatures for the purpose of e-invoicing is quite different from contract management or product data management, etc. In addition to various *topic areas* a system development approach is dependent on *sector* aspects. For example, the application of data protection legislation varies between the public and the private sectors of society. Furthermore, an implementation of electronic signatures in the public sector must take principles of openness and rules governing administrative procedures into consideration. Broadening the perspective even more, *jurisdictional* aspects need to be considered; will an implementation of electronic signatures be utilised only within the EU and/or in so called third countries? *Technical and organisational* matters have an impact also on the choice of system development approach; will transactions based on electronic signatures take place in open and/or closed networks?

A major task related to all the above mention aspects of system development approach is, of course, to ensure *legal validity* of electronic signatures.

3. System design

3.1 Conceptual model of legally relevant building blocks

After having captured an appropriate system development approach the next phase of an implementation of electronic signatures is *system design.* A *conceptual model of legally relevant building blocks* will support this process. Without going into any detailed (technical) explanations the list below comprises *core concepts (C) and actions (A)* related to electronic signatures:[7]

---

6) See e.g. Magnusson Sjöberg, Cecilia Critical Factors in Legal Document Management (Stockholm 1998).

7) See further illustrations in the Appendix.

- Electronic identity (C)
  - o States that a certain user is the holder of a specific public key, for instance, by using a certificate provided by a trusted third party (TTP)
- Electronic identification/authentication (A)
  - o Confirmation of electronic identity at a specific time, for instance, by using passwords Signature object (C)
  - o For example, an e-invoice, a contract or product data
- Electronic signing (A)
  - o Process comprising the calculation of data extract to be encrypted by a private key
- Electronic signature (C)
  - o Encrypted data extract attached to the signature object
- Electronic verification (A)
  - o Process comprising the calculation of data extract of signature object and decryption of signature data, and also comparison of hash sums
- Electronic encryption of signature object (A)
  - o Ensuring confidentiality
- Electronic decryption of signature object (A)
  - o Ensuring confidentiality

From the listing above it becomes clear that one should not be fooled by a *handwritten digital signature*, i.e. an image of a pencil drawn signature that has been transformed into a computer readable format, for example, by scanning. Such a signature is not dynamically related to the signature object in the way a digital signature is. This somewhat trivial comment points at the importance of grasping the *functionality* of electronic signatures (in a broad sense).

Electronics signatures may be implemented in many ways depending on the application area. A so called *Public Key Infrastructure (PKI)* is a model that has governed not the least the European Union normative initiative. From a general business point of view (including legal considerations) it is of vital importance to analyse which information security functions a chosen model supports. For instance, an implementation of electronic signatures based on a PKI supports authenticity, control of data integrity and non-repudiation (in a technical sense). It does not, however, support data integrity (protection of against distortion of data) and confidentiality (protection against unauthorised access to data).

In practice, not only the legal implications of the overall implementation model but each entry in the list of core concepts and actions (above) need to be considered. To exemplify, many e-business activities include a wide variety of *signature objects*. It is no doubt a worthwhile task to structure key signature objects according to their major characteristic from the point of view of signing. The list below illustrates a variety of possible signature objects.

- Record/Document
    - Fraction
    - Singular
    - Collection
- Case
    - Process oriented data
- Messages
    - E-mail
    - Attachments
- Transaction
    - Business oriented data
- Context
    - For example, authentication data
- Version
    - Content
    - Format
- Links
    - Internal
    - External

3.2 Extraction of application related legally relevant information

A conceptual model of legal building blocks may not only be taken advantage of for the purpose of a general analysis of core concepts and actions but also for extraction of *application related legally relevant information*. In the context of e-contracting, it is, for instance, important to uphold a distinction between an electronically signed invitation to treat on the one hand and an electronically signed binding offer on the other.[8] Furthermore, legal requirements may call for various security levels of how electronic signatures are implemented. Here reference should be made to the Signature Directive (1999/93/EC) that includes provisions defining (simple) electronic signatures, advanced and qualified ones.

3.3 Digital representation of legally relevant information

In order to make an implementation of electronic signatures running in a technical environment the application relevant information must be *digitally represented*. For this purpose there are, as mentioned above, several techniques available. PKI-

---

8) See further e.g. Edwards, Lilian and Waelde, Charlotte, Law & Internet: a framework for electronic commerce (Oxford 2000), Fejø, Jens, Nielsen, Ruth, and Riis, Thomas, Legal Aspects of Electronic Commerce (Copenhagen 2001), and Ramberg, Christina, Contracting on the Internet: Trends and Challenges (Stockholm 2002) pp. 109-116.

technologies, EDI-solutions,[9] data base technologies, information standards and web services[10] are just a few examples of components in today's technical infrastructures.

3.4 Legal user interfaces

One dimension of implemented electronic signatures that should not be underestimated concerns what may be labelled as *legal user interfaces*. In fact, this notion manifests the need for legal system management that was established already during the 70ies (see introduction above), which during the following two decades evolved into theories of legal system development and legal standards. Today, it is even possible to find legal user interfaces as an explicit goal of public agencies.[11] Basically, it has to do with an awareness of the advantages of integrating legal aspects not only into preparatory system design work, e.g. focusing on governing legal frameworks, but also to allow legal aspects to have an impact on the final technical work, including user dialogues. By doing so prospects of well-founded trust in information technology will increase.

An approach to legal user interfaces oriented towards electronic signatures could, for example, aim at, (a) an acceptable level of functionality, (b) a reasonable level of complexity, and (c) that information security is upheld. A successful implementation from this point of view might be that "you see what you sign", that user dialogues are comprehensible even for non-experts and that information security requirements are met not only from a technical point of view but also from a legal. These points may appear to be simple and easy to accomplish, but in practice taking current business applications into consideration, they are not.

3.5 Concluding remarks on system design

In a business environment an application involving electronic signatures involves various constellations of trusted as well as not trusted parties. These actors might be known as well as not known. Obviously, it is important to illuminate *different roles and authorities* as clearly as possible.

Furthermore, the notion of "electronic signatures" is not to be mistaken for a singular function as it implies a whole *process of actions* based on legal, technical as well as business oriented building blocks.

---

9) Electronic Data Interchange

10) See further e.g. Newcomer, Eric, Understanding Web Services (Boston 2002).

11) See further SAMSET (Samhällets elektroniska tjänster), i.e. a Swedish initiative within the area of e-supported public services, www.rsv.se/samset/samset/html

Although, PKI-technology did not meet the expectations that were raised when it was first introduced it is too early to out rule this approach completely. Rather, it appears to be time to revisit *PKI* techniques in combination with new methods for *identity management (IdM)*. A challenge in this context is no doubt to keep control of the level of *complexity*. This applies in particular to how electronic signatures are implemented from a user's point of view.

4. System management

4.1. An electronic signature strategy

A successful implementation of electronic signatures presupposes not only a system development approach and system design activities. After an application is up and running the phase of *system management* begins. This could be expressed also as a need for an *electronic signature strategy* (e-sig strategy for short).

To illustrate, one critical factor in such an e-sig strategy is to decide upon storage object(s). With this view in mind, it might be important to differentiate between *various kinds of signature objects*, such as an e-invoice, a contract, product data, etc. A key point in today's discussion is whether to store or not to store the electronic signature itself and/or signature data. Signature data are here to be understood as contextual information on conditions for applying a signature, e.g. time, roles and authorities of individuals involved. A closely related question concerns for how long time, if any, there is a need to save an electronic signature and/or signature data?

An e-sig strategy is governed by *legal requirements* as well as *business conditions* and available technical tools. There are, for instance, comprehensive rules and regulations demanding long term archival of original data within the pharmaceutical industry. Another reason for archiving electronic signatures has to with its potential as digital evidence in a future court trial.

Yet another incentive for an e-sig strategy may be found in business imperatives related to cost reduction or return on investments (Ro) as well as prospects of future business transactions.

4.2. An e-sig method

An e-sig strategy needs to be supplemented with an *e-sig method*. The purpose may be expressed in terms of long term management of electronically signed data objects. Such a method must be based on technical solutions in combination with organisational ones. More precisely, it will support archival functions by way of *attaching* or *detaching* signatures. As pointed out before, certain aspects of signature data may be relevant for archival purposes. Verification data can, for instance, function as support for security assurance (a kind of contextual meta data). An e-sig method could also provide measures for *resigning* signature objects. Not every application will, however, demand archival of electronic signatures (in a broad sense).

5. Challenges

5.1. Dynamic management of electronic signatures

The discussion above about system development approach, system design and system management boils down to a need for *dynamic management of electronic signatures*. Evidently, this is not trivial to accomplish. Just to mention a few *complicating factors* one individual may be associated with several organisational roles and at the same time be holder of a variety of authorities. Furthermore, a group of individuals may be authorised to sign the same signature object (e.g. an e-invoice, a contract, an electronically filed job application). One singular record may comprise a whole set of signed data fractions. In practice, many e-business applications are characterised by workflows of signed signature objects. Etc. One way of dealing with the challenges of electronic signatures is to *build trusted legal infrastructures*. The notion of legal infrastructure may be explained as those parts of a legal system that forms the basis and conditions for legal activities. Trust has become a common denominator for evaluation of IT-applications. A somewhat deepened analysis of the trust concept shows that from a legal point of view it is motivated to differentiate between well-founded trust, un-founded trust, well-founded mistrust and un-founded mistrust. *Legally applied information standards* is another step towards dynamic management of electronic signatures. In this context *proactive law* plays an important role. This is, however, not to be understood as legislative actions but rather to let law play an active role in IT-related activities. One example, worth mentioning of is the development of legally oriented vocabularies that take advantage of information standards.

Considering the rapid development of e-business applications based on information standards it is motivated to here (briefly) presentXML – Extensible Markup Language.[12] The core document markup standard XML is a W3C[13] Recommendation[14] with a whole family of related standards and vocabularies. For the purpose of document markup there is UBL (Universal Business

---

12) See also e.g. Lundblad, Nicklas and Magnusson Sjöberg, Cecilia, Making Money from Information Standards. In: XML Europe 2003, 5-8 May, 2003, London, Conference Proceedings. 22 pp. Electronically available at www.lisan.org (publications).

13) World Wide Web Consortium

14) See further www.w3.org/TR/REC-xml.

Language). ebXML (e-business XML) supports messaging and with the prospects of enhancing information security there are XML encryption, XML digital signatures and SAML (Security Assertion Markup Language).[15]

XML offers an expressiveness that enables contents markup etc. far beyond what is possible to accomplish with HTML (Hyper Text Markup Language). This is of vital importance considering that legal information is not just any kind of information.[16] The inherent possibility of validation of applied markup is a true advantage considering the special data quality demands related to the management of legal information.

An XML document can be well-formed or governed by either a so called DTD (Document Type Definition) or schema. The document instance comprises the encoded document containing subject oriented data (e.g. legal text), markup (element tags and attributes) and a DTD reference. The text below illustrates a marked up text unit in the Data Protection Directive (95/46/EC) including element tags and an attribute (ID).

```
<ARTICLE ID='A3-95-46-EC'><ARTTITLE>Scope
</ARTTITLE><ARTNO>Article 3 </ARTNO>
<PARA> 1.
    This Directive shall apply to the processing of personal data wholly or partly
by automatic means, and to the processing otherwise than by automatic means of
personal data which form part of a filing system or are intended to form part of a
filing system.> </PARA> ... </ARTICLE>
```

As a tool for digital signatures XML offers a variety of *signature methods*.[17] In comparison with conventional monolithic methods that do not allow for diversity XML based approaches are more selective. A major advantage is the possibility to take advantage of previously structured and marked up text unities. Of course, one has to consider the implications of signature implementation – attached/detached (see figures 1 and 2 below) – in this technical environment too. What are the consequences, with regard to, *storage requirements* depending on archival time, whether or not data must be unchanged, needs for data migration and accessibility requirements; who will use the signature data and how will it be used, etc.? All this will have an impact on the technical implementation in terms of software, operating system, network solutions, etc.

---

15) See further e.g. Ray, Erik T., Learning XML (Sebastopol 2003) and Chiu, Eric, ebXML Simplified. (New York 2002).

16) Introducing XML into the legal domain requires awareness of how different legal sources relate to each other according to their norm hierarchical status etc.

17) See further XML-Signature Syntax and Processing, www.w3.org/TR/xmldsig-core

```
<signature>
...
        <signature data>
                signature
        ...
                                  context
                <contents>
                Party A                     signed
                Party B                     part
                Party C

                Clause 1
                Clause 2
                Clause 3
```

```
<contents>
Party A
Party B
Party C
Clause 1
Clause 2
Clause 3
</contents>
<signature>
...
        <signature data>
        ...
        </signature
data>
```

Figure 1 Attached signatures

```
<Contents>
Part A
Part B
Part C
Clause 1
Clause 2
Clause 3
</Contents>
```

```
<signature>
...
   <signature data>
...
   </signature data>
</signature>
```

Figure 2 Detached signature

5.2. Working fora

Means and methods for managing electronic signatures do not evolve by themselves and there are working fora showing a specific interest in these kind of questions. Emerging legal networks in combination with research and development activities in the field of law and informatics[18] are just a few examples.

The network approach can be illustrated by LISA – Legal Information

18) The SLIM Project – Secure Legal Information Management – is one example hereof (see further www.juridicum.su.se/slim/). The Action Plan of SLIM can be summarised in the following focus points: (a) critical analysis of ICT-related security initiatives e.g. XML Digital Signatures, (b) exploring the use of language technology to enhance trust chains in legal information retrieval, and (c) conceptualisation of legal requirements with the prospects of security branding.

Standards Action Network.[19] It is an international non-commercial network with the overall purpose to support an in-depth understanding of the interaction of law and IT. The LISA network has an open agenda and functions as a supplementary arena for legal review and legal system design beyond formalised representation of legal expertise.[20] LISA focuses not only on system design issues but also on substantive law.

The action plan and goal for LISA can briefly be explained in the following way:

- Information standards need to be legally managed

  LISA takes responsibility forsharing information about the legal implications of information standards.
- The digital network society requires proactive law

  LISA plays a new role in the shaping of law in the information market. Major means and methods for LISAare to produce legal reviews of information standards and to contribute to ongoing debates as well as to support legal system design activities.
- Trust enhancement is the goal

Anyone interested in working with LISA is welcome to join the network as a member or observateur![21]

---

19) See further www.lisan.org

20) An umbrella network for the Swedish branch of LEXML (see e.g. www.lexml.de) which may be described as a European response to the US LegalXML initiative. Formally LegalXML is an OASIS Member Section (Organization for the Advancement of Structured Information Standards). that unites legal and technical experts in a common forum to create standards for the electronic exchange of legal data. There are quite a few technical committees associated to LegalXML: LegalXML Court Filing, LegalXML eContracts, LegalXML eNotary, LegalXML Integrated Justice, LegalXML Lawful Interception, LegalXML Legislative Documents, LegalXML Online Dispute Resolution, and LegalXML Legal Transcripts.

21) Collective positions are drawn up by a formalised procedure of Request for Comments (RFC) and Request for Position (RFP).

References

Chiu, Eric, ebXML Simplified: A Guide to the New Standard for Global E-Commerce. New York: Wiley, 2002.

Edwards, Lilian and Waelde, Charlotte, Law & Internet: a framework for electronic commerce. Second Edition (1997). Oxford: Hart Publishing 2000.

Fejø, Jens, Nielsen, Ruth, and Riis, Thomas, Legal Aspects of Electronic Commerce. Copenhagen: Jurist- og Økonomforbundets Forlag, 2001.

Lundblad, Nicklas and Magnusson Sjöberg, Cecilia, Making Money from Information Standards. In: XML Europe 2003, 5-8 May, 2003, London, Conference Proceedings. 22 pp. (electronically published on a CD).
See also http://www.lisan.org/li/docs/xmleurope/London03/02-05-06.pdf

Magnusson Sjöberg, Cecilia, Critical Factors in Legal Document Management.
Stockholm: Jure förlag, 1998.

Magnusson Sjöberg, Cecilia, Tillit i informationssamhället: Kejsarens nya kläder eller förändrade förutsättningar för rättsutvecklingen? In: Nordisk årsbok i rättsinformatik (NÅR) 2002, Anonymitet Övervakning Tillit pp. 107-125, Ed. Peter Blume. Stockolm: Jure förlag, 2003.

Magnusson Sjöberg, Cecilia, Rättsautomation: Särskilt om statsförvaltningens
datorisering. Stockholm: Norstedts juridik, 1992.

Newcomer, Eric, Understanding Web Services: XML, WSDL, SOAP, and UDDI.. Boston: Addison-Wesley, 2002.

Ramberg, Christina, Contracting on the Internet: Trends and Challenges. In: SOU 2002:112 (Swedish Government Official Reports), Law and Information Technology, Swedish Views, An anthology produced by the IT Law Observatory of the Swedish ICT Commission, pp. 109-116

Ray, Erik T., Learning XML (Second Edition 2001). Sebastopol: O´Reillly, 2003)

Schartum, Dag Wiese, Rettssikkerhet og systemutvikling i offentlig forvaltning.
Oslo: Universitetsforlaget, 1993.

Seipel, Peter, Computing Law: Perspectives on a New Legal Discipline. Stockholm: LiberFörlag, 1977.

The Legal and market Aspects of Electronic Signatures Jos Dumortier et.al. Study for the European Commission – DG Information Society, Service Contract Nr. C 28.400. Leuven: Interdisciplinary centre for Law & Information Technology, 2003.

Websites
SAMSET (Samhällets elektroniska tjänster)A Swedish initiative within the area of e-supported public services
www.rsv.se/samset/samset/html
XML W3C Recommendation
www.w3.org/TR/REC-xml.
XML-Signature Syntax and Processing
www.w3.org/TR/xmldsig-core
The SLIM Project – Secure Legal Information Management
www.juridicum.su.se/slim/
LISA – Legal Information Standards Action Network
www.lisan.org
LEXML
See e.g. the LEXML network in Germany
http://www.lexml.de/
LegalXML, part of the OASIS effort (Organization for the Advancement of Structured Information Standards). Legal XML's mission is to create open, non-proprietary standards for legal documents and applications.
http://www.oasis-open.org/home/index.php

Appendix

Illustrations of (a) electronic signing, (b) verification of signature and (c) Public Key Infrastructure (PKI)

(a) Electronic signing

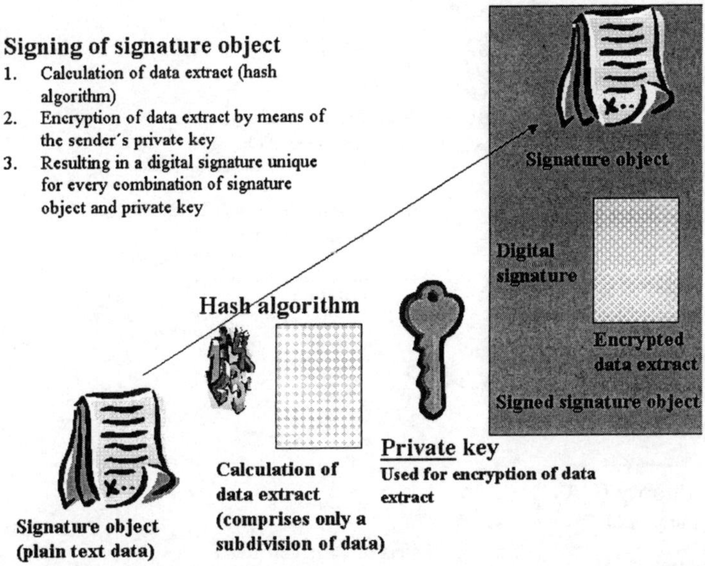

(b) Verification of signature

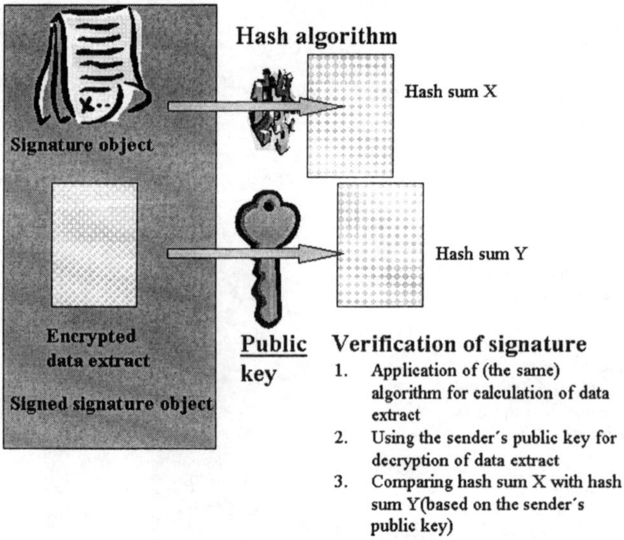

(c) Public Key Infrastructure (PKI)

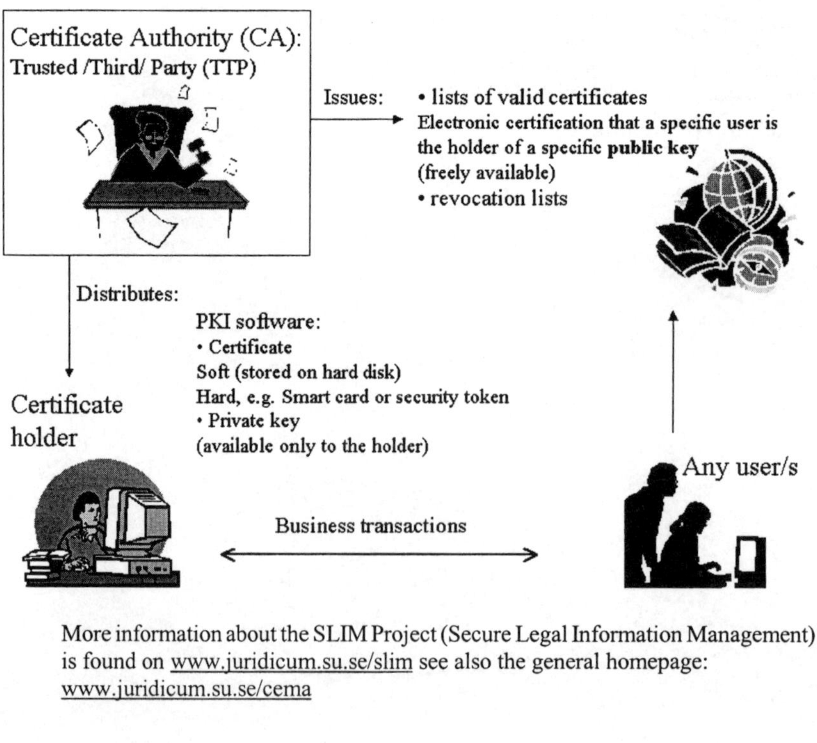

More information about the SLIM Project (Secure Legal Information Management) is found on www.juridicum.su.se/slim see also the general homepage: www.juridicum.su.se/cema

Principles of European Contract Law and the Formation of Contracts in the Information Society

by Katarzyna Kryczka*

1. Formation of electronic contracts – the need for harmonisation

The development of electronic communication technologies has created a new marketplace for the trade in goods and services worldwide. This is most notably true in the case of transactions concluded on the Internet. Modern technologies allow parties to enter into contracts in a manner that provides speed, ease, a mass scale and a cross-border range with which traditional means of contracting cannot easily compare. Contracting in the era of the Information Society is a new phenomenon and has resulted in the development of new models of commercial interaction. Contracts negotiated and concluded electronically can present difficult and sometimes novel questions for traditional contract law. One of the affected issues is contract formation – a problem that remains at the heart of legal considerations regarding electronic commerce.[1]

National legislators are currently seeking to provide their laws with solutions that will contribute to the predictability of a legal environment for electronic transactions and could answer the basic questions of "whether", "when", "where" and "on what terms" a contract is concluded when the

* The author is a Ph.D. researcher in Molengraaff Institute for Private Law, Utrecht University, the Netherlands. She prepares a doctoral thesis on Formation of Contracts in the Information Society under supervision of Professor Ewoud Hondius and Professor Willem Grosheide.

1) See e.g. Chissick M. Kelman A., *Electronic commerce – law and practice*, Sweet & Maxwell, London 1999; D'arcy L. et al., Schmithoff's Export Trade – The Law and Practice of International Trade, Sweet & Maxwell, London 2000; *Formation and Validity of On-line contracts*, a study by Institute for Information Law, Amsterdam, available at <http://www.imprimatur.net/contracts.htm>; Hoeren T., *Internetrecht*, available at: < http://www.uni-muenster.de/Jura.itm/hoeren/material/Skript/skript.pdf>; Nimmer R. T., *Principles of contract law in electronic commerce*, Schmithoff Symposium 2000, Session 4-6, available at: http:// www.ccls.edu/ eclu/ events/ Schmitthoff/SYMPOSIUM_Draft_4-6.html; Reed C., *Internet Law - text and materials*, Butterworths, London Edinburgh Dublin 2000; Rosenoer J., *Cyberlaw - the law of the Internet*, Springer-Verlag, New York, Berlin, Heidelberg 1996; Spindler G. Börner F. (eds), *E-commerce Law in Europe and the USA*, Springer-Verlag, New York, Berlin, Heidelberg 2001; Wright B. Winn J.K., *The Law of Electronic commerce*, Aspen Publishers 2000.

parties come into contact by means of electronic communications. However, transactions on the Internet often extend beyond the national level and a patchwork of particular local laws does not sufficiently eliminate the legal a survey conducted by the ICC Ad hoc Expert Group on electronic commerce,[2] the lack of harmonisation between different legal systems is considered by businesses to be an obstacle that may eventually hamper the development of electronic commerce. Also in case of consumer contracts the uncertainity whether and when a consumer enters into a legally binding contract constitutes one of the main barriers in building consumer confidence in e-commerce.

On the global level, the need to provide such harmonised rules which would regulate concluding contracts electronically has been recognised, among others, by UNCITRAL. It has introduced UNCITRAL Model Law on Electronic Commerce in 1996[3] and currently the UNCITRAL's Working Group on Electronic Commerce is working on developing of a new instrument, possibly a convention, dealing with specific issues of forming contracts by electronic means (UNCITRAL: Electronic contracting: Provisions for a Draft Convention).[4]

For Europe this means that at least between the Member States it would be desirable to introduce a uniform set of rules governing the issues of electronic contracting. This could result not only in facilitating cross-border contracting by electronic means within the EU but also contribute to the establishment of a common and strengthened negotiating position of Europe in international forums. An attempt to do so has to some extent already been made by the European Union by introducing, among other things, the EC Directive on Electronic Commerce,[5] the EC Directive on Distance Contracts[6] and the EC Directive on Electronic Signatures.[7] Nevertheless, as regards the mechanisms of contract formation (invitation to treat, offer, acceptance, time

---

2) Annex to ICC Expert Group Report on draft UNCITRAL convention on electronic contracting, available at http://www.iccwbo.org/home/e_business/-uncitral_ conven tion_report.asp.

3) UNCITRAL Model Law on Electronic Commerce 1996, General Assembly resolution 51/162 of 16 December 1996.

4) UNCITRAL: Electronic contracting: Provisions for a Draft Convention, document under preparation, working materials are available at: <www.uncitral.org.

5) Directive 2000/31/EC of the European Parliament and of the Council on certain legal aspects of information society services, in particular electronic commerce, in the Internal Market, OJ L 178, 17.7.2000.

6) Directive 1997/7/EC of the European Parliament and of the Council of 20 May 1997 on the protection of consumers in respect of distance contracts OJ L 144, 04/06/1997.

7) Directive 1999/93/EC of the European Parliament and of the Council of 13 December 1999 on a Community framework for electronic signatures OJ L 013, 19/01/2000.

and place of contract formation), the efforts undertaken while drafting the EC Directive on Electronic Commerce, aimed at harmonizing some of these issues (mainly the time when electronic contracts are formed), have eventually failed. As a result, the harmonisation of rules determining the formation of electronic contracts has not been achieved. [8]

Moreover, the approach adopted by the EC Directive on Electronic Commerce in respect of electronic contracts, based on a broad framework with details to be implemented on the local levels may not achieve the desired uniformity. It has been noticed that in seeking a harmonised supranational solution for electronic contracts there is a need for high-level agreement, not just on overarching principles, but also on some particular details. Differences in detail potentially frustrate the uniformity which is essential to the free flow of electronic commerce.[9]

The principles formulated in the literature[10] as ones that are indispensable for a legislative response in dealing with issues of electronic contracting include, among other requirements, the following:

the same legal effect should be given to contracts concluded electronically as to traditional, paper-based transactions (including the

---

8) For more on issues of electronic contracts in the E-commerce Directive, see, among a huge amount of literature, e.g.: Brownsword R. Howells G., *Europe's E-commerce Directive – a too hasty legislative rush to judgement?* Journal of Law and Information Science (2000) Vol. 11 No. 1 pp.77-88; Dickie J., *Internet and Electronic Commerce Law in the European Union*, Hart Publishing, Oxford 1999; Gavanon I. Lagarde-Bellec E., *What is new under the EC Directive on "Electronic Commerce"*, Revue de droit des affaires internationales (2001) No 6 pp. 723-740; Grosheide F.W., *The Legal Mapping and Tracking of Electronic Commerce – a view from the EU*, in: European Private Law, E-commerce issue, Articles on International Commercial Contracts and Intellectual Property, Molengrafica 1999/2000; Murray A.D., *Contracting Electronically in the Shadow of the E-Commerce Directive*, in: Edwards L. (ed), The New Legal Framework for E-Commerce, Hart Publishing, Oxford. (Forthcoming 2003); Lindholm P. Maennel F. M., *Directive on Electronic Commerce (2000/31/EC)*, Computer und Recht International (2000) Vol. 3 pp. 65-69; Lodder A. R., *Directive 2000/31/EC on certain legal aspects of information society services, in particular electronic commerce, in the Internal Market* in: Lodder A. R. Kaspersen H., eDirectives: Guide to European Union Law on E-commerce, Kluwer Law International, The Hague London New York 2002; Pearce G. Plattern N., *Promoting the Information Society: The EU Directive on Electronic Commerce*; European Law Journal (2000) Vol. 6, No. 4 pp.363-378; Ramberg C., *The E-commerce Directive and Formation of Contract in the Comparative Perspective*, in: Fejø J. Nielsen R. Riis T. (eds), Legal Aspects of Electronic Commerce (Jurist-og Økonomforbundets Forlag 2001).

9) O'Rourke M. A., *Progressing Towards A Uniform Commercial Code For Electronic Commerce Or Racing Towards Nonuniformity'* 14 Berkeley Technology and Law Journal 635, 641 (1999).

10) Poggi C. T., *Electronic Commerce Legislation: An Analysis Of European And American Approaches To Contract Formation* 41 Virginia. Journal of International Law 224, 277 (2000).

elimination of such obstacles as certain form requirements that are not suited to the electronic environment);

clear and predictable rules governing when and how contracts which are formed electronically should become legally binding and enforceable (preferably mirroring the rules for traditional contracts as far as possible and affirming the validity of the procedures that have already been established for electronic contracting);

legal provisions should be technology-neutral, that is, electronic commerce legislation should not have the purpose or effect of encouraging or mandating the use of one technology over another;

the same legal effect should be given to electronic messages originating in another nation or state as to domestic messages;

the rules should be consistent, practicable and based on common principles.

2. Harmonised European contract law – the Principles of European Contract Law

The discussion on the potential European harmonisation of rules determining the formation of electronic contracts should not, however, be totally detached from considerations with regard to the general harmonisation of contract law in Europe. After all, one of the points often raised in the debate on electronic contracts is that they are not believed to be (apart from certain technicalities that have to be considered) fundamentally different from contracts concluded by more traditional means.[11] It would not be desirable to apply rules for the formation of electronic contracts that would result in a duality of formation regimes depending on the technical means which are used for contracting.[12]

The trend towards harmonisation of contract law in Europe is strongly represented in contemporary legal thinking and also constitutes a part of the considerations of the European Commission. The most recent example thereof is the Communication from the Commission regarding an Action Plan for a more coherent European contract law.[13] Among the origins of this trend is an

---

11) Donnie L. Kidd Jr., William H. Daughtrey Jr. *Adapting Contract Law To Accommodate Electronic Contracts: Overview and Suggestions*, 26 Rutgers Computer and Technology Law Journal 215, 269 (2000) and further UNCITRAL Legal aspects of electronic commerce, Electronic contracting: provisions for a draft convention, Note by the Secretariat A/CN.9/WG.IV/WP.95 p. 5.

12) Similarly, Smith G., *Legislating for electronic transactions,* 8(3) Computer and Telecommunications Law Review 58, 58 (2002).

13) Communication from the Commission to the European Parliament and the Council, A More Coherent European Contract Law, An Action Plan, COM (2003) 68 final.

initiative launched by a group of academics who constituted the Commission of European Contract Law (also known as the Lando Commission). The Lando Commission - a body of academic lawyers from all the Member States of the European Union under the chairmanship of Professor Ole Lando - commenced its work in the early 1980s with the aim of developing a set of provisions that could be applied as uniform rules of contract law in the European Union. The working methodology focused on comparative research into the legal systems of the Member States, with the objective of identifying a common core of contract law in Europe that could serve as the basis for creating a workable uniform system.

Among the drafters were some of the most prominent contract law experts in Europe. Their work resulted in the creation of the Principles of European Contract Law (hereinafter referred to as "the PECL" or "the Principles") - a soft-law instrument that offers a carefully elaborated system of rules based on extensive comparative work.[14] The provisions of the Principles are derived from different legal systems combined into what were considered by the drafters to be the most appropriate solutions and sometimes new innovative rules have been proposed.[15] The PECL is believed to provide a bridge between the civil law and the common law by establishing rules designed to reconcile their differing legal philosophies (Introduction p. xxiii). Thus, the PECL constitute a satisfactory compromise which could be acceptable to the different legal systems of Europe.

Concerning the formation of contracts, the PECL contain a comprehensive regulation on these issues and remain in harmony with the

---

14) Principles of European Private Law, prepared by The Commission of European Private Law, ed. Lando O. Beale H., (Kluwer Law International 2000). The Principles are intended to be of service in a number ways to a wide range of institutions, enterprises or individuals. Among their stated purposes is to provide a legal foundation for measures taken by the organs of the European Union in the area of contract law, as well as to serve as a model for future harmonisation. Other aims include the express adoption of the Principles by the parties to govern their contract and serving as a modern *lex mercatoria* in Europe. Finally, the PECL could be a model for the judicial and legislative development of contract law. See Article 1:101 PECL and Introduction p. xxiii – xxiv.

15) For literature on the PECL, see e.g. Castronovo C., *Contract and the Idea of Codification in the Principles of European Contract Law* in: Fejø J. Nielsen R. (eds.), Festskrift til Ole Lando, Copenhagen 1997; Hartkamp A., *The UNIDROIT Principles for International Commercial Contracts and the Principles of European Contract Law*, European Review of Private Law (1994); Hesselink M. W. De Vries G.J.P., *Principles of European Contract Law*, Kluwer 2001; Lando O., *Principles of European Contract Law. An Alternative or a Precursor of European Legislation*, Rabels Zeitschr. (1992); Lando O., *Why codify the European Law of contract?*, European Review of Private Law (1997) Vol. 5 pp.525-536; Schelhaas H. (ed.) et al., *The Principles of the European Contract Law and Dutch Law*, Ars Aequi Libri, Nijmegen and Kluwer Law International, The Hague, London, New York 2002.

substantive contract laws of most of the Member States as well as the United Nations Convention for International Sale of Goods.[16]

3. The PECL and the formation of electronic contracts

Having regard to the above remarks it could be worth considering whether the PECL can be used as a point of departure for the European regulation of contract formation in electronic commerce. Their application (if found to be appropriate) would allow avoiding the duality of contract formation regimes depending on the means used for contract formation and would keep any differences (where necessary) to the essential minimum. Such an "Information Society-proof" analysis of the PECL should refer to their general principles and underlying values as well as to the specific legal provision contained therein.

The idea of the Commission of European Contract Law was to design rules which would provide maximum flexibility and could be accommodated in a range of different situations. The Principles should therefore be interpreted and developed in accordance with their purposes, with particular regard to promoting good faith and fair dealing, certainty in contractual relationships and uniformity of application (Article 1:106 (1) PECL). This is meant, first of all, to avoid a strict and narrow interpretation of their provisions, but also to be able to accommodate future developments in legal thinking in the field of contract law (Comment B). This "liberal" interpretation of the PECL, as established by its drafters, has a static and dynamic aspect (Comment C). The former envisages situations which might occur when the PECL were drafted but which have been overlooked or omitted, the latter refers to new situations that could not then be imagined. Moreover, the PECL contain a rule for their supplementation, which allows certain legal issues, remaining within the scope prescribed for the Principles, but not expressly settled by them, to be solved in accordance with the ideas underlying the Principles (Article 1:106 (2) PECL). This flexible approach should thus allow the PECL to be applied, by means of their appropriate interpretation, to such a new phenomenon as contracting with the use of information technologies. The Principles even include some considerations regarding electronic communications e.g. in its definition of writing.

The Principles are based on freedom of contract (mainly limited by good faith and fair dealing as well as certain mandatory rules established by the PECL), and nothing within them shall preclude the parties from concluding their contracts by means of their choice, including electronic communication.

16) United Nations Convention on Contracts for the International Sale of Goods (Vienna 1980).

The PECL also do not establish any form requirements which condition the valid conclusion of a contract. Specifically, such communications as an offer and an acceptance are categorised in the Principles as notices. Notices can be made in any form which is appropriate in the circumstances (Article 1:303 (1)). The examples enumerated in the Comments to the Article expressly include, among others, notices made by electronic mail. The fact that this catalogue refers to such means of communication as electronic mail shows that the drafters intended to take into account new technical developments (also other than electronic mail e.g. communication through an interactive website) that can conceivably be used by parties for contracting purposes. As a result, under the PECL electronic contracts should be given, in principle, the same legal effect as contracts concluded by traditional means.

Another feature that could be important in the context of electronic commerce is the significance that the PECL attribute to practices and usages. Usages may be described as a course of dealing or line of conduct which is and for a certain period of time has been gradually adopted by those engaged in trade or in a particular trade. Practice is a state of affairs arising as a result of a previous conduct under a particular transaction or a particular sort of transactions between the parties (Article 1:105, Comment B). Under the PECL, both practices and usages, when applicable to the contract, have priority over the rules of law (including those of the PECL) that would otherwise apply (Article 1:105). This leaves space for parties to use (while the PECL could remain a general framework governing their contract) codes of conduct or other self-regulation instruments, which are often considered to be the most suitable tools for addressing specific issues of the electronic commerce regulation.

Furthermore, although they contain a thorough regulation of the formation model based on offer and acceptance, the PECL are also applicable to contracts concluded by alternative methods. The Principles expressly recognize that agreements are often made in circumstances where it is impossible to analyse the process of offer and acceptance. This can be of particular importance in electronic commerce where the relationship between the parties can often include a great deal of communication which does not necessarily fit within the traditional analysis of the offer and acceptance model. The PECL have noted that, even if the rules on offer and acceptance cannot always be applied to such alternative contracting models, sometimes it is possible to do so. Examples of rules that can be applied include provisions concerning the following: acceptance, non-acceptance by silence, rejection, modified acceptance. In such cases the provisions of the PECL should be applied with appropriate adaptations (Article 2:211).

The PECL are applicable both to transactions between professionals as well as to consumer contracts, which are of ever-increasing importance in contracting on the Internet. They are confined, however, to the general law of contractual obligations and they do not make special provisions for consumer contracts which, as was decided, raise policy issues more appropriately determined by Community law and national legislations (Introduction p. xxv). Nothing in the text of the PECL affects the protection of consumers, neither does it prevent the application of provisions aimed at additional consumer protection that could be enacted on the national, supranational or international level. In such a case the resulting solution would be a common legal framework applicable for both types of transactions in question, which, however, would not be exhaustive, as far as consumer contracts are concerned. The details regarding additional consumer protection would have to be dealt separately. [17]

The above general remarks will be complemented by a brief presentation of a few selected provisions of the PECL in the field of contract formation which are of relevance for electronic commerce.

Invitation to treat compared to an offer

One of the main problems in the formation of electronic contracts is that of determining whether offering goods or services via the Internet constitutes in fact an offer to enter into a contract.[18]

This can be true, above all, in the case of websites featuring not only a presentation of goods or services but also technical means for their purchase. It is in particular the interactive character of communication that may lead to the situation where electronic transactions may not fit easily within the established distinction between an offer and a mere "invitation to treat." From one point of view, the procedure of contracting with the use of interactive applications, may quite reasonably lead the second party to assume that he faces an offer and when he accepts it by placing an order and following the payment instructions he is validly concluding a contract at that point in time (this could be of particular importance for purchase orders for securities, commodities or other items with a strongly fluctuating price). On the other

---

17) At the European level the examples of such additional measures can be found e.g. in provisions of the EC Directive on Electronic Commerce and the EC Directive on Distance Contracts. They include extensive information duties, a cooling-off period for the consumer or an obligation to confirm the receipt of the consumer's order. They are not contrary to the provisions of the PECL but rather have a supplementary nature.

18) For reference, see notes 1 and 7 above as well as: Davies L., *Contract Formation on the Internet – Shattering Few Myths* in: Edwards L. Waelde Ch. (eds), Law & the Internet – regulating cyberspace, Hart Publishing, Oxford 1997; Glatt C., *Comparative Issues in the Formation of Electronic Contracts*, International Journal of Law and Information Technology (1998) Vol. 6 No. 1 pp.34-68; Mehrings J., *Vertragsabschluß im Internet*, Multimedia und Recht (1998) No. 1; Murray A.D., *Entering into Contracts Electronically: the Real W.W.W.* in: Edwards L. Waelde Ch. (eds), Law & the Internet – a framework for electronic commerce, Hart Publishing, Oxford – Portland Oregon 2000.

hand, a commercial proposal displayed on the Internet has a global range and can be accessed by an indefinite number of customers. If such a proposal is to be treated as an offer the provider of goods or services could find himself obliged to conclude an unpredictable number of contracts, which could be beyond his stock capacity or intended range of activity (e.g. geographically) or even intended conditions (e.g. in the case of a pricing error).

Under the PECL, as in most of the national legal systems, an offer has to be distinguished from an invitation to treat by the fact that it demonstrates the party's intention to be bound. The PECL recognize that the offer can be communicated not only to one or more specific persons but also to the public at large (Article 2:201 (2)), the latter being usually the case of proposals made on the Internet (e.g. websites). Proposals made to the public such as advertisements, posters, circulars or window displays are to be treated as offers if they are sufficiently definite and can be accepted by anybody (no regard is made to the second party's specific features) (Comment C). The PECL contain also an express provision stating that a proposal to supply goods or services at stated prices by a professional supplier in a public advertisement or a catalogue, or by a display of goods, is presumed to be an offer to sell or supply at that price until the stock of goods, or the supplier's capacity to supply the service, is exhausted (Article 2:201 (3)). Proposals displayed on the website of an e-commerce shop seem to fall within this category.

The above provision is rather interesting from the electronic commerce point of view. Concerning offering goods or services via the Internet, the PECL establish the presumption that, where an online seller states the price of goods or services, he issues a binding offer. His offer is limited, though, by his capacity to supply the offered goods or services. The advantageous feature for electronic commerce is here introduced by the fact that, instead of leaving it only to interpretation, the PECL establish a certain presumption, thereby offering a simple and fast rule which is so desirable for electronic contracting. This provision gives a customer a certain degree of certainty (in principle, this is a customer who, through his acceptance, decides whether the contract is concluded) but also recognizes the fact that the supplier who makes an offer to the public cannot be bound by contracts beyond his capacity to provide. On the other hand, it does not take into account other reasons for which an online seller would like to retain a right of final approval of the contract. The rule, however, is indeed flexible since the presumption can be rebutted when an intention to the contrary follows from the advertisement or the circumstances of the case. It does not therefore prevent the online seller from stating, as is often the case in current business practice, that he is not bound by the displayed information or that his offer is conditional and, as a result, the customer's orders are subject to further acceptance.

Receipt of electronic messages

Electronic contracting is characterised by the fact that the parties exchange messages in an electronic form. In the context of contract formation the most prominent examples of such messages are an offer and an acceptance. Establishing when such an offer and/or an acceptance in an electronic form become effective determines not only the conclusion of the contract but also the time and place of its formation.[19] In order to ascertain the legal effectiveness of communications in the form of electronic messages it is crucial to determine the notions of their receipt and dispatch.

As already mentioned, under the PECL such communications as an offer and an acceptance fall within the category of notices. The general rule is that a notice becomes effective when it reaches the other party (Article 1:303 (3)). It is further explained that a notice reaches the addressee when it is delivered to him or to his place of business or mailing address, or, if he does not have a place of business or mailing address, to his habitual residence (Article 1:303 (4)). The Principles do not require that the notice should actually have come to the addressee's attention provided it has been delivered to him in a normal way (e.g. a letter has been put in his letter box, a message has been sent to his telex or fax machine).

In this respect the PECL are not really well suited to electronic messages. This is true even if a general rule regarding the effectiveness of communications based on the "receipt theory" (as envisaged by the PECL) should also be acceptable to electronic contracts.[20] However, taking into consideration the specific character of technologies used for the transmission of electronic data, the traditional notions determining that a message "reaches", "is delivered" or "is received" by the recipient are difficult to apply. Also the references to the place of business or mailing address used in the PECL can be ambiguous concepts within the electronic environment.

Therefore, for the purposes of electronic communications it would be desirable to have additional rules specifying the notion of receipt in electronic contracts. These rules should take into account the technical particularities of the means of communication used.

On the European level, the principle introduced in this respect is that of Article 11 of the EC Directive on Electronic Commerce. It provides that the order of the customer, as well as the acknowledgement of its receipt made in

---

19) On this issue, apart from the literature referred to in notes 1,7 and 18, Niemann J. M., *Cyber Contracts – A Comparative View on the Actual Time of Formation,* Communications Law (2000), Vol. 5 No. 2, pp.48-53.

20) See an interesting analysis on that in: Eiselen S., *Electronic Commerce and the UN Convention on Contracts for the International Sale of Goods (CISG) 1980*, The EDI Law Review (1999) Vol. 6, pp. 24-28.

an electronic form, are deemed to be received when the parties to whom they are addressed are able to access them. Such a solution is, however, not sufficient not only because it refers merely to such messages as the order and the confirmation of its receipt. It is also the use of the notion of accessibility that can be ambiguous in the context of electronic communications.

An example of the appropriate provision may be found rather in the UNCITRAL Model Law on Electronic Commerce. In order to determine when an electronic message is received Article 15 of the Model Law focuses on the notion of "entry" into an information system used by a recipient. The entry of the message into an information system is indicated by the fact that it becomes available for processing within that information system. This provision establishes a nuanced structure distinguishing whether the recipient has designated an information system to receive electronic messages (if so, in order to be received a message has to enter the designated information system, if not – any information system of the recipient) and whether this system was used by the sender (in such a situation, a receipt is deemed to occur when the electronic message is retrieved by the addressee). It has been felt that these rules reflect the reality of solutions found by business entities that routinely use electronic communications. Useful as they are, the discussed rules can seem somewhat complex and are in their spirit totally different from the Articles of the PECL.

However, a simpler solution can also be found. The US Uniform Electronic Transactions Act[21] formulates an analogical rule regarding the receipt of a message in electronic form referring only to prerequisites that the message has entered the recipient's information processing system and is capable of being processed.

It seems that for the purposes of electronic commerce it could be useful to have a similar rule in the PECL. Such a rule does not necessarily have to be in the form of an Article of the PECL, if it is considered to be too technical, but could for example be contained in the Comments, which in the PECL accompany and explain each provision.

Form requirements

As already mentioned, the PECL do not include any form requirements which condition the valid formation of contracts and preclude the use of electronic

21) Uniform Electronic Transactions Act drafted by the National Conference of Commissioners on Uniform State Laws, Section 15 (b) Unless otherwise agreed between a sender and the recipient, an electronic record is received when: (1) it enters an information processing system that the recipient has designated or uses for the purpose of receiving electronic records or information of the type sent and from which the recipient is able to retrieve the electronic record; and (2) it is in a form capable of being processed by that system.

messages in the process of contracting. However, the Principles often refer to writing as the appropriate form for the parties to use for notices of major importance. (Article 1:303, Comment B). A written statement is e.g. required for the purpose of Article 2:106 (time-limit for acceptance) and Article 2:210 (a professional's written confirmation) of the PECL.

According to the PECL, written statements include communications made by telegram, telex, telefax and electronic mail as well as other means of communication capable of providing a readable record of the statement on both sides (Article 1:301(6)). In cases of telecommunications other than a telegram, telex and telefax the statement is considered to be in writing if it is possible to provide a readable record of the message as transferred on both sides (Comment F). Thus, the definition of "writing" under the PECL places particular emphasis on two elements: the message must be readable and it has to be able to constitute a record of statements contained in it, which should mean that it ought to be available for further reference. Provided that the two above-mentioned conditions are met, a message in an electronic form can be used when "writing" is required (it should suffice that the message is displayed on the computer screen, or even mobile phone, subject to the condition that it can be saved). The conditions envisaged in the discussed provision are comparable with the requirements set by the UNCITRAL Model Law on Electronic Commerce for the functional equivalence of electronic messages with "writing". Thus, the PECL, in fact, also formulate a rule providing for such a functional equivalence - even if they were not drafted specifically for the needs of electronic commerce like the UNCITRAL Model Law was.

Use of automated systems for contracting

Nowadays, an increasing phenomenon in the process of the negotiation and formation of contracts is the use of automated computer systems. Within the parameters of its programming such a system is capable of initiating, responding or interacting with other parties or their computer systems without the further attention of that party once it has been activated. Such systems vary from the simple software performing automated tasks to the complex systems that are able to act autonomously not only on the basis of their instructions but also on the "experience" gained and can even device new instructions for their behaviour (so called intelligent agents).

Nothing in the PECL in fact prohibits the use of automated systems for contract conclusion. As a rule, the Principles accept that parties can set up their own ways of contracting. Moreover, the practice established between the parties (e.g. that they use automated systems) can set aside the provisions of the PECL where they are not in accordance with this practice. Thus, it seems that under the Principles the parties are free to establish an automated communication scheme if they so wish.

However, the PECL do not regulate the paramount issue connected with the application of such systems, that is whether, and to what extent, actions of an automated system, that has been programmed and used by people but acts without human supervision, could bind the user of the system. It could be argued that such a rule is not necessary since the question of attribution of acts of the automated system to the person using it can be solved under general rules of law.[22] Moreover, nowadays it seems to be rather widely accepted that in principle the actions of an automated computer system should be attributed to the person or legal entity using such a system (the opinions regarding the grounds for such attribution and consequently the scope of liability of the employer of the automated system differ, however).[23] Nevertheless, since this issue is relatively new, a rule which provides some solutions to that effect could contribute to certainty and uniformity.

An additional concern could be whether the conceptual approach of the PECL, referring on many occasions to such notions as the intention of the parties or their good faith, can be easily applied in the case of transactions made not by humans but by machines. Nevertheless, these notions, which, at first glance, may seem to be somewhat subjective, have to undergo, according to the PECL provisions, the test of reasonableness, which turns them into objective concepts. Hence, the intention is to be determined from the party's statements or acts and they have to be interpreted as they reasonably appear to the other party (Article 2:102). Similarly, the notion of good faith and fair dealing used in the PECL has two sides: the subjective element of good faith, which refers to honesty and fairness in mind, and the objective one i.e. fair dealing that should be understood as the observance of fairness in fact (Article 1:201 Comment E). Consequently, no particular problems should arise when interpreting the concepts of intention or good faith and fair dealing in automated transactions. They should be construed according to the objective

22) Cavanillas S. Nadal A., *Research paper on contract law, Electronic Commerce Legal Issues Platform (ECLIP) report. Deliverable 2.1.7 bis* and Finocchiaro G., *The conclusion of the electronic contract through software agents'. A false legal problem? Brief considerations,* Computer Law and Security Report (2003) Vol. 19 No. 1 pp. 20-24. This is true in particular if we assume that such systems should be treated merely as tools. In such a situation it is only reasonable that the employer of a tool is responsible for the results obtained by its use since the tool has no independent volition of its own.

23) See e.g. Weitzenbock E.M., *Electronic Agents and Formation of Contracts* International Journal of Law and Information Technology (2001) Vol. 9 No. 3 pp. 204-234; Allen T. Widdison R., *Can computers make contracts?* 9 Harvard Journal of Law and Technology 25; Davies L. supra note 18.

criteria, in the light of acts performed by the automated system used by the party.[24]

4. Hard and fast rules?

As follows from the analysis of both general principles and values underlying the PECL, as well as some of their provisions, the norms of the PECL should be considered sufficiently open and flexible to be also applicable to the formation of electronic contracts. Subject to some exceptions, which could be modified, the interpretation of the PECL provisions allows one to attain the results which are necessary to enable the functioning of electronic contracts. The PECL represent the main concerns of the modern law of contract which include, on the one side, the emphasis on the facilitation of entering into contractual relationships and, on the other, the need for protection of reasonable expectations of the parties. These concerns, as noticed in the literature,[25] remain crucial also when the parties use electronic means for conclusion of the contract.

However, even if electronic contracts are not believed to be essentially different from paper-based contracts, electronic commerce does not fully reproduce contracting patterns used in contract formation through more traditional means. The mechanics of electronic contracting cover a range of situations that existing rules and concepts address without contemplating electronic commerce. This brings about a number of practical questions that require specific attention.

These questions challenge the usual ways of interpretation and the attempts to solve them through extensive recourse thereto can result in the disparity of judicial decisions. Thus, the risk of disharmony in the legal

---

24) In the literature it has even been suggested that an objective understanding of good faith and fair dealing principles can be used to lay down general criteria for determining how the contracting parties should behave. The identified behavioural criteria could be subsequently applied as requirements to be fulfilled by electronic agents involved in contract formation. See Weitzenbock E.M., *Good faith and fair dealing in the context of contract formation by electronic agents*, Proceedings of the AISB 2002 Symposium on Intelligent Agents in Virtual Markets, 2-5 April 2002, Imperial College London. Other authors also refer to notions of good practices or good faith and fair dealing for electronic agents' behaviour, see Brazier F. Oskamp A. Schellekens M. and Wijngaards N., *Can agents close contracts?* Proceedings of the Law and Electronic Agents workshop (LEA'03) available also at <http://www.iids.org/publicationdata/db/lea03_contract/pubdetail> and Schafer B., *It is just not cricket – RoboCup and fair dealing in contract*, Proceedings of the Law and Electronic Agents workshop (LEA'03) available also at http://www.iids.org/projectfolder/alias/events/ProgramLEA2003.htm.

25) So, raising, however, some reservations: Brownsword R. Howells G., *When surfers start to shop. Internet commerce and contract law*, Legal Studies Vol. 19 (1999) pp. 287-315.

solutions for electronic contracting issues is increased and the harmonisation effect could be jeopardised. Therefore, in order to accommodate the needs of electronic commerce some modifications or specifications of traditional rules on contract formation would be needed (e.g. defining the notions of dispatching and receiving of the electronic message, regulating issues connected with the application of automated systems for concluding contracts). On the other hand, these adjustments must continue to fit the purposes underlying the rules of contract law.

The Articles of the PECL do not contain provisions that would be specifically tailored for electronic commerce and would focus on the technicalities of contracting via electronic means. This follows not so much from the fact that the drafters were not aware of the problem as from the intended character of the Principles as a general part of contract law. It is understandable that in the text of the Articles there are no special provisions dealing with, in particular, one selected type of communication used for contracting, even one having such a potential as electronic communication.

Yet, for the sake of the smooth development of electronic commerce there is a need for such specific solutions. Therefore, the application of the PECL to issues related to the formation of electronic contracts may require their supplementation by technical rules which are more suited to realities of electronic communication. Some of such rules could be included in Comments on the relevant Articles in order to provide some guidance as to their interpretation in the context of electronic commerce and to ensure that the applied solutions are uniform. Additionally, since the PECL place great emphasis on the relevance of usages and practices between parties, the specific technical provisions, that would nevertheless operate within the framework created by the PECL and would have a supplementary character, could be contained in the self-regulatory instrument, preferably one operating on the supranational level.

5. Conclusion

In order to encourage the development of the pan-European electronic commerce and to build the position of Europe as the competitive digital economy, the harmonisation of a legal framework governing the formation of electronic contracts would be desirable. The achievement of a uniform solution in this respect is not easy, as demonstrated e.g. by the history of drafting the EC Directive on Electronic Commerce. It seems, though, that elaborating such common rules could be more feasible when based on a set of provisions that has been already recognised as an acceptable compromise for Europe regulating the formation of contract in general. The norms of the PECL, which contain comprehensive regulation on contract formation and are consistent with the legal systems of the Member States, do offer, in principle, a good starting point to flesh out a harmonised solution regarding also the formation of electronic contracts. The PECL could serve here as an inspiration or, more specifically, constitute a basis on which such a uniform solution may be shaped (and, preferably, in the framework of which it should fit so as to remain within the common core of European contract law). Nevertheless, in order to create a modern legislation responding to the specific problems and needs of electronic contracting, a fair amount of elaboration would be indispensable.

Jurisdiction and Enforcement in the Information Society

by Peter Mankowski

I. Introduction

1. Outline

Questions of private international law are widely believed to have seen their relevance and importance augmented by the rise of the Internet. They are believed to have gained momentum. Hence, every symposium on e-commerce law or legal matters of the Internet appears to be incomplete without an internationalist dwelling upon his subject in relation to e-commerce or the Internet. The organisers rightly identified that the foremost question to be answered first, is the question of jurisdiction as it marks the important border-line between a home and an away game for the respective parties concerned: When is a court competent to hear and decide a case which comprises at least some cross-border elements and which is not purely domestic? The answer will be given in three subdivisions relating to jurisdiction in contract (see II *infra*), jurisdiction in consumer contract (see III *infra*) and jurisdiction in tort (see IV *infra*) on the ground mainly of the Brussels I Regulation.[1] I will refrain from referring to the national law of particular states. The last genuinely legal part is devoted to the enforcement of judgements in an online environment (see V *infra*). The concluding remarks venture to name some reasons why cross-border business was not augmented as significantly by the rise of the Net to the extent as generally expected in the 1990s (see VI *infra*).

2. No influence on jurisdiction from the E-Commerce-Directive

To deal with a possible miscue at the outset: The rules on jurisdiction have not been affected by the E-Commerce-Directive. Inasmuch as Art. 1 (4) E-Commerce Directive is incorrect insofar as it states that the Directive does not contain

---

1) Matters of injunctory relief or other protective or provisional measures will not be dealt with specifically. Artt. 31 Brussels I Regulation; 24 Brussels and Lugano Convention however refer in principle to national rules on jurisdiction including the Brussels system.

conflicts rules,[2] inasmuch the very same Art. 1 (4) is correct insofar as it states that the Directive does not contain rules on jurisdiction.[3] The respect for the then forthcoming Brussels I Regulation (which was negotiated during virtually the same time-stretch as the E-Commerce-Directive) simply prohibited any other course to be taken than to refrain from tackling the intricate topic of rules on jurisdiction. Hence, the E-Commerce Directive does not inflict damage on the proven jurisdictional system.

II. Jurisdiction in contract: business as usual

1. General jurisdiction under Art. 2 in connection with Art. 60 Brussels I Regulation

Art. 2 in connection with Art. 60 Brussels I Regulation vests general jurisdiction in the courts of the state, where the defendant company has its statutory seat or real seat or principal place of business. Both times the "or" has to be read as a disjunctive "and/or": It entirely suffices if one of this connecting factors can be located in a given state to vest jurisdiction in the courts of this particular state.[4] Neither the Information Society nor the rise of the Internet have fundamentally

---

2) Cf. *Peter Mankowski,* Das Herkunftslandprinzip als internationales Privatrecht der e-commerce-Richtlinie, Zeitschrift für vergleichende Rechtswissenschaft (ZvglRWiss) 100 (2001), 137; *id.*, Das Herkunftslandprinzip der E-Commerce-Richtlinie als Internationales Privatrecht, Europäisches Wirtschafts- und Steuerrecht (EWS) 2002, 401; *id.*, Herkunftslandprinzip und deutsches Umsetzungsgesetz zur e-commerce-Richtlinie, Praxis des Internationalen Privat- und Verfahrensrechts (IPRax) 2002, 257.

3) *Peter Mankowski,* Wettbewerbsrechtliches Gerichtspflichtigkeits- und Rechtsanwendungsrisiko bei Werbung über Web-sites, Computer und Recht (CR) 2000, 763 at 768 et seq.; *Peter Stone,* Internet Consumer Contracts and European Private International Law, (2000) Information and Communication Technology Law (Info. & Comm. Tech. L.) 5 at 6; *Adrian Moerel,* E-Commerce vanuit Europees perspectief, Ondernemingsrecht 2000, 202 at 209; *Barry Rodger,* The Communitarisation of International Private Law: Reform of the Brussels Convention by Regulation, 2001 Juridical Review 69 at 74; *Marc Fallon/Johan Meeusen,* Le commerce électronique, la directive 2000/31/CE et le droit international privé, Revue critiqu de droit international privé (Rev. crit. dr. int. pr.) 91 (2002), 435 at 471; *Annette Kur,* Das Herkunftslandprinzip der E-Commerce-Richtlinie – Chancen und Risiken, in: Festschrift für Willi Erdmann, Cologne/Berlin/Bonn/Munich 2002, 629 at 635.

4) Cf. only *Hans-W. Micklitz/Peter Rott,* Vergemeinschaftung des EuGVÜ in der Verordnung (EG), Nr. 44/2001, Europäische Zeitschrift für Wirtschaftsrecht (EuZW) 2001, 325 at 327; *Jan Kropholler,* Europäisches Zivilprozessrecht, 6th ed. Heidelberg 2002, Art. 60 EuGVVO note 2; *Burghard Piltz,* Vom EuGVÜ zur Brüssel I-Verordnung, Neue Juristische Wochenschrift (NJW) 2002, 789 at 792; *Ansgar Staudinger,* in: *Thomas Rauscher* (ed.), Europäisches Zivilprozessrecht, Munich 2003, Art. 60 Brüssel I-VO note 1.

or even incidentally changed any of the three relevant concepts.[5] They have not brought forward novel notions of statutory seat, real seat or principal place of business as opposed to the concepts applied previously. Companies might operate on-line, but they do not exist in a legal *vacuum* or under the sovereignty of a supposed Cyberspace. They still must register with real world registrars or courts. Both real seat and principal place of business are real world factual concepts. That the notion of place of business has not been altered substantially, is supported by the definition of place of business in the E-Commerce-Directive. Even in this Act, specifically designed to deal with online-affairs, the European legislator refrained from letting a server, other technical devices, a web-site or other electronic means suffice in order to constitute a place of business as Art. 2 lit. c E-Commerce Directive unambiguously asserts. Still, a permanent establishment in the real world is firmly required.

2. Special jurisdiction vested in courts at the place of performance of the contract

Under Art. 5 no. 1 lit. b Brussels I Regulation in its two indents special jurisdiction in contract is vested in the courts at the place where the goods have been delivered or are expected to be delivered according to the contract if the relevant contract is a contract of sale or anothe kind of contract for the delivery of goods, or where the services have been provided or are expected to be provided according to the contract if the relevant contract is a contract for services. Consequently, the question to be answered reads: Where are goods expected to be delivered, or services expected to be rendered under the contract?

a) Delivery of tangible goods under a sales contract

A traditional sales contracts for the delivery of real world goods does not pose any specific problem. Real world goods require real world delivery. The mode of contracting is irrelevant for the place of delivery and thus performance. Hence, only the goods contracted for are relevant for determining their place of the delivery according to the terms of the contract. There is nothing peculiar about this kind of contract.

b) A matter of classification: Are software or information "goods"?

Hence, tangibles are easy. More difficult is the next step forward: Must software or information be regarded as "goods" for the purposes of Art. 5 No. 1 lit. b first

---

5) *Simone van der Hof,* Internationale on-line overeenkomsten, Tilburg 2002, 54 et seq.

indent Brussels I Regulation? In the first place, this comes down to a matter of classification. Perhaps surprisingly the better arguments can be raised in favour of an affirmative answer at least for standard software.[6] Despite the naturalistic impression at first glance that both software and information are intangibles, the notion of "goods" ought not to be restricted to tangibles.[7] For software there is a line of argument relating back to the interpretation of the CISG. Under the CISG the almost general opinion subjects standard software (i.e. software not specifically designed to meet the customer's individual orders and requirements) to the notion of "goods" for it should not make a fundamental difference whether the software is delivered on a hard disk or on-line.[8] Not the hard disk as the mere wrapping matters, but the content. The wrapping cannot determine the nature of the entity itself.[9] Historically anything started with the hard disk and software thus was believed to be covered by the CISG. Alterations possibly following technological progress were rejected. A justification to treat someone who buys standard software on a hard disk or CD more preferential insofar as an additional ground for jurisdiction is opened in his favour, compared to someone who buys the software in digitised mode can hardly be found.[10]

Other digitised products could possibly follow an analogy to the standard/individual software divide. Mostly, matters of licensing and transferring usage rights under intellectual property law could be the most imminent cause and

---

6) *Oliver Klimek/Susanne Sieber,* Anwendbares Recht bei Vertrieb digitalisierbarer Waren über das Internet am Beispiel der Softwareüberlassung, Zeitschrift für Urheber- und Medienrecht (ZUM) 1998, 902 at 906 et seq.; *Karsten Thorn,* Verbraucherschutz bei Verträgen im Fernabsatz, IPRax 1999, 1 at 3; *Peter Mankowski,* Das Internet im Internationalen Vertrags- und Deliktsrecht, RabelsZ 63 (1999), 203 at 232 et seq.; *id.,* Internet und besondere Aspekte des Internationalen Vertragsrechts (I), CR 1999, 512 at 515.

7) *Contra Matthias Terlau,* in: *Hans-Werner Moritz/Thomas Dreier* (eds.), Rechts-Handbuch zum E-Commerce, Cologne 2002, Part C note 59.

8) Cf. only Oberlandesgericht (OLG) Koblenz September 17, 1993 – Case 2 U 1230/91, Recht der Internationalen Wirtschaft (RIW) 1993, 934 at 936; OLG Köln (Cologne) August 26, 1994 – Case 19 U 282/93, RIW 1994, 970 at 974; *Frank Diedrich,* Autonome Auslegung von Internationalem Einheitsrecht, Baden-Baden 1994, 174-323; *id.,* Anwendbarkeit des Wiener Kaufrechts auf Softwareüberlassungsverträge, RIW 1993, 441 at 452; *Peter Mankowski,* Internet und besondere Aspekte des Internationalen Vertragsrechts (II), CR 1999, 581 at 586; *Hans Markus Wulf,* UN-Kaufrecht und eCommerce, Frankfurt etc. 2003, 42-51.

9) *Peter Mankowski,* Das Internet im Internationalen Vertrags- und Deliktsrecht, RabelsZ 63 (1999), 203 at 232 et seq.

10) Cf. *Matthias Terlau,* in: *Hans-Werner Moritz/Thomas Dreier* (eds.), Rechts-Handbuch zum E-Commerce, Cologne 2002, Part C note 235.

purpose for contracting. Perhaps this can be reflected in classification.[11] Information, however, has never had a tangible form and can thus not be treated as a "good".[12] Allowing a database research, however, would constitute a "supply of services", *a fortiori* conducting such a research as a kind of shopping or research agent;[13] hence, such activity would enter the realm of Art. 5 No. 1 lit. b Brussels I Regulation not by the first, but by the second door.[14]

c) Services provided on-line

One intricate and intriguing question requires an answer: Where are services performed online rendered? As nothing happens online without input either by men or by machine programmed by men, the notion that the service is rendered in a legal vacuum, should be easily disposed off. Thus it comes down to the alternative whether the up-loading by the content provider (literally taken: the service provider[15]), or the down-loading by the customer bears more weight.[16] On one hand wc have the activity and the making available of the result, on the other hand we have the mere extraction of the result. Drawing an analogy to the delivery of goods would slightly favour the completion of the service, i.e. the result passing into the customer's sphere. Playing with words would place reliance and emphasis on the wording of Art. 5 no. 1 lit. b 2nd lemma Brussels I Regulation that the services have to be "provided", as this wording does not

---

11) Cf. *Morten Foss/Lee Bygrave,* International Consumer Puchases through the Internet: Jurisdictional Issues pursuant to European Law, (2000) 8 International Journal of Law and Information Technology (Int. J. L. & Info. Tech.) 99 at 109-112; *Peter Mankowski,* Internet und besondere Aspekte des Internationalen Vertragsrechts (I), CR 1999, 512 at 516 et seq.

12) *Peter Mankowski,* Internet und besondere Aspekte des Internationalen Vertragsrechts (II), CR 1999, 581 at 586.

13) *Morten Foss/Lee Bygrave,* International Consumer Puchases through the Internet: Jurisdictional Issues pursuant to European Law, (2000) 8 Int. J. L. & Info. Tech. 99 at 113; *Anastasia Papathoma-Baetge/Stefanie Nehrenberg/Tilmann Finke,* in: *Bert Kaminski/Thomas Henßler/Helge F. Kolaschnik/Anastasia Papathoma-Baetge* (eds.), Rechtshandbuch E-Business, Neuwied/Kriftel 2002, Part 2 A note 84; *Veronika Mochar/Simone Seidl,* Internationales Verbraucherschutzrecht und e-commerce, Österreichische Juristenzeitung (ÖJZ) 2003, 241 at 243; *Hans Markus Wulf,* UN-Kaufrecht und eCommerce, Frankfurt etc. 2003, 34-37.

14) *Simone van der Hof,* Internationale on-line overeenkomsten, Tilburg 2002, 57.

15) Since in an internet-context ISP (Internet Service Provider) is often used invariably and as a kind of synonym for Access Provider, here „content provider" as the more neutral denomination is used deliberately in order to avoid misunderstandings.

16) The alternative is formulated e.g. by *Stefania Savini,* Delocalizzazione del contratto stipulato su Internet – Problemi di giurisdizione e legge applicabile, Contratto e impresa/Europa 2002, 1131 at 1147.

employ "performed". "Performed" could point a little further towards the activity whereas "provided" brings the customer's perspective in the picture more prominently. Providing services gives an eye to the customer receiving the services.[17] The natural reflection could point to the provider's place at least insofar as research or teaching efforts are at stake.[18]

Another concept puts forward the submission that in case of doubt the place where the service is provided, should be equated with the place where the person providing the service has its relevant place of business; allegedly a comparative survey is said to support such a submission.[19] This would, however, be tantamount to re-introducing normative concepts[20] into Art. 5 No. 1 lit. b Brussels I Regulation through the backdoor in spite of the fact that this rule was developed as a deviation and as opposed to normative concepts (in particular like those in Tessili)[21] and thus is bound to revert to a factual concept.[22] Dropping any reasoning which refers to legal concepts of a specific law, a rebuttable presumption that the service is provided at the relevant place of business of the service provider, could offer some help.[23] In particular it could avoid difficulties

---

17) Cf. also *Simone van der Hof,* Internationale on-line overeenkomsten, Tilburg 2002, 58.

18) *Jean-Paul Béraudo,* Le Règlement (CE) du Conseil du 22 décembre 2000 concernant la compétence judiciaire, la reconnaissance et l'exécution des décisions en matière civil et commerciale, Clunet 128 (2001), 1033 at 1047.

19) *Stefan Leible,* in: *Thomas Rauscher* (ed.), Europäisches Zivilprozessrecht, Munich 2003, Art. 5 Brüssel I-VO note 54.

20) As *Peter Schlosser,* EU-Zivilprozessrecht, 2nd ed. Munich 2003, Art. 5 EuGVVO note 10b openly does.

21) Proposal for a Council Regulation on Civil Regulation and Enforcement of Judgements in Civil and Commercial Matters, submitted by the Commission on April 17, 1999, COM (1999) 348 final, Bundesrats-Drucksache 534/99, 15.

22) Cf. only *Jan Kropholler/Michael v. Hinden,* Die Reform des europäischen Gerichtsstands am Erfüllungsort (Art. 5 Nr. 1 EuGVÜ), in: Gedächtnisschrift für Alexander Lüderitz, Munich 2000, 401 at 409 et seq.; *Thomas Pfeiffer,* Rechtsdurchsetzung im internationalen Rechtsverkehr, in: *Giorgios Gounalakis* (ed.), Rechtshandbuch Electronic Business, Munich 2003, § 13 note 38.

23) *Peter Mankowski,* Internationale Zuständigkeit, in: *Gerald Spindler/Andreas Wiebe* (eds.), Internet-Auktionen, Munich 2001, ch. H note 24; *Alfonso Luis Calvo Caravca/Javier Carrascosa González,* Conflictos de leyes y conflictos de jurisdicción en Internet, Madrid 2001, 53 et seq.; cf. also *Beate Gsell,* Autonom bestimmter Gerichtsstand am Erfüllungsort nach der Brüssel I-Verordnung, IPRax 2002, 484 at 491; *Dietmar Czernich,* in: *Dietmar Czernich/Stefan Tiefenthaler/Georg Kodek,* Europäisches Gerichtsstands- und Vollstreckungsrecht, 2nd ed. Vienna 2003, Art. 5 EuGVVO note 42.

which were to be encountered if one referred to the factual place of uploading.[24]

Nevertheless, if parties to the contract do for which ever reason not want to resort to jurisdiction clauses, it is strongly recommended that they should expressly spell out in the contract which place they want to become the place of performance of the relevant services. Pursuant to the opening words of Art. 5 No. 1 lit. b Brussels I Regulation such a contractual determination is paramount to any objective search for the place of performance and effective precludes such a search. One minor but nevertheless important qualification should be observed:[25] The contractually determined place of performance should have some objective relationship with the performance itself; otherwise it will be treated as a jurisdiction clause.[26]

3. Special jurisdiction vested in courts at the place of a branch or other place of business

Another head of special jurisdiction is to be found in Art. 5 No. 5 Brussels I Regulation, Brussels and Lugano Convention respectively. Special jurisdiction is vested in the courts at the place of a branch or other place of business. Another time, any modification of general notions with regard to online-affairs appears unnecessary. This is thoroughly supported by Art. 2 lit. c E-Commerce-Directive.[27]

4. The traditional and still appropriate device: jurisdiction clauses

a) Jurisdiction clauses as means of effective contract planning

Traditionally, well advised businessmen resort to a particular device in order to solve, or even better: to avoid, any sort of dispute on jurisdiction. This well-known device is the jurisdiction clause. E-commerce has not changed the basic

---

24) As described by *Georges A.L. Droz/Hélène Gaudemet-Tallon,* La transformation de la Convention de Bruxelles du 27 septembre 1968 en Règlement du Conseil concernant la compétence judiciaire, la reconnaissance et l'exécution des décisions en matière civil et commerciale, Rev. crit. dr. int. pr. 90 (2001), 601 at 636.

25) Cf. only *Jan Eltzschig,* Art. 5 Nr. 1 b EuGVO: Ende oder Fortführung von forum actoris und Erfüllungsortbestimmung lege causae?, IPRax 2002, 491 at 493.

26) ECJ February 20, 1997 – Case C-106/95, Rep. 1997, I-911 at 943 et seq. paras. 31-35 – Mainschifffahrts-Genossenschaft eG (MSG)/Les Gravières Rhénanes SARL; ECJ September 28, 1999 – Case C-440/97, Rep. 1999, I-6307 at I-6351 et seq. para. 28.

27) Cf. only *Simone van der Hof,* Internationale on-line overeenkomsten, Tilburg 2002, 60-62.

content of contracts nor the entire mode of contracting nor the appropriateness of contractual devices previously held in the highest regard. Thus, jurisdiction clauses are still to be recommended. In daily contractual practice they still appear in their shades for the simple reason that the vast majority of enterprises did not alter their General Conditions. E-commerce did not demand to alter the basics, the truly general parts of those General Conditions. Hence, jurisdiction clauses developed for ordinary real world business but contained in the General Conditions still form part of contracts even if they are concluded on-line or deal with genuine on-line business. And they are up to their job. They execute. As there is no Cyberspace and enterprises still have their seats or places of business in the real world,[28] a jurisdiction clause destining the court at one party's seat or place of business as the court competent to hear all suits arising from the contract, still is an appropriate solution. Companies do not disappear into Cyberspace, hence their interest in contracting for a home game is still vital. In the end jurisdictional management comes down to the old tune: Jurisdiction clauses, jurisdiction clauses, and once again jurisdiction clauses - or arbitration clauses instead.

b) Formal requirements under Artt. 23 Brussels I Regulation; 17 Brussels or Lugano Convention

Pursuant to Art. 23 (1) Brussels I Regulation jurisdiction clauses must be in writing or orally with written confirmation (lit. a) or in accordance with practices that have been established between the parties (lit. b) or in accordance with a usage in international trade or commerce (lit. c). The time might not be appear ripe yet to assert jurisdiction clauses in e-mail correspondence or in another electronic form as conforming to a usage in international trade or commerce.[29] But at least lit. b applies from the third electronic contract between the parties onwards. The first two are needed to establish the individual practice as between the parties.[30] However, a courageous interpretation of lit. a, the requirement of writing, might render the best service and provide the most helpful hand: In the

---

28) See II *supra*.

29) *Peter Mankowski,* Das Internet im Internationalen Vertrags- und Deliktsrecht, RabelsZ 63 (1999), 203 at 219; *Miriam Mann,* Besonderer Teil zu Fragen des Internationalen Vertragsrechts, in: *Fabian Schuster* (ed.), Vertragshandbuch Telemedia, Munich 2001, ch. 19 note 13; *Matthias Terlau,* in: *Hans-Werner Moritz/Thomas Dreier* (eds.), Rechts-Handbuch zum E-Commerce, Cologne 2002, Part C note 20.

30) Cf. *Peter Mankowski,* Das Internet im Internationalen Vertrags- und Deliktsrecht, RabelsZ 63 (1999), 203 at 219; *Matthias Terlau,* in: *Hans-Werner Moritz/Thomas Dreier* (eds.), Rechts-Handbuch zum E-Commerce, Cologne 2002, Part C note 19; *Thomas Pfeiffer,* Rechtsdurchsetzung im internationalen Rechtsverkehr, in: *Giorgios Gounalakis* (ed.), Rechtshandbuch Electronic Business, Munich 2003, § 13 note 94.

light of Art. 7 (2) 2 1985 UNICTRAL Model Law on International Commercial Arbitration[31] and the subsequent rise of the so-called durable medium in Community legislation,[32] "writing" might not be interpreted strictly but expected to include at least e-mails.[33] A parallel can be found in the dynamic interpretation[34] of Art. II (2) of the 9158 New York Convention on International Arbitration. Further support is granted by the legislative history of Art. 17 (1) 2 Lugano Convention.[35]

However, the discussion about the meaning of "writing" is of greater importance for Art. 17 (1) lit. a Brussels or Lugano Convention than for Art. 23 Brussels I Regulation: Art. 23 (2) Brussels I Regulation puts beyond any doubt that electronically concluded jurisdiction clauses suffice and fulfil the formal requirements.[36] Jurisdiction agreements made by e-mails are not expressly mentioned, but are envisaged with sincerity.[37] They provide for the required

---

31) UN Doc. A/40/17 and A/RES/72.

32) In particular Art. 5 (1) 1 Directive 97/7/EC of the European Parliament and the Council of 20 May 1997 on the protection of consumers in respect of distance contracts, OJ EC 1997 L 144/19.

33) *Gabrielle Kaufmann-Kohler,* Internet: mondialisation de la communication – mondialisation de la résolution des litiges?, in: *Katharina Boele-Woelki/Catherine Kessedjian* (eds.), Internet – Which Court Decides? Which Law Applies? Quel tribunal décide? Quel droit s'applique?, The Hague/London/Boston 1998, 89 at 127-131; *Peter Mankowski,* Das Internet im Internationalen Vertrags- und Deliktsrecht, RabelsZ 63 (1999), 203 at 218 et seq.; *Abbo Junker,* Internationales Vertragsrecht und Internet, RIW 1999, 809 at 813; *Oliver Arter/Florian S. Jörg/Urs P. Gnos,* Zuständigkeit und anwendbares Recht bei internationalen Rechtsgeschäften über Internet unter Berücksichtigung unerlaubter Handlungen, Aktuelle Juristische Praxis (AJP) 2000, 277 at 279; *Pascal Grolimund,* Geschäftsverkehr im Internet – Aspekte des internationalen Vertragsrechts, Zeitschrift für schweizerisches Recht (ZSR) 119 (2000), I 339 at 354; *Katharina Boele-Woelki,* Internet und IPR: Wo geht jemand ins Netz?, Berichte der Deutschen Gesellschaft für Völkerrecht (BerDGesVR) 36 (2000), 307 at 322; *Pedro Alberto de Miguel Asensio,* Derecho privado de Internet, 3rd ed. Madrid 2002, 452-455 paras. 332 et seq.

34) In particular *Jasna Arsic,* International Commercial Arbitration on the Internet – Has the Future Come Too Early?, (1997) 14 J. Int. Arb. 209 at 216.

35) See in detail *Peter Mankowski,* Das Internet im Internationalen Vertrags- und Deliktsrecht, RabelsZ 63 (1999), 203 at 218. Rather sceptical and restricting the equivalent to writing to qualified electronic signatures *Matthias Terlau,* in: *Hans-Werner Moritz/Thomas Dreier* (eds.), Rechts-Handbuch zum E-Commerce, Cologne 2002, Part C note 18.

36) Cf. only *Christian Frank,* in: *Peter Bräutigam/Andreas Leupold* (eds.), Online-Handel, Munich 2003, Part B III note 88; *Peter Mankowski,* in: *Thomas Rauscher* (ed.), Europäisches Zivilprozessrecht, Munich 2003, Art. 23 Brüssel I-VO note 38.

37) Proposal for a Council Regulation on Civil Regulation and Enforcement of Judgements in Civil and Commercial Matters, submitted by the Commission on April 17, 1999, COM (1999) 348 final, Bundesrats-Drucksache 534/99, 19.

opportunity of durability and unaltered reproduction.[38] Qualified electronic signatures are not necessary.[39] Even a link in an e-mail leading to the Standard Terms of the respective party including the jurisdiction clause can suffice.[40]

III. Jurisdiction with regard to consumer contracts: really that frightening?

1. The general picture: consumer-friendly

The most heavily debated issue of all jurisdictional matters concerning e-commerce was the jurisdiction in consumer contracts. In the battle of Brussels the country of destination-principle fought against the country of origin-principle – or in other words: General Directorate SanCo[41] was challenged by General Directorate Internal Market. Whilst SanCo favoured the country of destination-approach which is both traditional and prevailing in issues of consumer protection, Internal Market promoted their eternal champion, the country of origin-principle. The burden was on Internal Market as Art. 13 (1) Brussels Convention already sported the country of destination-approach (and the same does Art. 5 (1), (2) Rome Convention). The very outcome of the battle of Brussels is Art. 15 Brussels I Regulation – and the perhaps surprising result after heaviest lobbying previously unheard of in PIL: SanCo wins! The new criterion to be found in Art. 15 (1) (c) Brussels I Regulation reads: directing commercial or professional activities to the consumer's home country. This is designed as a wide concept. This holds in particular true with regard to B2C e-commerce, an issue that was at the very core of the discussion. But has anything relevant changed in this point[42] compared to Art. 13 (1) no. 3 Brussels Convention? The answer

---

38) *Pedro Alberto de Miguel Asensio,* Derecho privado de Internet, 3rd ed. Madrid 2002, 455 para. 333; *Peter Mankowski,* in: *Thomas Rauscher* (ed.), Europäisches Zivilprozessrecht, Munich 2003, Art. 23 Brüssel I-VO note 38; *Thomas Pfeiffer,* Rechtsdurchsetzung im internationalen Rechtsverkehr, in: *Giorgios Gounalakis* (ed.), Rechtshandbuch Electronic Business, Munich 2003, § 13 note 100.

39) *Stefan Tiefenthaler,* in:*Dietmar Czernich/Stefan Tiefenthaler/Georg Kodek,* Europäisches Gerichtsstands- und Vollstreckungsrecht, 2nd ed. Vienna 2003, Art. 23 EuGVVO note 27.

40) *Alfonso Luis Calvo Caravca/Javier Carrascosa González,* Conflictos de leyes y conflictos de jurisdicción en Internet, Madrid 2001, 44.

41) Health, Sanitary and Consumer Protection.

42) With regard to two other aspects, certainly substantial changes have been implemented: The regime for consumer contracts has been extended in principle to all kinds of contracts regardless of their subject. Hence, loans without a specified purpose, the sale of information and buying securities are included contrary to Art. 13 (1) Brussels Convention where those matters were excluded or at least arguably excluded (as was the case with loans). The only exceptions apply where a case comes within Art. 15 (3) Brussels I Regulation or is covered

heavily depends on the stance one takes in interpreting Art. 13 (1) no. 3 Brussels Convention. If a web-site is regarded as advertising under Art. 13 (1) no. 3 Brussels Convention,[43] no material changes have been implemented, but only slight alterations and clarifications in the wording.

2. Should there be a differenciation between active and passive web-sites?

However, one specific points deserves closer examination: Does one have to distinguish between active and passive web-sites? At least, the Commission so opines[44] (although it in other aspects regards the same concept as too narrow[45]).

a) Support from competition law?

This approach appears to derive some backing from the quarters of competition law, namely Para. 51 Guidelines on Vertical Restraints[46].[47] But one should not

---

by the rules on exclusive jurisdiction contained in Art. 22 Brussels I Regulation, e.g. establishing a tenancy on land. The other substantial change is the deletion of the additional requirement previously appearing in Art. 13 (1) no. 3 Brussels Convention that the consumer had to take the necessary steps to conclude the contract on his side, in his home country, i.e. that the consumer had to express (even more precisely: to issue the expression of) his consent in his home country.

43) So e.g. Österreichischer Oberster Gerichtshof (Austrian Supreme Court) May 15, 2001 – 7 Nd 507/01, August 2, 2001 – 7 Nd 510/01 and February 12, 2002 – 10 Nd 501/02.

44) Proposal of the Commission for a Council Regulation (EC) on civil jurisdiction and the recognition and enforcement of judicial decisions in civil and commercial matters, OJ 1999 L 376/17; cf. also *Thomas Pfeiffer,* Grenzüberschreitende Internetverträge, in: *Michael Hohl/Stefan Leible/Olaf Sosnitza* (eds.), Vernetztes Recht, Stuttgart/Munich etc. 2002, 21 at 42; *id.,* Anwendbares Recht, in: *Giorgios Gounalakis* (ed.), Rechtshandbuch Electronic Business, Munich 2003, § 12 note 75 and *Graham J. H. Smith,* Internet Law and Regulation, 3rd ed. London 2002, paras. 6-060 et seq.

45) Amended Proposal of the Commission for a Council Regulation (EC) on civil jurisdiction and the recognition and enforcement of judicial decisions in civil and commercial matters, COM (2000) 689 final p. 6.

46) Commission Notice - Guidelines on Vertical Restraints (October 2000), OJ EC 2000 C 291/1, issued pursuant to Commission Regulation (EC) No. 2790/1999 of December 22, 1999 on the application of Article 81 (3) of the Treaty to categories of vertical agreements and concerted practices (Block Exemtion Regulation), OJ EC 1999 L 336/1

47) Cf. *Georges A.L. Droz/Hélène Gaudemet-Tallon,* La transformation de la Convention de Bruxelles du 27 septembre 1968 en Règlement du Conseil concernant la compétence judiciaire, la reconnaissance et l'exécution des décisions en matière civil et commerciale, Rev. crit. dr. int. pr. 90 (2001), 601 at 639 and *Marc Fallon/Johan Meeusen,* Le commerce électronique, la directive 2000/31/CE et le droit international privé, Rev. crit. dr. int. pr. 91 (2002), 435 at 447 et seq.

miss the important difference, that competition law is concerned with effects on a market and thus operates necessarily at a more abstract level not taking into account the single contract as such whereas consumer contract law counts on every single contract. The yardsticks in the two fields of the law inevitably do not run entirely parallel but must reflect the different regulatory purposes pursued. Hence, the support for the divide from the alleged support by competition law is rather weak and buckles if subjected to closer examination and scrutiny.

b) The dangers of partially importing American concepts

Howsoever, to distinguish between active and passive web-sites appears tantamount to importing certain American concepts into Europe. Distinguishing between (inter-)active and passive web-sites relates back, and is intrinsically linked, to the American decisions *Zippo*[48] and *Cybersell*[49]. Many rather technical arguments can be made against such an import: Firstly, the *Zippo*-approach appears not to be the favoured (and even less the sole) approach of the American courts anymore.[50] In fact, criticism of it grew by the time.[51] In particular, guidelines for the middle category of active web-sites are lamented to be missing.[52] In the case law, a certain shift away from *Zippo* can be discerned.[53]

---

48) *Zippo Manufacturing Co. v. Zippo Dot Com, Inc.* 952 F. Supp. 1119 at 1124 (W.D. Pa. 1997).

49) *Cybersell, Inc. v. Cybersell, Inc.* 130 F. 3d 414 at 418 (9th Cir. 1997).

50) Although *Zippo* was followed e.g. in *Mink. v. AAA Development L.L.C.* 190 F. 3d 333 (5th Cir. 1999); *Soma Media International v. Standard Chartered Bank* 196 F. 3d 1292 (10th Cir. 1999); *Blumenthal v. Drudge* 992 F. Supp. 44 (D. N.J. 1998); *Citigroup v. City Holding Co.* 97 F. Supp. 2d 549 (S.D.N.Y. 2000); *America Online, Inc. v. Huang* 106 F. Supp. 2d 848 (E.D. Va. 2000); *American Eyewear, Inc. v. Peeper's Sunglasses and Accessories, Inc.* 106 F. Supp. 2d 895 (N.D. Tex. 2000); *Tech Heads, Inc. v. Desktop Service Countor, Inc.* 105 F. Supp. 2d 1142 (D. Oreg. 2000); *Biometrics, LLC v. New Womyn, Inc.* 112 F. Supp. 2d 869 (E.D. Mo. 2000); *Nida Corp. v. Nida* 118 F. Supp. 2d 1223 (M.D. Fla. 2000).

51) Cf. *Brian E. Doughdrill,* Personal Jurisdiction and the Internet: Waiting for the Other *Shoe* to Drop on First Amendment Concerns, 51 Mercer L. Rev. 919 (2000); *Michael Geist,* Is There a There There? Toward Greater Certainty for Internet Jurisdiction, 16 Berkeley Tech. L.J. 1345 (2001); *Paul Berman Schiff,* The Globalization of Jurisdiction, 151 U. Penn. L. Rev. 311 (2002), all with further references.

52) Cf. *Dagesse v. Plant Hotel NV* No. CV-98-713-B (D. N.H. 2000).

53) Cf. *Bancroft & Masters, Inc. v. Augusta National, Inc.* 223 F. 3d 1082 (9th Cir. 2000); *Millenium Enterprises, Inc. v. Millenium Music L.P.* 33 F. Supp. 2d 907 (D. Oreg. 1999)*Blakey v. Continental Airlines, Inc.* 751 A. 2d 538 (D. N.J. 2000); *Nissan Motor Co. Ltd. v. Nissan Computer Corp.* 89 F. Supp. 2d 1154 (C.D. Cal. 2000); *Uncle Sam's Safari Outfitters, Inc. v. Uncle Sam's Army Nay Outfitters – Manhattan, Inc.* 96 F. Supp. 2d 919 (E.D. Mo. 2000) *Euromarket Designs, Inc. v. Crate & Barrel Ltd.* 96 F. Supp. 2d 924 (N.D. Ill. 2000); *People Solutions, Inc. v. People Solutions, Inc.* No. Civ. A.399-CV-2339-L, 2000

Secondly, underlying the notion are American concepts of personal jurisdiction which do not have counterparts in the European system, for instance that personal jurisdiction based on doing business is general jurisdiction only based on some minimum requirements and requiring some counter-balancing.[54] Taking only one element from a foreign (if not alien) system and importing it into the European system could lead to severe frictions.[55] One slight indication: The third branch of the system constructed in *Zippo*, namely the so-called integral web-site, has not been imported. Thirdly, recurring to notions of activity and passivity of web-sites bears the inherent danger of confusing these notions with the concepts of activity and passivity of consumers.[56] Fourthly, the factual difficulty of distinguishing is immense.[57] The web-site comprising an electronic order form must be distinguished from the web-site asking to contact the seller via a traditional phone-line. More concerning is the lack of justification for an entirely different treatment of these two web-sites in each other's close vicinity.[58] At the very end it would come down to a rather subjective assessment by the judge hearing the case. Thus, security would vanish. Activity and passivity are nothing more than ciphers concealing the underlying concepts.[59] Fifthly, the approach places too

---

WL 1030619 (N.D. Tex. July 25, 2000); *Winfield Collection, Ltd. v. McCauley* 105 F. Supp. 2d 746 (E.D. Mich. 2000); *Neogen Corp. v. Neo Gen Screening, Inc.* 109 F. Supp. 2d 724 (W.D. Mich. 2000), rev'd on other grounds 282 F. 3d 883 (6th Cir. 2002); *Search Force, Inc. v. DataForce International, Inc.* 112 F. Supp. 2d 771 (S.D. Ind. 2000).

54) Cf. *Millenium Enterprises, Inc. v. Millenium Music L.P.* 33 F. Supp. 2d 907 at 923 (D. Oreg. 1999) and also *Gaetano Iorio Fiorelli,* Contratti telematici, strumenti di diritto internazionale privato e prospettive di armonizzazione della disciplina materiale, Diritto di commercio internazionale (Dir. comm. int.) 2003, 427 at 436.

55) *Catherine Kessedjian,* Internet et le règlement de différends, Molengrafica 1999/2000, 69 at 89 et seq.; *Jean-Paul Béraudo,* Le Réglement (CE) du Conseil du 22 décembre 2000 concernant la compétance judiciaire et l'exécution des decisions en matière civile et commerciale, Clunet 128 (2001), 1033 at 1056; *Peter Mankowski,* Internationaler Verbraucherschutz und Internet, in: Internet und Recht, Vienna 2002, 191 at 199.

56) *Peter Mankowski,* Internationaler Verbraucherschutz und Internet, in: Internet und Recht, Vienna 2002, 191 at 200.

57) *Anton K. Schnyder,* Internationalprivatrechtliche Aspekte des E-Commerce, in: *Walter Trüeb* (ed.), Aktuelle Rechtsfragen des E-Commerce, Zurich 2001, 103 at 109; *Stephan Bücker,* Internetauktionen, Münster/Hamburg 2003, 137.

58) *William Blair/David Quest,* Jurisdiction, Conflict of Laws and the Internet, in: *Guido Ferrarini/Klaus J. Hopt/Eddy Wymeersch* (eds.), Capital Markets in the Age of the Euro, The Hague/London/New York 2002, 153 at 158.

59) *Brian E. Doughdrill,* Personal Jurisdiction and the Internet: Waiting for the Other *Shoe* to Drop on First Amendment Concerns, 51 Mercer L. Rev. 919 (2000); *Peter Mankowski,* Internationaler Verbraucherschutz und Internet, in: Internet und Recht, Vienna 2002, 191 at 199 et seq.

much reliance on, and focuses too much, on technicalities and technology.[60] Furthermore, it would give rise to a necessity between different techniques and technical modes of advertising not easily to be reconciled with the general notion of advertising.[61] Sixthly, restricting the application of Art. 15 (1) lit. c Brussels I Regulation would be contrary to the clear intention of extending or at least not going back behind the level of consumer previously reached with Art. 13 (1) No. 3 Brussels Convention.[62] Also one should consider the general trend in European legislation to enhance consumer protection, with particular emphasis on B2C contracts concluded online, as it is most prominently indicated by the very existence of the Distance Contracts Directive 97/7/EC.[63]

c) The angler, the fish and the fishing rod

But the most imminent argument against distinguishing, carrying the greatest weight with it, is best illustrated by the comparison to an angler and his fishing-rod:[64] Every web-site, be it active or passive, can be regarded as a means of advertising and thus compared to a fishing-rod.[65] The angler throws it out and just waits for fish to swim by and bite on. Every time, even with the most passive fishing-rod throwing out the fishing-rod is the first step by the seller towards the consumer. Afterwards, it is the consumer's part to get ignited and to get carried to contact the seller. It does not make any difference in commercial terms whether this contact is established by fast e-mailing back or by phone. The interesting and decisive aspects are: The seller takes the initiative, and the consumer responds.

---

60) *Michael Geist,* Is There a There There? Toward Greater Certainty for Internet Jurisdiction, 16 Berkeley Tech. L.J. 1345 (2001); *Simone van der Hof,* Internationale on-line overeenkomsten, Tilburg 2002, 76.

61) *Jean-Paul Béraudo,* Le Règlement (CE) du Conseil du 22 décembre 2000 concernant la compétence judiciaire, la reconnaissance et l'exécution des décisions en matière civil et commerciale, Clunet 128 (2001), 1033 at 1056.

62) *Hans-W. Micklitz/Peter Rott,* Vergemeinschaftung des EuGVÜ in der Verordnung (EG) Nr. 44/2001, EuZW 2001, 325 at 331; *Matthias Terlau,* in: *Hans-Werner Moritz/Thomas Dreier* (eds.), Rechts-Handbuch zum E-Commerce, Cologne 2002, Part C note 238.

63) *Gabrielle Kaufmann-Kohler,* Internet: mondialisation de la communication – mondialisation de la résolution des litiges?, in: *Katharina Boele-Woelki/Catherine Kessedjian* (eds.), Internet – Which Court Decides? Which Law Applies? Quel tribunal décide? Quel droit s'applique?, The Hague/London/Boston 1998, 89 at 139.

64) *Peter Mankowski,* Review on Norbert Reich/Annette Nordhausen, Verbraucher und Recht im elektronischen Geschäftsverkehr (eG) (Baden-Baden 2000), MMR 3/2001, XXI at XXII; cf. also *Stephan Bücker,* Internetauktionen, Münster/Hamburg 2003, 134 et seq.

65) This comparison was originally and for the first known time developed in *Superguide Corp. v. Kegan* Docket Shelby Div. 4:97cv181-C (W.D. N.C. July 28/Oct. 7, 1997).

The all important first contact generating the consumer's interest is made by the seller. Every web-site aims at triggering other people's interest. Behind every commercially run web-site there lies this commercial interest to attract or generate business. The fish might bite on the hook – but throwing out the fishing rod is the first activity. The consumer is not the originally active person in the communication process.[66] He does not physically take steps towards the seller, but only seizes technical means and he does not leave his home country physically.[67] The world is visiting him, and not the other way round.

The web-site might be deemed dormant unless it is activated by the consumer.[68] But the same applies to an advertisement in a newspaper: it remains dormant until the reader opens the relevant page after having bought or else acquired the newspaper. And the same is true with regard to TV commercials. The individual consumer is not confronted with them unless he switches to the channel where they are broadcasted. No-one would deny that both the advertisement in the newspaper or the TV commercial are commercial advertisements. Hence, "dormancy" is irrelevant. Why should matters be judged differently with regard to web-sites?[69] The consumer has to choose the respective medium to become receptive to advertising; that stems from the very notion of advertising and can not be regarded as a detrimental "activity" on the consumer's side.[70] Additionally it should not be overlooked that if the consumer does not hit the web-site, we do not have jurisdictional problems in consumer *contract* at all simply because no contract will be concluded.[71]

These fairly simple observations also squash every attempt to exclude cases where the consumer used search machines. The use of search machines does not

---

66) But cf. e.g. *Rufus Pichler,* Internationale Gerichtszuständigkeit im Online-Bereich, Jahrbuch Junger Zivilrechtswissenschaftler 1998, 229 at 245; *Stéphanie Francq,* The Impact of EC Legislation for a Service Provider Established in the United States, 60 Louisiana L. Rev. 1071 at 1074 (2000).

67) *Simone van der Hof,* Internationale on-line overeenkomsten, Tilburg 2002, 199 et seq.

68) Cf. *Christoph Glatt,* Vertragsschluss im Internet, Baden-Baden 2002, 142 et seq.

69) Cf. only *Peter Mankowski,* Das Internet im Internationalen Vertrags- und Deliktsrecht, RabelsZ 63 (1999), 203 at 240; *Morten Foss/Lee Bygrave,* International Consumer Puchases through the Internet: Jurisdictional Issues pursuant to European Law, (2000) 8 Int. J. L. & Info. Tech. 99 at 115; *Christoph Glatt,* Vertragsschluss im Internet, Baden-Baden 2002, 146.

70) *Peter Mankowski,* Das Internet im Internationalen Vertrags- und Deliktsrecht, RabelsZ 63 (1999), 203 at 241; *Matthias Terlau,* in: *Hans-Werner Moritz/Thomas Dreier* (eds.), Rechts-Handbuch zum E-Commerce, Cologne 2002, Part C note 238 and cf. even *Gerald Spindler,* Internationales Verbraucherschutzrecht im Internet, MMR 2000, 18 at 20.

71) *Peter Mankowski,* Review on Christoph Glatt, Vertragsschluss im Internet (Baden-Baden 2002), Computer und Recht (CR) 2003, 307 at 308.

alter the basic fact that the web-site as a kind of advertisement is directed at the consumer.[72] A comparison between typing the Internet address of a certain business and making a phone call to the same company[73] disregards the important difference and misses the point: In the latter case there is no active step towards the consumer by the business whereas a web-site goes beyond simply existing and being accessible as a supplier. The opportunity to establish in conjunction with the display of the goods or services offered goes also beyond the entry in a telephone directory like the Yellow Pages.[74] A comparison of a web-site to the display window of an ordinary real world shop[75] fails either. Such windows are not at all able to visit the consumer at home nor does it transgress borders.[76] By far better fits the comparison to a mail-order catalogue sent to the consumer's home.[77] And finally, a last counter-argument has some force namely that no distinguishing is demanded by the very wording of Art. 15 (1) lit. c Brussels I Convention as the active/Passive divide has not be implemented in the wording.[78]

---

72) *Contra William Blair/David Quest,* Jurisdiction, Conflict of Laws and the Internet, in: *Guido Ferrarini/Klaus J. Hopt/Eddy Wymeersch* (eds.), Capital Markets in the Age of the Euro, The Hague/London/New York 2002, 153 at 158 et seq.

73) For such a comparison cf. *Tapio Puurunen,* Choice of Law in European Business-to-Consumer Electronic Commerce – A Trail out of a Political Impasse, Zeitschrift für Europäisches Privatrecht (ZEuP) 2003, 789 at 796.

74) *Kurt Siehr,* Telemarketing und Internationales Recht des Verbraucherschutzes, Jahrbuch des Schweizerischen Konsumentenschutzrechts (JKR) 1998, 151 at 169.

75) Cf. *Reinhard Schu,* The Applicable Law to Consumer Contracts Made over the Internet: Consumer Protection through Private International Law?, (1997) 5 Int. J. L. & Info. Tech. 192 at 213.

76) Additionally, one could attack the underlying argument that display windows and shop fronts never could constitute advertising; cf. *Morten Foss/Lee Bygrave,* International Consumer Puchases through the Internet: Jurisdictional Issues pursuant to European Law, (2000) 8 Int. J. L. & Info. Tech. 99 at 115.

77) *Jens Haubold,* Doing E-Business in the European Union – The Non-Member State Perspective: A Snapshot of Private International Issues in E-Commerce, in: International Bureau of the Permanent Court of Arbitration (ed.), Strengthening Relations with Arab and Islamic Countries through International Law, The Hague/London/Boston 2002, 109 at 122.

78) *Jean-Paul Béraudo,* Le Règlement (CE) du Conseil du 22 décembre 2000 concernant la compétence judiciaire, la reconnaissance et l'exécution des décisions en matière civil et commerciale, Clunet 128 (2001), 1033 at 1056.

3. Are the jurisdiction rules really that frightening?

a) The missing evidence

Doesn't this sound frightening, to say the least? To legal advisors of enterprises involved in B2C commerce it might even sound appalling or outright nightmarish. At first sight this appears to look like a lethal threat for cross-border B2C consumer business. Quite accordingly, some alarmists accused PIL to be the undertaker of cross-border B2C e-commerce. However, one should not join these alarmists, be they hired guns, be they simply not perfectly informed and thus overly concerned. From the outset, one should in the first place simply ask how many published court cases concerning cross-border consumer contracts concluded on the Internet have unearthed so far. The astonishing and surprising answer reads: none. Not a single case in total Europe has reached the law reviews yet. On closer examination, some reasons underlying this phenomenon might be identified.

b) The natural and commercially sound choice: suing the consumer at his domicile

Looking at steps to be taken against the consumer in order to enforce contractual claims first, there is but one simple question: Where else would you sue a consumer that at this domicile if you were a sound commercial-man? This is where his assets are, supposedly. You avoid any need to run an enforcement procedure in a second state. Hence, Art. 16 (2) Brussels I Regulation is not an onslaught on the prospects of legal enforcement against the consumer.[79] The alternative for a commercial-man would go like this: First sue in you own home state. Expect to get a judgement by default as it is very likely that the consumer will not appear in court. Then take the judgement rendered and try to enforce it in the consumer's home state. Endeavour the pleasures of enforcing a default judgement at all (although this would be facilitated by the implementation of Art. 41 Brussels I Regulation). Experience that with a rather high probability the consumer will appeal to the second instance and defend himself successfully relying on Art. 45 (1) in connection with Art. 35 Brussels I Regulation. *Cet animal est tres mechant – quand on l'attaque il se defend.* You simply can not avoid one kind or the other of an away game against the consumer in his home state. If you play at home in the first leg you will have the away game (in the form of the enforcement procedure) in the second leg. And your chances of winning might be better if you attack him at home from the outset as Art. 45 (1) in connection with Art. 35 Brussels I Regulation surmounts to a pretty high

---

79) *Peter Mankowski,* E-Commerce und Internationales Verbraucherschutzrecht, MMR-Beilage 7/2000, 22 at 32.

burden to be overcome at second instance if the consumer appeals in the enforcement procedure. All the effort spend might be rendered futile at a very late stage of the proceedings.

Admittedly, the probability of a seller suing a consumer has to be assessed rather low as consumers mostly are contractually bound to make payments in advance (e.g. via a credit card debt). But there still remain cases of mere part instalments and part payments only[80] or cases of the money being deposited with a trusted third party where it might prove necessary to sue the consumer either to extract the money itself or to obtain the consumer's consent to the money being released by the trusted third party.

c) Why consumers do not sue sellers established abroad

Now we have to take the reverse angle and should ask why there are no published cases in which consumers sued on-line sellers. It might be appropriate to stress that the argument connected with reversing the angle is a rather complex one: Sellers complain that the rules on jurisdiction in consumer contract load an almost unbearable burden on them. But if in reality consumers do rather not make use of the rules designed to protect them, the burden on business can in fact not be that high. Also it should be kept in mind that eventually sellers have to back their case before any legislative change can be successfully recommended.[81] Hence, the following purports as its eventual aim to pierce the veil of lobbyism and to attribute its proper weight to the mentioned complaint.

i) Too small amounts at stake

The first and main reason another time is a rather simplistic one: In the majority of possible instances, for the consumer it is not worth to fight because ordinarily the amounts at stake are way too small to properly consider commencing a lawsuit.[82] As a Danish consumer you simply do not sue a company established in Italy for dkr 150 nor for dkr 500. As a German consumer you do not sue a company established in Spain for € 20 nor for € 50 nor for € 100. It's not worth the gamble. It's not worth the effort. Litigation would be too expensive and too

---

80) The bulk of these cases might even fall within Art. 15 (1) lit. a Brussels I Regulation.

81) *Peter Mankowski,* Das Grünbuch zur Rom I-Verordnung, ZEuP 2003, 483 at 486.

82) *Peter Mankowski,* E-Commerce und Internationales Verbraucherschutzrecht, MMR-Beilage 7/2000, 22 at 32; *Julie Guttenberg,* Internet et la protection du consommateur dans la résolution des litiges contractuels, Revue du droit de l'Union Européenne (Rev. dr. UE) 2002, 513 at 522.

time-consuming.[83] You internalise your loss and will react economically:[84] In the future you will refrain from buying from this seller (or, going one significant step further, from sellers of this type) and will advise your friends and acquaintances accordingly, thus inflicting damage on the seller's reputation in the market. No legal action is taken, no legal resources are wasted, and no court is concerned with such cases.

ii) The deterring prospect of proceedings abroad

Consumers lack information about international law. Even the prospect of having to commence proceedings in another state than their own home state deters them. The "promising" endeavours of cross-border enforcement, thought to eat up at least time and effort,[85] add to this considerably, at least they do not diminish the fear of being involved in some kind of proceedings abroad.[86] The whole matter might even start at an earlier stage with the factual difficulties of having to serve the seller abroad.

iii) The additional deterring effect of jurisdiction clauses

To this one should add an effect not often discussed but nevertheless of some importance:[87] Jurisdiction clauses in consumer contracts might not be legally binding upon the consumer pursuant to Artt. 17 Brussels I Regulation; 15 Brussels and Lugano Conventions. However, more often than not they still star in the final clauses of consumer contracts and vest by their very letter exclusive jurisdiction to decide all matters arising out, or in relationship with, the contract in the court at the seller's seat or place of business. Factually they exert a

---

83) Admitted by *Tapio Puurunen*, Choice of Law in European Business-to-Consumer Electronic Commerce – A Trail out of a Political Impasse, ZEuP 2003, 789 at 790 with an interesting reference to a telling study prepared in 1995 in fn. 8.

84) *Peter Mankowski*, Das Grünbuch zur Rom I-Verordnung, ZEuP 2003, 483 at 486.

85) Since costs for the enforcement procedure are awarded in accordance with the law of the state where enforcement is sought by this state's court, money might be added to the list if even successful applicants can not recover their costs from their opponents (as the law stands e.g. in France). Money might also be lost if after winning in the enforcement procedure, the defendant company does not have enough assets as to provide for a reimbursement.

86) *Peter Mankowski*, E-Commerce und Internationales Verbraucherschutzrecht, MMR-Beilage 7/2000, 22 at 30; *Julie Guttenberg*, Internet et la protection du consommateur dans la résolution des litiges contractuels, Rev. dr. UE 2002, 513 at 522.

87) Cf. *Peter Mankowski*, Internationales Privatrecht, in: *Gerald Spindler* (ed.), Vertragsrecht der Internet-Provider, 2nd ed. Cologne 2004, Part III note 23.

deterring effect on the unadvised consumer's mind and prevent the consumer who did not seek legal advice, from commencing a lawsuit in his own home state. "Haven't you read the contract you undersigned (or you consented to)" might be a very apt first line of retreat where the seller might successfully entrench himself counting on the consumer being uninformed and on the consumer's reluctance to seek legal advice with a lawyer. Art. 17 Brussels I Regulation is way too specific to form part of common knowledge. The law can long for one result, but clever use of psychology might lead to another outcome. The clause is legally invalid - but this does not mean it is ineffective in reality.

iv) Who is my seller anyway – and where to reach him?

The consumer-buyer might have to encounter and to overcome yet another difficulty: In order to sue his seller he first has to identify the seller. Then he has to find out the seller's seat or place of business just in order to enable service of the writ on the seller. The most dubious culprits notably hide behind PO boxes and turn out to be mere mailbox companies. They play hide and seek or "catch me - if you can" with their puzzled customers when things get ugly for them. They are not after repeat business and after building a reputation in the market, but after the fast money. They (or in fact the persons behind them) take the money and run. The possibility in running into such trouble generated by rogues in the market is not promising for consumers and does definitely not prompt them into commencing lawsuits.

v) Rational apathy as consumers' preferred strategy

For all these reasons, consumers adapt rational apathy as their preferred strategy. For consumers, it might be rational not to pursue their goals actively. The burden of first having to invest in information about the law and their respective rights appears to high. To this one should add the generally high threshold before consumers actively access the law and the additional obstacles created by enterprises not interested in
building a reputation.

d) Calculating or assessing probabilities

Hence, rationally acting enterprises have to calculate the probability with which they might be sued by the consumer in the consumer's home state. This musters amongst the utmost demands of proper risk assessment and thus goes to the very core of a sound legal risk management. Legal risk management includes not getting overly frightened by remote possibilities. The more remote the probability of being sued the better a flexible approach becomes as the proper answer to consumers' complaints. Sellers should strike the finely balanced line between caution and overcautiousness. However, the better way might be not to wait for being sued but to negotiate with the consumer over his complaint. The risk-neutral and not risk-adverse seller might decide that he will take chances and risks as they come. This includes resolving complaints internally without letting them go to court. Good business perform the vast majority of transactions without any dispute arising; the remaining minority or fraction then should be internally resolved.[88] A further advantage of adopting this line is another time a market-related commercial one: It might help building reputation in the market. The consumer might feel tempted to buy from the company in question repeatedly or will recommended this companies to his friends and acquaintances for its customer-friendly case-handling. Sellers must make up their own mind whether they prefer preventive risk control on one hand or subsequently dealing with risks as and when they are realised, on the other hand.[89] The relevant risks are simply not uncontrollable.[90]

e) Last but not least: contractual risk management as the appropriate device

i) Contractual risk management

One further point must not be overlooked: In the present context we are dealing with jurisdiction in consumer *contract*, with a particular emphasis on *contract*. Contract requires mutual consent – and this includes and comprises consent by the seller. Hence, a seller who is unwilling to run in jurisdictional risks might reject an contract offer by a prospective customer siting in a country with which the seller does not want to do business. The seller has the choice between accepting both the offer and its inherent risk or alternatively turning down the offer and thus negating the inherent risk. You simply cannot have the cake and eat it at the same time. If you want to enhance the geographical ambit of your business, you have to take the risks intrinsically and almost inevitably linked with

88) Cf. *Robert Coleman* (Director General of GD SanCo), Address Concerning Consumers and the Internet at the AIM Brand Forum 2001 http://europa.eu.int/comm/dgs/health_consumer/library/speeches/speech134_en.pdf> and also *Tapio Puurunen*, Choice of Law in European Business-to-Consumer Electronic Commerce – A Trail out of a Political Impasse, ZEuP 2003, 789 at 790.

89) *Peter Mankowski*, Internationaler Verbraucherschutz und Internet, in: Internet und Recht, Vienna 2002, 191 at 213.

90) *Brigitta Lurger*, Internationaler Verbraucherschutz im Internet, in: *Stefan Leible* (ed.), Die Bedeutung des Internationalen Privatrechts im Zeitalter der neuen Medien, Stuttgart etc. 2003, 33 at 42.

this enhancement.[91] If you want to become global or international, you can not expect that you will be treated as an entirely local dealer when it comes down to establishing jurisdiction. You have the opportunity to decide whether you accept offers by consumers from "unwanted" or "undesired" countries. If you have deprived yourself of this opportunity by employing clickwrap- or browsewrap-techniques comprising binding offers to the general public you cannot complain if you are held responsible for your own miscalculation and for not having established yourself the necessary contracting procedures to protect yourself.[92] In contract, the commercial seller has every opportunity to protect himself by contractual means. He is in driver seat. He can exercise contracting control in order to reduce and to minimise his jurisdictional risk.[93] He is in control of the mode of contracting. If he decides not to exercise such control, this might turn out to his detriment. He unwillingly contracted not well advised and eventually at too high a cost. Who as a professional seller has all devices of self-defence at his liberty but does not use them can not complain afterwards. The more since this kind of contractual risk management is supposed to be the most cost efficient way

---

91) *Peter Mankowski,* Das Internet im Internationalen Vertrags- und Deliktsrecht, RabelsZ 63 (1999), 203 at 236-239; *id.,* Internationales Privatrecht, in: *Gerald Spindler* (ed.), Vertragsrecht der Internet-Provider, 2nd ed. Cologne 2004, Part III note 33; *Abbo Junker,* Internationales Vertragsrecht und Internet, RIW 1999, 809 at 816; *Pascal Grolimund,* Geschäftsverkehr im Internet – Aspekte des internationalen Vertragsrechts, ZSR 119 (2000), I 339 at 368; *Miriam Mann,* Besonderer Teil zu Fragen des Internationalen Vertragsrechts, in: *Fabian Schuster* (ed.), Vertragshandbuch Telemedia, Munich 2001, ch. 19 note 85; *Thomas Hoeren/Henning Große Ruse,* Immaterialgüter-, Wettbewerbs- und Verbraucherschutz-Kollisionsrecht sowie gerichtliche Zuständigkeiten bei Internet-Sachverhalten, in: *Michael Lehmann* (ed.), Electronic Business in Europa, Munich 2002, ch. K note 49; *Ulrich Magnus,* E-Commerce und Internationales Privatrecht, in: *Christian Graf/Marian Paschke/Rolf Stober* (eds.), Das Wirtschaftsrecht vor den Herausforderungen des E-Commerce, Cologne/Berlin/Bonn/Munich 2002, 19 at 27.

92) *Peter Mankowski,* E-Commerce und Internationales Verbraucherschutzrecht, MMR-Beilage 7/2000, 22 at 25; *id.,* Internationaler Verbraucherschutz und Internet, in: Internet und Recht, Vienna 2002, 191 at 214; *id.,* Internationales Privatrecht, in: *Gerald Spindler* (ed.), Vertragsrecht der Internet-Provider, 2nd ed. Cologne 2004, Part III note 34.

93) *Peter Mankowski,* Das Internet im Internationalen Vertrags- und Deliktsrecht, RabelsZ 63 (1999), 203 at 248-250; *id.,* E-Commerce und Internationales Verbraucherschutzrecht, MMR-Beilage 7/2000, 22 at 25-27; *id.,* Internationaler Verbraucherschutz und Internet, in: Internet und Recht, Vienna 2002, 191 at 213-218; *Pascal Grolimund,* Geschäftsverkehr im Internet – Aspekte des internationalen Vertragsrechts, ZSR 119 (2000), I 339 at 367 et seq.; *Anastasia Papathoma-Baetge/Stefanie Nehrenberg/Tilmann Finke,* in: *Bert Kaminski/Thomas Henßler/Helge F. Kolaschnik/Anastasia Papathoma-Baetge* (eds.), Rechtshandbuch E-Business, Neuwied/Kriftel 2002, Part 2 A note 88; *Marc Fallon/Johan Meeusen,* Le commerce électronique, la directive 2000/31/CE et le droit international privé, Rev. crit. dr. int. pr. 91 (2002), 435 at 454; *Stefania Savini,* Delocalizzazione del contratto stipulato su Internet – Problemi di giurisdizione e legge applicabile, Contratto e impresa/Europa 2002, 1131 at 1155.

to mitigate the legal risks[94] as ordinarily the controlling measures are cheap and in place since most of them are already demanded by conventional mercantile wisdom.[95] You might err on the side of caution,[96] but the underlying cause is your own risk-adversity. You might deprive the consumers of an enlargement of their opportunities, but this can be reconciled with the general goal of consumer protection:[97] A supplier is not forced or obliged to enter the market. Talking about risk management the opportunity to control with whom you are contracting heavily influences the decision whether it is fair to the seller to subject him to certain risks generated by a certain interpretation of the direction of online-activities.[98] Suppliers operating only locally, regionally or at the utmost nation-wide, will in their own paramount interest establish modes of contracting control just in order to avoid becoming stretched beyond the limits of their logistics and blowing their calculation of fair prices; disturbing the calculation would lead to a lack of amortisation.[99]

A precautionary warning should be added: Simply inserting a disclaimer on the web-site that the web-site is directed solely and exclusively at certain listed countries or that the web-site is not directed at certain listed countries, does not do the trick. Nor would a so-called country-specific design of a web-site do.[100] The seller who afterwards concludes contracts with consumers from "unwanted"

---

94) *Jan Trzaskowski,* Cross-Border Law Enforcement in the Information Society (v. 0.82), Julebog 2003, 233 at 243.

95) *Peter Mankowski,* Internationaler Verbraucherschutz und Internet, in: Internet und Recht, Vienna 2002, 191 at 217.

96) Cf. *Jens Haubold,* Doing E-Business in the European Union – The Non-Member State Perspective: A Snapshot of Private International Issues in E-Commerce, in: International Bureau of the Permanent Court of Arbitration (ed.), Strengthening Relations with Arab and Islamic Countries through International Law, The Hague/London/Boston 2002, 109 at 123.

97) *Contra Georg Borges,* Lokalisierung von Angeboten beim Electronic Banking, Wertpapier-Mitteilungen (WM) 2001, 1542 at 1546; *id.,* Verträge im elektronischen Geschäftsverkehr, Munich 2003, 715.

98) Countering *Markus Fallenböck,* Internet und Internationales Privatrecht, Vienna/New York 2001, 123.

99) *Peter Mankowski,* Internationaler Verbraucherschutz und Internet, in: Internet und Recht, Vienna 2002, 191 at 219 et seq. This is not properly recognized by *Markus Fallenböck,* Internet und Internationales Privatrecht, Vienna/New York 2001, 121.

100) Apparently *contra Jaime Pérez Renovales,* Ley y jurisdicción applicabile, in: *Rafael Mateu de Ros/Juan Manuel Cendoya Méndez de Vigo* (eds.), Derecho de Internet, Madrid 2000, 339 at 350; *Alfonso Luis Calvo Caravca/Javier Carrascosa González,* Conflictos de leyes y conflictos de jurisdicción en Internet, Madrid 2001, 89 et seq.; *Tapio Puurunen,* Choice of Law in European Business-to-Consumer Electronic Commerce – A Trail out of a Political Impasse, ZEuP 2003, 789 at 797.

or "undesired" countries, himself diminishes and reduces his own disclaimer to a mere and unreliable *protestatio facto contraria*. He does not obey his own alleged rules. There should not be any incentive for cheating with disclaimers.[101] Regulation must not allow professionals to tamper with consumer protection unilaterally.[102] Hence, only the combination of disclaimer and obeyance to it suffices to protect the seller whereas a simple disclaimer without consequential contract management would not reach the threshold.[103] On the other hand, one should not negate nor neglect the deterring effect of a disclaimer on consumers located in "unwanted" or "undesired" countries: It diminishes the likelihood that such consumers will contact the seller.[104]

ii) Gathering the necessary information

Sellers might feel tempted to raise the objection that they do not have the necessary information on their customers' whereabouts as to make an informed decision whether to conclude the contract or not. However, acquiring such information does not require an overwhelming effort. If nothing can be detected from the single customer's e-mail-address at first glance, the seller can simply ask his prospective customer where the customer lives. This is a plain and perfectly understandable question which does not give rise to misunderstandings deriving from the use of legal notions as domicile or habitual residence.[105] If a contract for the delivery of real world goods, i.e. genuine tangibles, is intended, the seller desperately needs such data for another vital purpose too: He ought to know

---

101) *Veronika Mochar/Simone Seidl,* Internationales Verbraucherschutzrecht und e-commerce, ÖJZ 2003, 241 at 248.

102) Cf. *Peter Mankowski,* Internationaler Verbraucherschutz und Internet, in: Internet und Recht, Vienna 2002, 191 at 216; *Ulrich Magnus,* E-Commerce und Internationales Privatrecht, in: *Christian Graf/Marian Paschke/Rolf Stober* (eds.), Das Wirtschaftsrecht vor den Herausforderungen des E-Commerce, Cologne/Berlin/Bonn/Munich 2002, 19 at 27.

103) *Peter Mankowski,* Das Internet im Internationalen Vertrags- und Deliktsrecht, RabelsZ 63 (1999), 203 at 245; *Anton K. Schnyder,* Internationalprivatrechtliche Aspekte des E-Commerce, in: *Walter Trüeb* (ed.), Aktuelle Rechtsfragen des E-Commerce, Zurich 2001, 103 at 108; *Markus Fallenböck,* Internet und Internationales Privatrecht, Vienna/New York 2001, 128; *Brigitta Lurger,* Internationaler Verbraucherschutz im Internet, in: *Stefan Leible* (ed.), Die Bedeutung des Internationalen Privatrechts im Zeitalter der neuen Medien, Stuttgart etc. 2003, 33 at 43; *Stephan Bücker,* Internetauktionen, Münster/Hamburg 2003, 133.

104) Cf. only *Nina Wernicke/Vera Hoppe,* Die neue EuGVVO – Auswirkungen auf die internationale Zuständigkeit bei Internetverträgen, MMR 2002, 643 at 647.

105) *Peter Mankowski,* E-Commerce und Internationales Verbraucherschutzrecht, MMR-Beilage 7/2000, 22 at 31. But cf. *Gerald Spindler,* Internationales Verbraucherschutzrecht im Internet, MMR 2000, 18 at 22 et seq.

where to deliver the goods. Hence, he will pose the question beforehand.[106] Not acquiring the relevant data about the customer also could do severe harm to the seller's own prospects as it effectively disposes of any opportunity to run an advance check on the customer's standing and liquidity.[107]

This finally leaves the case of the deceptive customer who wilfully misleads the seller as to his own whereabouts.[108] The solution of this problem is fairly straightforward: The deceiving consumer acting fraudulently does not deserve protection by the law.[109] He who comes to justice, must come with clean hands.

IV. Jurisdiction in tort: a boondoggle for lawyers?

Special jurisdiction in tort under Art. 5 no. 3 Brussels I Regulation follows the so called principle of ubiquity: Jurisdiction can be found both where the incriminated action takes places and/or where the protected interest is affected.[110] The latter does not include the place where consequential damage is sustained.[111]

---

106) *Peter Mankowski,* E-Commerce und Internationales Verbraucherschutzrecht, MMR-Beilage 7/2000, 22 at 26; *Markus Fallenböck,* Internet und Internationales Privatrecht, Vienna/New York 2001, 122; *Brigitta Lurger,* Internationaler Verbraucherschutz im Internet, in: *Stefan Leible* (ed.), Die Bedeutung des Internationalen Privatrechts im Zeitalter der neuen Medien, Stuttgart etc. 2003, 33 at 42.

107) *Peter Mankowski,* E-Commerce und Internationales Verbraucherschutzrecht, MMR-Beilage 7/2000, 22 at 26; *id.,* Internationales Privatrecht, in: *Gerald Spindler* (ed.), Vertragsrecht der Internet-Provider, 2nd ed. Cologne 2004, Part III note 34.

108) Cf. *Gerald Spindler,* Internationales Verbraucherschutzrecht im Internet, MMR 2000, 18 at 22.

109) *Peter Mankowski,* Das Internet im Internationalen Vertrags- und Deliktsrecht, RabelsZ 63 (1999), 203 at 249; *id.,* E-Commerce und Internationales Verbraucherschutzrecht, MMR-Beilage 7/2000, 22 at 27; *id.,* Internationaler Verbraucherschutz und Internet, in: Internet und Recht, Vienna 2002, 191 at 217 et seq.; *Rolf H. Weber,* E-Commerce und Recht, Zurich 2001, 45; *Nina Wernicke/Vera Hoppe,* Die neue EuGVVO – Auswirkungen auf die internationale Zuständigkeit bei Internetverträgen, MMR 2002, 643 at 647; *Simone van der Hof,* Internationale on-line overeenkomsten, Tilburg 2002, 200; *Brigitta Lurger,* Internationaler Verbraucherschutz im Internet, in: *Stefan Leible* (ed.), Die Bedeutung des Internationalen Privatrechts im Zeitalter der neuen Medien, Stuttgart etc. 2003, 33 at 42 et seq.; cf. also *Luca Radicati di Brozolo,* Jurisdiction, Conflict of Laws and the Internet, in: *Guido Ferrarini/Klaus J. Hopt/Eddy Wymeersch* (eds.), Capital Markets in the Age of the Euro, The Hague/London/New York 2002, 165 at 166 et seq.

110) Leading case: ECJ November 30, 1976 – Case 21/76, Rep. 1976, 1735 – Handelskwekerij Bier BV/Mines de Potasse d'Alsace SA.

111) Leading cases: ECJ January 11, 1990 – Case 220/88, Rep. 1990, I-49 - Dumez France SA/Hessische Landesbank; ECJ September 19, 1995 – Case C-364/93, Rep. 1995, I-2719 – Antonio Marinari/Lloyd's Bank plc and Zubaidi Trading Co.

Economic efforts made to repair damaged goods do not constitute jurisdiction with the place where the account is held from which the respective money is taken. Art. 5 No. 3 Brussels I Regulation does quite rightly not contain a sub-rule specifically designed for torts committed on-line. Hence, the generally applied standards have to be applied.[112]

1. Where the incriminated action took place

To identify where the incriminated action took place, might pose a difficulty. The plaintiff only exceptionally will have the necessary information since the action as such was entirely in the defendant's internal sphere. Only going back from the later outcome could provide some clues. Hence, it may be proposed to overcome such an unpleasant deadlock with a rebuttable presumption: It may be presumed that a person acts where he has his habitual residence, or in the case of a company, where this company has its principal place of business. If the business in question is generally delegated to a certain branch, it may be presumed that the relevant act took place where this particular branch is located. Such a presumption might give the alleged victim a helping hand. On the other side, it does not inflict all too much harm on the alleged wrong-doer: As it usually leads to the country of a person's habitual residence or the principal place of business of the defendant company, special jurisdiction in tort based on this first limp might not lay very often since these connecting factors either establish, or normally concord with the factors[113] establishing, general jurisdiction under Art. 2 in connection with Art. 59 or Art. 60 Brussels I Regulation respectively and according to the opening words of Art. 5 Brussels I Regulation, special jurisdiction can not be vested in the courts of the country which already has general jurisdiction.

2. Where the protected interested is affected

a) Locating the affected interest

The more controversial head of jurisdiction is the second part under the principle of ubiquity, namely the place where the protected interest is affected. There is one

---

112) A thorough analysis of existing UK case law on online-torts is provided by *Graham J. H. Smith*, Internet Law and Regulation, 3rd ed. London 2002, paras. 6-032 to 6-056.

113) Art. 2 in connection with Art. 59 Brussels I Regulation employs a normative concept of domicile referring to national law for determining a person's domicile whereas the habitual residence is a factually determined connecting factor. This might lead to some slight divergences.

paramount task: to identify the localisation of the interest affected. To reformulate a once famous song: Tell me where the interests are... Torts committed on and via the Internet generally do not affect tangible goods. But even this suffers an important exception: Inserting viruses damaging hardware inflicts damage to tangible and corporeal goods. Nevertheless, the affected interests ordinarily are intangibles as reputation or databases.

Tentatively, another rebuttable presumption might help, but this time a different one: It may be presumed that a person holds the bulk of his reputation at the place and in the country where he is living, or clad in legal terms, where he has his habitual residence,[114] or in the case of a company, where this company has its principal place of business. However, centering interests this way mainly helps in cases of defamation or other kinds of attacks on a person's reputation but might prove less helpful and appropriate in cases where other intangibles are concerned.

b) The "mosaic principle" as an effective device against *forum shopping*

The nightmare opposite to not presenting the victim with a proper forum at all is inviting the alleged victim to sue for the entire damage wherever he holds even part of the intangible allegedly affected. This would jeopardise the alleged wrongdoer's prospects severely as it would result in world-wide or at least Europe-wide *forum shopping*. To the rescue comes the ECJ. In *Shevill* it established the so-called "mosaic principle": The plaintiff can at the place where the protected interest is affected, only recover the part of the overall damage which was suffered in the state of the forum.[115] Hence, the forum at the place where the protected interest is affected, does not provide a forum for recovering all the damage suffered world-wide.[116] If the plaintiff wants to recover his world-wide damage he has to file writs in all the different states where he suffered damage for the respective partition (or with the forum of the place where the defendant has his domicile or where the incriminated action took place).

The mosaic principle provides a very effective counter-incentive against forum shopping by supposed or alleged victims and thus effectively safeguards the legitimate jurisdictional interests on the alleged wrongdoer's side.[117] That he would have to commence litigation in every state concerned in order to collect

114) *Peter Mankowski,* Das Internet im Internationalen Vertrags- und Deliktsrecht, RabelsZ 63 (1999), 203 at 274.

115) ECJ March 7, 1995 – Case C-68/93, Rep. 1995, I-415 at I-462 paras. 31, 33 – Fiona Shevill/Presse Alliance SA.

116) ECJ March 7, 1995 – Case C-68/93, Rep. 1995, I-415 at I-462 paras. 31, 33 – Fiona Shevill/Presse Alliance SA.

117) *Peter Mankowski,* Das Internet im Internationalen Vertrags- und Deliktsrecht, RabelsZ 63 (1999), 203 at 276.

part of the damage, is too expensive, too costly and thus not attractive for the alleged victim.[118] Fairness is safeguarded and guaranteed by the two other elements of the over-all system: The alleged victim still has any opportunity to sue the alleged wrongdoer at the wrongdoer's domicile of at the place where the incriminated action took place, in order to recover his world-wide damage.[119] The victim is not without protection and not without a forum where he can claim all in one. Therefore the mosaic principle should not be restricted to defamation cases, but extended or better: withheld generally, particularly with regard to online torts.[120]

3. Identifying the wrongdoer as the paramount factual problem

Before you can sue someone you first have to identify this particular someone. This trite sentence addresses the mostly overlooked but utmost problem of jurisdiction in online-tort. People doing wrongs online only seldom hand over, or leave, their card. The occasional e-mail "Hello, I just hacked you" followed by a full (and true!) signature and address is a white raven. Hackers in particular own a profession in making themselves untraceable. Who inserts viruses, worms or Trojans also tries to conceal his identity. In defamation cases wrongdoers also might hide behind a veil of pseudonyms, *nomes de plum* or *nomes de guerre*. The major problem in all these instances reads: You have to identify the wrongdoer in the first place. This is no specific shortcoming of the jurisdictional rules, but a far more general factual problem.[121]

---

118) *Rufus Pichler,* Internationale Gerichtszuständigkeit im Online-Bereich, in: *Thomas Hoeren/Ulrich Sieber* (eds.), Handbuch Multimedia-Recht, Munich looseleaf 1999 onwards, Part 31 note 189 (December 1998).

119) ECJ March 7, 1995 – Case C-68/93, Rep. 1995, I-415 at I-462 para. 32 – Fiona Shevill/Presse Alliance SA.

120) *Peter Mankowski,* Das Internet im Internationalen Vertrags- und Deliktsrecht, RabelsZ 63 (1999), 203 at 274-276; *Thomas Pfeiffer,* Rechtsdurchsetzung im internationalen Rechtsverkehr, in: *Giorgios Gounalakis* (ed.), Rechtshandbuch Electronic Business, Munich 2003, § 13 note 60. But *contra* e.g. *Gabrielle Kaufmann-Kohler,* Internet: mondialisation de la communication – mondialisation de la résolution des litiges?, in: *Katharina Boele-Woelki/Catherine Kessedjian* (eds.), Internet – Which Court Decides? Which Law Applies? Quel tribunal décide? Quel droit s'applique?, The Hague/London/Boston 1998, 89 at 113 et seq.

121) *Peter Mankowski,* Das Internet im Internationalen Vertrags- und Deliktsrecht, RabelsZ 63 (1999), 203 at 285.

In on-line fraud (for instance the infamous Nigeria connections with their lots of allegedly dead uncles and alleged Nigerian lawyers asking for advance payments) the problem is a little different in the factual setting but displays only another facet of the picture in its entirety. In these cases the victim might have a wrongdoer's name, but on closer examination the name proves to be a sham. Hence, the victim is another time left with empty hands unable to identify the people extracting the benefits.

4. Jurisdiction in matters of unfair commercial practices

a) Factual outset

If one hay to predict a single key area where jurisdiction in tort for Internet appearances will really matter it ought to be unfair commercial practices. In this area one has not to overcome insurmountable problems of identifying the possible wrongdoer regularly. Advertisements ordinarily allow to identify the company advertising as they are aimed at attracting business in favour of this particular company. If prospective customers would not know whereto to turn for the advertised good or service, the whole exercise of advertising would be rendered meaningless and futile.[122] The infamous mass spamming, the ocean of abundant spam mails looking to entice innocent victims to buy Viagra from obscure sources (to which spam we all have unwillingly become costumed to) provide but one exception. Those "sellers" are not reputable players in a market to be taken seriously.

b) Jurisdictional rule: principle of ubiquity or marketplace rule?

However, it might sound surprising that the next step would be to identify the jurisdictional rule to be applied and its content. Taking Art. 5 no. 3 Brussels I Regulation literally this rule does not contain a sub-rule specifically designed for unfair commercial practices. Hence, the question appears to be answered once it is raised: Art. 5 no. 3 Brussels I Regulation applies as clad in its usual terms, without modification or adaptation.[123] But learned conflicts lawyers might hesitate

---

122) *Peter Mankowski,* Besondere Formen von Wettbewerbsverstößen im Internet und Internationales Wettbewerbsrecht, Gewerblicher Rechtsschutz und Urheberrecht Internationaler Teil (GRUR Int.) 1999, 995 at 1003.

123) Cf. only *Thomas Hoeren/Henning Große Ruse,* Immaterialgüter-, Wettbewerbs- und Verbraucherschutz-Kollisionsrecht sowie gerichtliche Zuständigkeiten bei Internet-Sachverhalten, in: *Michael Lehmann* (ed.), Electronic Business in Europa, Munich 2002, ch. K note 54.

before concluding this as the final result. At the back of their mind they have the traditional rule in private international law specifically designed for unfair commercial practices, namely the so-called marketplace rule.[124] The PIL of unfair commercial practices does not follow the principle of ubiquity, but developed an own rule. Applying the ordinary principle of ubiquity when jurisdiction in unfair commercial practices has to be judged, does thus not coincide with the revered PIL rule. One could argue that the jurisdictional rule is still inchoate and needs refinement in order to reach the higher echelon and more elevated level the PIL has already reached. To reconcile PIL and jurisdiction, one could feel tempted to instrumentalise a purpotive interpretation of Art. 5 No. 3 Brussels I Regulation in order to establish the marketplace rule.[125] But practitioners should be warned that this has not been affirmed by reliable authority yet.[126] The likelihood of differing results using the different approaches is not all too high in any event. The marketplace can be described as the place where the incriminated action took place,[127] or the place where the protected interested, namely fair competition with regard to consumers or customers, is affected.[128] To operate both approaches

---

124) Its latest emanation is Art. 5 (1) of the Amended Proposal for a Council Regulation on the law applicable to non-contractual obligations, submitted by the Commission on July 22, 2003, COM (2003) 427 final, the so-called Rome II Regulation.

125) In favour of such an approach *Catherine Kessedjian,* Competition, in: *Campbell McLachlan/Peter Nygh* (eds.), Transnational Tort Litigation - Jurisdictional Principles, Oxford 1996, 171 at 184-187; *Bernd Schauer,* Electronic Commerce in der EU, Vienna 1999, 257; *Haimo Schack,* Internationale Urheber-, Marken- und Wettbewerbsrechtsverletzungen im Internet – Internationale Zuständigkeit, MMR 2000, 135 at 137. But sceptical e.g. *Helmut Rüßmann,* Wettbewerbshandlungen im Internet – Internationale Zuständigkeit und anwendbares Recht, Kommunikation und Re

126) *Thomas Pfeiffer,* Rechtsdurchsetzung im internationalen Rechtsverkehr, in: *Giorgios Gounalakis* (ed.), Rechtshandbuch Electronic Business, Munich 2003, § 13 note 60.

127) So e.g. *Rolf Sack,* Das internationale Wettbewerbs- und Immaterialgüterrecht nach der EGBGB-Novelle, Wettbewerb in Recht und Praxis (WRP) 2000, 269 at 272; *Winfried Veelken,* Sachnormzwecke im Internationalen Wettbewerbsrecht, in: Aufbruch nach Europa - Festschrift 75 Jahre Max-Planck-Institut für Privatrecht, Tübingen 2001, 293 at 315 et seq.; *Peter Mankowski,* in: *Christian v. Bar/Peter Mankowski,* Internationales Privatrecht, Vol. I: Allgemeine Lehren, 2nd ed. Munich 2003, § 7 note 61.

128) So e.g. *Walter F. Lindacher,* Zum Internationalen Privatrecht des unlauteren Wettbewerbs, WRP 1996, 645 at 648; *Rufus Pichler,* Internationale Gerichtszuständigkeit im Online-Bereich, Jahrbuch Junger Zivilrechtswissenschaftler 1998, 229 at 249.

properly one has to introduce an additional requirement of minimum market relevance[129] whichever approach is preferred.

c) Utility of disclaimers

In the field of unfair commercial practices disclaimers might serve a useful purpose. Other than in contract where the individual contract could defy the general statement,[130] in unfair commercial practices a generalisation has to be implemented. Disclaimers indicate the spatial ambit of the web-site[131] but only insofar as the advertising person himself generally pays due regard to his own disclaimer and complies with it.[132] That a handful of contracts is concluded with consumers from an "unwanted" or "undesired" country over a longer period does not render the disclaimer ineffective as such an indication. To apply the law of the place where it is issued, to the disclaimer[133] appears to be an unnecessary complication and divides closely related issues. More precisely, it would elevate the disclaimer beyond its proper rank making the disclaimer an issue of its own. But since the disclaimer only provides nothing more than a mere indication, its validity is not an issue at stake.

V. The enforcement side: Nothing new under the sun yet

1. The present situation: Courts are still courts, judgements are still judgements, enforcement proceedings are still enforcement proceedings

The rise of the Information Society as such has changed nothing at all with regard to the recognition and enforcement of judgements. This holds true for one simple

---

129) Guidelines for, and elements of, designing such restriction are provided by *Peter Mankowski,* Internet und Internationales Wettbewerbsrecht, GRUR Int. 1999, 909 at 916-918; *id.,* Wettbewerbsrechtliches Gerichtspflichtigkeits- und Rechtsanwendungsrisiko bei Werbung über Web-sites, CR 2000, 763.

130) See III 3 e i) *supra.*

131) OLG Frankfurt on Main May 31, 2001 – Case 6 U 240/00, MMR 2001, 751 at 752 with note by *Peter Mankowski*; Landgericht (LG) Frankfurt on Main August 10, 2001 – Case 3/12 O 96/01, CR 2002, 222 with note by *Jochen Dieselhorst.*

132) OLG Frankfurt on Main May 31, 2001 – Case 6 U 240/00, MMR 2001, 751 at 752 with note by *Peter Mankowski*; *Peter Mankowski,* Internet und Internationales Wettbewerbsrecht, GRUR Int. 1999, 909 at 919 et seq.

133) As proposed e.g. by *Luca Radicati di Brozolo,* Jurisdiction, Conflict of Laws and the Internet, in: *Guido Ferrarini/Klaus J. Hopt/Eddy Wymeersch* (eds.), Capital Markets in the Age of the Euro, The Hague/London/New York 2002, 165 at 167.

reason: Judgements are rendered by courts – and the courts rendering judgements are the same regardless whether the case at hands concerns online- or offline-matters. They are the same and eversame "Old World" courts. The Information Society has not brought forward its own court system nor the slightest trace of a specific judiciary sitting in Cyberspace. Genuine Cybercourts simply do not exist. Cyberspace as an independent sovereign with an own legal system or own courts does not exist.[134] Any dreams of or towards such a sovereign Cyberspace[135] have faltered years ago. They utterly failed and dismantled themselves just as – dreams. The commercialisation of the Net killed the early enthusiasts' utopia of declaring "the Net" independent. There were some projects of developing so-called Cybercourts, but neither of them succeeded eventually. In fact, those so-called Cybercourts could be described as arbitration panels, not as courts in the strict sense. In essence the same applies to the growing number of attempts to establish different kinds of on-line dispute resolution (ODR), be they aimed at arbitration, conciliation, mediation, mini-trials or ombudsmanship. Courts in the strict sense of the word are still state-run courts. Every court belongs to a particular state. Its judges are appointed by this very state, and it obeys the procedural rules of this very state. And whilst a court is still a court, a judgement is still a judgement. Judgements rendered abroad are still judgements rendered by courts of foreign states.[136] As court judgements in matters related to Internet business or Web affairs are on their face indiscernible from "ordinary" court judgements concerned with real world affairs, no special regime of enforcement rules specifically designed has been developed. Such judgements are in foreign country, i.e. another country than the forum State, confronted with the general rules on recognition and enforcement. For instance, freedom of speech might matter as a matter of the public policy in the State where enforcement is sought. That is the lesson of the American part of the famous *Yahoo!* case.[137] But as usual not such random cases are the obstacles, but the delay, the cost and the effort connected with having to endure a new set of proceedings in a second state. A judgement debtor can still hide behind the inefficiency of the judiciary in the

---

134) See in more detail *Peter Mankowski,* Wider ein transnationales Cyberlaw, Archiv für Presserecht (AfP) 1999, 138.

135) The most prominent one was dreamed by *David R. Johnson/David G. Post,* Law and Borders – The Rise of Law in Cyberspace, 48 Stanford L. Rev. 1367 (1996).

136) Just for the sake of clarification I would like to stress that this is not (repeat: not) to state that nothing at all has changed in the law of enforcement itself. Quite to the contrary, Artt. 41; 44 Brussels I Regulation have been a major step, a quantum leap forward in the history of enforcement procedures, greatly enhancing creditors' prospects. But there are not the least specifically online-related.

137) *Yahoo!, Inc. v. Ligue contre le Racisme et l'Antisemitisme* 169 F. Supp. 2d 1181 (N.D. Cal. 2001); most interestly commented on by *Horatia Muir Watt, Yahoo!* Cyber-Collision of Cultures: Who Regulates?, 24 Michigan J. Int'l. L. 673 (2003).

country where he holds his assets. He might even think of hiding his assets in so-called enforcement havens[138] (all of which are outside the EU).

2. The future: the European enforcement order for uncontested claims

Only the forthcoming project of the European enforcement order (or Single European Judgement) might change the overall picture dramatically. The pending Proposal concerned with uncontested claims[139] seeks to abolish any specific enforcement proceedings in this regard. A Single European Judgement will be regarded and accepted like an judgement rendered by its own courts in every Member State. The restriction to judgements on uncontested claims sounds consoling but does not on its face reveal the fact that according to a recent survey[140] some 90 percent of judgements for which enforcement is sought, deal with uncontested claims. At the core of the matter, it is all about the weight, force and power of default judgements. This might be explained rather easily: Usually a defendant who lost his case actively pursued and defended in court, will honour the judgement rendered. Most genuine disputes between professional or commercial businesses do not go to court, but end in arbitration. Hence, judgements on uncontested claims might be a kind of remainder but provide the bulk of enforcement cases.[141] The main issue at stake in the discussion is whether cases concerning consumer contracts shall be covered and to which extent Art. 35 Brussels I Regulation will be lifted.[142] However, once again this will in its entirety be a general development without specific links to, or restrictions to, e-commerce.

---

138) Cf. *Thomas Hoeren,* Rechtsoasen im Internet, MMR 1998, 297; *Katharina Boele-Woelki,* Internet und IPR: Wo geht jemand ins Netz?, BerDGesVR 36 (2000), 307 at 320.

139) Amended Proposal for a Council Regulation creating a European enforcement order for uncontested claims, submitted by the Commission on June 11, 2003, COM (2003) 341 final.

140) Opinion of the Economic and Social Committee, OJ EU2003 C 85/1 Introduction sub 3.1

141) *Astrid Stadler,* Das Europäische Zivilprozessrecht – Wie viel Beschleunigung verträgt Europa? – Kritisches zur Verordnung über den Europäischen Vollstreckungstitel und ihrer Grundidee, IPRax 2004, 2 at 6.

142) *Erik Jayme/Christian Kohler,* Europäisches Kollisionsrecht 2003: Der Verfassungskonvent und das Internationale Privat- und Verfahrensrecht, IPRax 2003, 485 at 489.

VI. An epilogue: The Internet – really a new spark for B2C cross-border business?

Back in the "old ages" in the mid of the 1990s almost everyone expected the Internet to spark cross-border business and to enhance the volume of international trade considerably. Fantasies of billions and billions of Dollars or Euros revenue by cross-border B2C-business raised on the Net were dreamed all over the world. The international, the border-less medium was expected to generate international contracts in their shades. It grew in people's mind until it was believed to be, and heralded as, some kind of messianic saviour or the *perpetuum mobile* or, even better, both in one. Even before the burst of the Internet Bubble in 2000, a more realistic examination could reveal that those expectations were grossly over-exaggerated. This was in particular true with regard to B2C-business. The Net might be international – but consumer business generally remained local, regional and national. The early days of trans-Atlantic shipping of books by Amazon.com are but one of the few exceptions to the rule.

To the contrary, Amazon provides a fine example for another, much more dominant trend: Successful enterprises establish branches or subsidiaries in relevant countries. The language barrier and the delay in shipping goods rank among the most important factors why cross-border B2C-business did not take off. Local branches overcome these barriers.

And yet another dominant trend should be identified: To a remarkable extent, the winners in the battle for B2C-business were and are well-known and well-established "Old World" players with a high reputation and a resounding reliability index. Behind their success two factors are the most prominent: Firstly, they easily outdid anyone else in the battle for "lighthouses", i.e. the recognisable signposts on the coast of the ocean, the signposts in the vast informational overkill of the Internet. They did not need to make their own name (i.e. to establish it from the scratch) – as they already owned a "name". They did not need to establish themselves as known and recognised entities – as they were already so established. Secondly, they had the necessary logistics already in place.[143] By employing the Net as an additional channel for doing business only, they profited from genuine synergy. However, even those winners in terms of revenue are only scarcely involved in B2C-transactions across a border. Taking one leaping step out of the immanent picture, one can easily detect that legal rules for international business did not have a major stake in these developments. Not only did they not star – they simply did not matter.

143) *Peter Mankowski,* E-Commerce und Internationales Verbraucherschutzrecht, MMR-Beilage 7/2000, 22 at 35.

Legal Risk Management in Cross-Border E-Commerce

by Jan Trzaskowski[1]

The Internet has made it easier to do business across borders. It may still involve considerable investment to do so, but the need for physical establishment in the targeted markets is reduced.

When businesses use the Internet for marketing or contracting purposes, are the activities by default available to all Internet users around the globe. There are no official standards for how a business can delimit its Internet activities in order to avoid economical loss deriving from infringement of the law of other states.

This paper focuses on possibilities in cross-border law enforcement and how businesses can manage legal risks deriving from states where its Internet activities are available. The article establishes a distinction between Traditional Law Enforcement and Alternative Law Enforcement.

This paper is elaborated in connection to a project presentation at Copenhagen Business School's international research conference on EU E-Commerce Law in November 2003. This paper is like the conference presentation meant as a project presentation, which means that it contains ideas and possible solutions without reaching conclusions.

1. Legal Risk Management

A Legal Risk can be defined as a potential economical loss deriving from the infringement of a legal norm. The loss can derive from a sanction or the deprival of possible advantages. Infringing behavioural norms may cause pecuniary penalties or tort claims, whereas infringement of norms regarding contracting may lead to unenforceable claims, damages or performance obligations. Infringement of legal norms may also lead to economical loss caused by damaged reputation.

Legal Risk Management is about how businesses should handle Legal Risks. Legal Risk Management concerns both economical based choices and practical implementation of strategies. This project deals only with the economical choices concerning legal risks deriving from the infringement of

---

1) jan@extuto.dk, www.legalriskmanagement.com.

legal norms in states where the subject, a business, is established. It is assumed that the business complies with the law of the state in which it is established.

The assessment of a Legal Risk entails a number of uncertainties, including the risk of detection and actual legal action, litigation costs, the magnitude of a possible judgement and reputation consequences. This project examines only the economical effect of the possibility of law enforcement across borders.

The expected loss due to the infringement of a legal norm can be calculated by multiplying the potential loss with the probability of the loss being suffered. If no sanctions can be carried out, the probability is zero and the expected loss is consequently zero. Even if the expected loss is not zero, may it be efficient for a business to breach the law. The somewhat controversial question of efficient breach is further elaborated on in the project presented in this article.

The purpose of the project is to present and discuss various ways of enforcing law in order for businesses to assess Legal Risks deriving from cross-border Internet activities. A second purpose is to evaluate certain risk mitigating techniques that can enable businesses mitigate Legal Risks. These risk mitigation techniques are presented below.

1.1. Cross-Border Law Enforcement

Cross-border law enforcement can be defined as imposing sanctions on a business in another state than the state in which the law enforcer is established.[2] It is assumed that the sanction is imposed due to the infringement of the law of the state in which the law enforcer is established and that that law is different from the law in the state where the business is established.

This article contains a division between Traditional Law Enforcement (direct law enforcement) and Alternative Law Enforcement (indirect law enforcement). Traditional law enforcement is sanctions imposed on the primary offender (the business) through the Judiciary, whereas Alternative Law Enforcement comprises other sanctions, such as imposing joint liability on intermediaries (secondary offenders), employ technical measures or using market forces.[3]

Under both traditional and alternative law enforcement are sanctions carried out on the initiative of an aggrieved party or a party who is authorized or

2) See Trzaskowski, Jan, Cross-Border Law Enforcement in the Information Society, Julebog 2003, Jurist- og Økonomforbundets forlag, 2003.

3) See in general also cross-border law enforcement; Mankowski, Peter, Behördliche Eingriff und grenzüberschreitende Online-Dienste, Die Bedeutung des Internationalen Privatrechts im Zeitalter der neuen Medien, Richard Doorberg Verlag, 2003, p. 51.

obliged to take actions on behalf of collective interest. Law enforcers can be divided into private law enforcers and public law enforcers.

> The division between private and public law enforcers is neither sharp nor consistent in an international perspective. A division of common parties can be:
>
> Public law-enforcers: the Public Prosecutor and public organs such as health and consumer authorities, including ombudsmen.
>
> Private law-enforcers: Business partners, costumers, competitors and private organisations pursuing collective interest (e.g. consumer and business organisations)

2. Traditional Law Enforcement

2.1. Private Law and Public Law

In the western world, states carry a distinction between private law and public law (criminal and administrative law). There are similarities in this distinction among states but the distinction is far from uniform. Public law and private law may also be defined as being penal and compensatory respectively.[4]

In this article public law is legislation that is normally enforced by public authorities exercising public powers. Private law is legislation normally enforced by private parties or governments acting as such.[5] A law can have both a private and a public nature.

There are different sanctions and procedural rules attached to private and public law respectively. Private law is normally sanctioned by damages, contractual obligations, specific performance etc., whereas public law enforcement normally implies sanctions such as custodial penalties (imprisonment), pecuniary penalties (fines) and disqualifications. Court orders such as injunctions and commands are found under both private and public law.

Some legislation can clearly be placed under either private or public law. Legislation may however fall within both private and public law. That is for example the case for a number of laws regulating businesses' market behaviour.

---

4) Black, Donald, The Behaviour of Law, Academic Press, Inc., 1976, p. 5.

5) Civil law gives private parties rights to take legal actions, whereas public law gives public authorities acting on behalf of society as such right to take legal actions. See also the case, Verein für Konsumenteninformation vs. Karl Heinz Henkel, ECJ Case C-167/00 (1 October 2002) regarding the 1968 Brussels Convention.

> The distribution between public and private law sanction differs from state to state. Most states have legislation against misleading advertising. The types and magnitude of sanctions differs substantially. Legislation on misleading advertising may be sanctioned by e.g. fines, damages or contractual consequences. In some situations public law offences is also subject to private prosecution.

It is not the purpose of this article to establish an exact division of the content of the law. The purpose is to present and discuss procedural characteristics of the enforcement of private and public law respectively to provide guidelines for businesses' Legal Risk Management in international e-commerce.

2.2. Cross-Border Law Enforcement

The legal field of conflicts of law (private law) consist of three layers: Choice of law, jurisdiction (choice of forum) and recognition/enforcement of foreign judgements. The function of public law can be described by the same three elements, but with far less flexibility than in private law.

All three layers play an important role in cross-border law enforcement. Recognition and enforcement of foreign judgements is linked both to the jurisdiction applied and the subject matter of the judgement. Traditional cross-border law enforcement can be carried out in three ways:

- The state where the business is established applies the law of the enforcer's state and grant the enforcer access to sue in its courts
- The state where the sued business is established recognise or enforce foreign judgements from the state where the enforcer sues
- The state where the business is established extradites the person(s) running the business to prosecution in the state of the enforcer.

A fourth situation exists where a court applies the law of the defendant and that law prescribe sanctions for actions carried out abroad. This situation is not dealt with in this article since it is assumed that the business complies with the law of the state in which it is established.

2.2.1. Applying Foreign Law

The first situation of cross-border law enforcement requires that the enforcer (plaintiff or prosecutor) brings proceedings in the business' homecourt. In order to do so the Judiciary of that state needs to recognise the enforcer by granting litigation capacity.

When a judgement is entered in the offender's state can actual enforcement be carried out by the legal system of that state since states normally enforce judgements entered within the state's own courts.

2.2.1.1. Litigation Capacity

Private persons will normally have litigation capacity in foreign courts. Public authorities and private organisations may however not be correspondingly recognised by foreign courts. Especially public law enforcers will most likely be reduced to ask local authorities to bring proceedings.

The 1998 EU Injunction Directive[6] provides within the Internal Market certain qualified bodies with litigation capacity to seek injunctions in the homecourt of the offender. The directive deals however only with infringement of some specific directives – i.e. a harmonised area.

2.2.1.2. Private Law

Most states can apply foreign law in private law suits. The starting point of private international law is the contacts approach, which provides that the law with the closest connection to the matter should be applied. Most states also accept the contracting parties' freedom to choose the applicable law.

In Europe the main provisions for choice of law in contract are found in the 1980 Rome Convention.[7] Besides laying down the parties autonomy and the contacts approach as key principles, the convention contains special choice of law rules for inter alia certain consumer contracts and contracts on sale of goods and services.

2.2.1.2.1. Consumer Contracts

Consumers often benefit from legal protection. In the 1980 Rome Convention consumers are awarded with a mandatory rule, which designate the consumer's substantive law in certain consumer contracts.[8]

It is a prerequisite for designating the consumer's law under article 5 of the 1980 Rome Convention that the contract concerns the supply of goods or

---

6) Directive 98/27/EC on injunctions for the protection of consumers' interests (19 May 1998).

7) Convention on the Law Applicable to Contractual Obligations, consolidated version (98/C 27/02).

8) See e.g. Mankowski, Peter, E-Commerce und Internationales Verbracherschutzrecht, MultMedia und Recht-Beilage, vol. 7 (22), 2000, Foss, Morten and Bygrave, Lee A., International Consumer Purchases through the Internet: Jurisdictional Issues pursuant to European Law, International Journal of Law and Information Technology, Vol. 8, No. 2, 2000, Øren, Joakim ST., International Jurisdiction over Consumer Contracts in e-Europe, ICLQ vol 52, July 2003, p. 665 and Debusseré, Frederic, International Jurisdiction over E-Consumer Contracts in the European Union: Quid Novi Sub Sole?, International Journal of Law and Information Technology, Vol. 10 No. 3, 2002.

services to a person ('the consumer') for a purpose which can be regarded as being outside his trade or profession, or a contract for the provision of credit for that object and:

- if in that country the conclusion of the contract was preceded by a specific invitation addressed to him or by advertising, and he had taken in that country all the steps necessary on his part for the conclusion of the contract, or
- if the other party or his agent received the consumer's order in that country, or
- if the contract is for the sale of goods and the consumer travelled from that country to another country and there gave his order, provided that the consumer's journey was arranged by the seller for the purpose of inducing the consumer to buy.[9]

It follows from the 1980 Rome Convention that while maintaining the parties freedom to choose the applicable law, the choice of law may not have the result of depriving the consumer of the protection afforded to him by the mandatory rules of the law of the state in which the consumer resides, provided the requirements above are satisfied.[10]

It is possible to object to the choice of law by questioning the material validity of the contract[11] or if the choice is manifestly incompatible with the public policy ('ordre public') of the forum.[12]

2.2.1.2.2. Tort

The 1980 Rome Convention does not apply to tort cases. In multinational tort-cases, most states apply the concept of lex loci delicti in various manners. In

9) The requirements listed are identical to the coherent requirements in the Brussels convention. When the 1980 Rome Convention will be "converted" into a EU regulation, the text may be expected to be adjusted along the line of the above mentioned requirements in the 2000 Brussels Regulation.

10) The provision does not apply to contract of carriage and contract for the supply of services where the services are to be supplied to the consumer exclusively in a country other than that in which he has his habitual residence, except for contracts which, for an inclusive price, provides for a combination of travel and accommodation.

11) Article 8. As a starting point the designated law shall determine the existence and validity of a contract. However may a party rely upon the law of the country in which he has his habitual residence to establish that he did not consent if it appears from the circumstances that it would not be reasonable to determine the effect of the designated law. The law of the country in which the consumer has his habitual residence governs the formal validity of a consumer contract. Article 9 (5).

12) Article 16.

the EU there is an ongoing work on the EU Rome II Regulation, which is to approximate the choice of law in tort.[13]

The principle of lex loci delicti means that sanctions under a foreign law can be imposed on a business if it is sued in its own homecourt. States may apply a liberal approach to weighing up different contacts and may also refuse to apply foreign law if it would be incompatible with the public policy of the forum.

The 2000 EU E-Commerce Directive introduced the country of origin principle, which provides that within the Internal Market, business should as a starting point only fulfil the legal requirements in the state of establishment. Consumer contracts are exempt from the scope of application, but the country of origin principle may conflict with the concept of lex loci delicti.

A business established in the Internal market can reasonably (and most likely with success) argue that applying (the stricter) tort law of another state than that, in which the business is established, is in contravention of the country of origin principle and the free movement of information Society Services as defined in the 2000 EU E-Commerce Directive.[14]

2.2.1.3. Public Law

Choice of law is normally not discussed within public law since state's courts only apply their own public law. The aggrieved party is therefore reduced to ask the public prosecutor of the state of establishment to initiate proceedings. Such a request is however not likely to be carried out if the underlying activity is not unlawful under the law of the state where the business is established.

The 1998 EU Injunction Directive ensures litigation capacity to certain parties, but the directive does not determine the applicable law.[15] It is unlikely that a state will apply foreign public law, whereas a state may do so in private law cases. There is no harmonisation of the rules on choice of law in this field.

---

13) The officially presented draft is based on the principle of lex loci delicti for a number of situations. Text available at http://europa.eu.int/comm/justice_home/news/consulting_public/rome_ii/news_hearing_ rome2_en.htm in connection to written hearing of 3 May 2002.

14) Second part of recital 23 states, "provisions of the applicable law designated by rules of private international law must not restrict the freedom to provide information society services as established in this Directive". See also Mankowski, Peter, Das Herkunftlandprinzip als Internationales Privatrecht der e-commerce-rechlinie, Zeitschrift für vergleichende Rechtswissenschaft, 2001, p. 137.

15) Article 2 (2) of the directive only that the directive is without prejudice to the rules of private international law, with respect to the applicable law, thus leading normally to the application of either the law of the Member State where the infringement originated or the law of the Member State where the infringement has its effects.

The country of origin principle of the 2000 EU E-Commerce Directive comprises a principle of home country control, which obliges the EU member states to ensure that a service provider established on its territory comply with the national provisions applicable in the Member State in question which fall within the directives coordinated field.

2.2.2. Recognition and Enforcement of Foreign Judgements

A judgement is recognised in the state in which the judgement has been rendered, but no state is by default obliged to recognise foreign judgments. Cooperation between regional states has led to agreements on recognition of certain foreign judgements. Recognition of foreign judgement is more accepted in private law than public law.

In order to be characterized as cross-border law enforcement, the judgement should be entered under a law other than the defendant's. This may in particular be of importance for considering the compatibility with the public order of the recognising state.

2.2.2.1. Private Law

The most important acts on recognition of foreign judgements in Europe are the 2000 EU Brussels Regulation[16] and 1988 Lugano Convention.[17] The acts regulate both jurisdiction (choice of forum) and mutual recognition of judgements. These acts provide 'free movement' of private judgements within EU and EFTA States respectively.

The European free movement of judgements is only applicable to judgements from courts within EU and EFTA. Enforcement of judgements can be refused only on procedural grounds or by invoking that recognition is incompatible with the public order of the recognising state.

---

16) Council regulation No 44/2001 of 22 December 2000 on jurisdiction and the recognition and enforcement of judgements in civil and commercial matters. This regulation replaces the EC Convention on Jurisdiction and Enforcement of Judgements in Civil and Commercial Matters (1968 Brussels Convention) from 27 September 1968. Changing the convention into an EU regulation brings the principles into a part of the EU legislation whereas the Brussels convention was an independent multilateral agreement. Denmark is as the only EU states not bound by the 2000 Brussels regulation and therefore the 1968 Brussels convention still apply between Denmark and either of the other EU member states.

17) The EC and EFTA Lugano Convention on Jurisdiction and the Enforcement of Judgements Civil and Commercial Matters from 16 September 1988.

Outside these obligations each state can decide whether to recognise a foreign judgement. The forthcoming of states varies from no recognition (as in Denmark) to recognition in respect of cooperation among sovereign nations.[18]

At a more global level is the 1958 UN New York Convention[19] of interest for European businesses. This convention provides a more globally adopted system for recognition of arbitral awards.[20] A similar convention for judgements seems to be emerging out of a previously more ambitious project under the Hague Convention.[21]

Like the 1958 UN New York Convention, the draft Hague Convention on Recognition of Civil or Commercial Judgements only deals with situations where the parties have chosen a forum.[22] The recognition of a judgement from another contracting state may only be refused on grounds similar to what is described above regarding the 2000 EU Brussels Regulation.

2.2.2.2. Public Law

Traditional judicial cooperation in criminal matters is based on a variety of international legal instruments, which are overwhelmingly characterised by a principle of request which implies that one sovereign state makes a request to another sovereign state, which then determines whether it will comply with the request.[23]

The Treaty of the European Union article 31 (a) deals with judicial cooperation between EU member states and a programme of measures to implement the principle of mutual recognition of decisions in criminal matters has been adopted.[24]

---

18) European civil law states seem to be more reluctant to recognise foreign judgement than common law states. Most courts in the United States recognise foreign judgements as a matter of mutual respect and cooperation among sovereign nations ('Comity'), provided that that the recognising state find the rendering state to have proper jurisdiction and that fair procedures has been employed. See Kay, Herma Hill, Conflict of Laws, Harcourt Brace Legal and Professional Publications, Inc., 1998, p. 152.

19) United Nations Convention on the Recognition and Enforcement of Foreign Arbitral Awards, New York, 10 June 1958.

20) More than 120 states have adopted the convention, including the USA.

21) See http://www.hcch.net/e/workprog/jdgm.html.

22) ftp://ftp.hcch.net/doc/jdgm_pd22e.doc.

23) Communication from the Commission to the Council and the European Parliament on Mutual Recognition of Final Decisions in Criminal Matters, COM (2000) 495 final (26 July 2000), p. 2.

24) Official Journal of the European Communities C12/10 (15 January 2001).

Since mutual recognition[25] of criminal decisions requires mutual trust in the concerned foreign states, harmonisation is required to ensure inter alia the rights of the indicted. Mutual recognition may however require extensive harmonisation of several substantial and procedural areas.

In Europe the two most important conventions on mutual recognition in criminal matters is the 1970 Hague Convention on the International Validity of Criminal Judgement[26] and the 1991 Brussels Convention on the Enforcement of Foreign Criminal Sentences.[27] Both conventions are however poorly ratified in the EU.[28]

A basic principle of the two mentioned conventions and international cooperation on criminal law in general is the principle of dual criminality, which requires the act to be criminal under both the state of the prosecutor and the defendant. Furthermore are the conventions equipped with a number of exemptions including for situations where the recognition would contravene with the public order of the recognising state.

Freedom to establishment and provide goods and services are fundamental principles of the Internal Market, which may restricts the application of national law – including public law. See for example Piergiorgio Gambelli (case C-243/01) where the court established that:

> *"National legislation which prohibits on pain of criminal penalties the pursuit of the activities of collecting, taking, booking and forwarding offers of bets, in particular bets on sporting events, without a licence or authorisation from the Member State concerned constitutes a restriction on the freedom of establishment and the freedom to provide services provided for in Articles 43 and 49 EC respectively."*

Restrictions on the freedom to establishment and provide goods and services may however be justified by a public-interest objective, which take precedence over the requirements of the free movement. The European Court of justice established for example in the DocMorris[29] that a ban on mail order

---

25) Mutual recognition can appear in the form that the state just enforce the foreign decision or it may be required that the state converts the foreign decision to a national decision which is hereafter enforced.

26) Council of Europe, European Treaty Series No. 70 (28 May 1970).

27) Convention of 13 November 1991.

28) Communication from the Commission to the Council and the European Parliament on Mutual Recognition of Final Decisions in Criminal Matters, COM (2000) 495 final (26 July 2000), p. 6.

29) Case C-322/01.

sale of medicinal product subject to prescription was justified – unlike for medicinal products not subject to prescription.

The country of origin principle in the 2000 EU E-Commerce Directive has supplemented these principles. The freedom to provide Information Society Services[30] in the 2000 EU E-Commerce is wider than for services in general under the EU Treaty. Unlike the EU Treaty, the 2000 EU E-Commerce Directive designates the law of establishment (country of origin principle), whereas the EU Treaty may only limit the application of legislation that may restrict the function of the Internal Market.

2.2.3. Extradition

Extradition of an offender is also cross-border law enforcement. Extradition is based on either a case-to-case request structure or international agreements between states. Extradition is only used in more severe crimes involving custodial sanctions, i.e. public law. Businesses that are carried out by legal persons (companies) can for obvious reasons not be extradited, but extradition can be relevant for natural persons who carry out business or are responsible for a company's activities.

Like for other international cooperation in the field of criminal law is extradition based on dual criminal and respect of public order of the state, which is requested to extradite a person. The main convention in Europe on extradition is the 1957 Paris Convention.[31] This convention is also based on dual criminality, which means that a person will not be extradited for prosecution if the activities are not illegal in the requested state.

2.2.3.1. Alternatives to extradition

In American cases against two Russian hackers, Vasiliy Gorshkov and Alexey V. Ivanov, the FBI persuaded the two men to travel to the Unites States in order to participate in job interviews in a fictitious computer security company in Seattle created by the FBI.[32] During the meeting, the FBI recorded evidence against the hackers and obtained, through a demonstration by the hackers, access to search and copy evidence from the hackers' computers in Russia.

---

30) "Any service normally provided for remuneration, at a distance, by means of electronic equipment for the processing (including digital compression) and storage of data, and at the individual request of a recipient of a service". See EU Directives 98/34 and 98/84.

31) European Convention on Extradition of 13 December 1957.

32) U.S. Department of Justice, www.usdoj.gov/criminal/cybercrime. See also Bellia, Patricia L, Berman, Paul Schiff and Post, Davis G., Cyberlaw – Problems of Policy and Jurisprudence in the Information Age, Thomson West, 2003, p. 183.

The mentioned approach led to conviction on a number of counts of conspiracy, various computer crimes and fraud. Since the two hackers conveniently enough were staying in the USA, the sentences could easily be enforced within U.S. territory. Though such undercover enforcement approaches may be effective, they are not allowed in a number of states.

A Legal Risk can also potentially restrict a businessman's freedom of movement if the businessman has ground to fear prosecution in certain states. Such a restriction in freedom to travel for either business or pleasure purposes may be significant for a person and thus should be considered when pursuing international e-commerce.

3. Alternative Law Enforcement

Alternative Law Enforcement is about imposing sanctions on secondary offenders (intermediaries) or on primary offenders by other sanctions than those carried out through the Judiciary. This article focuses only on joint liability and law enforcement through the market and by technical means. Alternative Law Enforcement does not require judicial cooperation between states and may therefore be more effective in cross-border situation than Traditional Law Enforcement.

3.1. Intermediaries and Joint Liability

In situations where it may be difficult to sue the primary offender in the enforcing state, a law enforcer may be successful in suing intermediaries. Suing intermediaries is often used when it is pointless to sue the primary offender or when the purpose of the lawsuit can be achieved easier that way, for example if the intermediary is established in the same state as the law enforcer.[33]

Joint liability can for example be imposed on users in for example gambling activities, on the executives of a company or business partners. Payment intermediaries such as credit card issuers may also play an important role in the law enforcement.

Joint liability is of significance from a Legal Risk Management perspective when sanctions on secondary offender can affect the business (the primary offender). That can be in situations where the intermediary may have recourse against the business or where the business is dependent on the intermediary's operation.

---

33) The 2000 EU E-Commerce Directive prescribes some limitations to the possibility to apply joint responsibility on certain kinds of intermediaries. The directive however does not exclude such law enforcement.

In a number of situations will the cooperation between the business and an intermediary be regulated by contract, which may contain distribution of liability. In these situations is it relatively easy to understand the Legal Risk. This can e.g. be the relationship between the business and a payment intermediary (bank or credit card issuer) or content intermediaries (for example banner-ad carriers).

3.2. Law Enforcement Through the Market

Market forces are a well-known effective regulator. Most businesses are to some extent vulnerable to unfavourable commenting, thus using the media can for some purposes be an alternative to enforcement through the Judiciary. In the wake of the Information Society the character and credibility of information and media has changed, but information can still be a powerful tool.

A party enforcing the law can take advantage of the possibility to influence the market through information. Information has the advantage that it can have an effect on foreign businesses without being dependent on recognition. To influence the market, the party enforcing the law may however need both credibility and access to a medium.

The market can be used to put pressure on businesses carrying out illegal activities by influencing the businesses' goodwill through for example warning potential costumers. It has however been seen that businesses have managed to turn such situations to their own advantage, which makes the consequences of unfavourable commenting less predictable.

The market can also be used positively by approving or evaluating certain businesses or activities in some form of trustmark scheme. As long as the information under the hallmark scheme has some significance in the market, business will have an incentive to comply with the scheme and thereby inter alia observe the law of the state in question.

The market forces can be applied in order to deter infringement, but can also be applied to punish businesses to the extent the business is vulnerable to such enforcement. Enforcement through unfavourable commenting by for example a public authority may have a greater effect than traditional law enforcement. The credibility of information may however be diluted if the media is being used too intensively or in cases without wide support.

3.3. Technical Law Enforcement

The Internet requires electricity and connections in order to function. A sovereign state can choose not to connect the state to the Internet. Between this extreme and full access lie a number of possible solutions for effective law enforcement. No sovereign state is obliged to allow access to material, which is deemed unlawful in that state, unless otherwise agreed between states.

The Internet provides effective means of control.[34] If a sovereign state chooses to give access to the Internet, the state has possibilities to block out access to certain material or material from certain destinations.[35] Existing blocking techniques may not be 100% effective, but like for most other laws full compliance is not necessary in order to have effective law enforcement.

Blocking requires control over providers of Internet access. Since access providers are normally established within the state where access is provided, the access provider will also be within the state's control. Technical enforcement can be put into an automated system, which will not impose unreasonable burdens on the access providers.

Blocking will have the effect that users in the state in question cannot access the illegal material and will then mitigate the effect of the activity. Blocking causes however no further punishment than the hindrance of availability and can notably not be used to compensate injured parties.

Technical law Enforcement can also be carried out through the Domain Name System, which is an important point of control in the Internet environment. The Internet Corporation For Assigned Names and Numbers (ICANN) manage the Domain Name System[36] and its centralised nature makes it an obvious measure for technical law enforcement.[37] The Domain Name System already plays an important role in the enforcement of decisions concerning domain name disputes.[38]

4. Mitigating Legal Risks

An important part of Legal Risk Management is to mitigate Legal Risks. Business can take a number of measures to mitigate Legal Risks in electronic commerce. This article present four approaches, viz. 1) geographical delimitation, 2) contractual regulation, 3) substantive adjustment and 4) controlling litigation initiative.

---

34) See Zittrain, Jonathan, Internet Points of control, Havard Law School Research paper No. 54, Boston College Law Review.

35) See Dornseif, Maximillian, Government mandated blocking of foreign Web content, md.hudora.de.

36) www.icann.org.

37) See in general Mueller, Milton L., Ruling the Root: Internet Governance and the Taming of Cyberspace, The MIT Press, 2002.

38) See http://ecommerce.wipo.int/domains/.

4.1. Geographical Delimitation

The most cost efficient approach to mitigate legal risks will normally be to geographically delimit the marketing material, including especially access to enter contracts. In absence of international standards for defining the targeted states, businesses may want to divide their websites into different regions from which the user has to choose.[39] Thereby business can at least to some extent control whereto which material is disseminated.[40]

Systems for technical delimitation are possible to elaborate in a way that users from non-targeted states will not obtain access to the business' marketing material or specific parts thereof. This can be done if for example a country code is connected to the user information sent in Internet communication.[41] Such delimitation will probably be more effective than the above-mentioned solution.

It should be noted that geographical delimitation within the Internal Market might become incompatible with EU law due to a proposed directive on services in the Internal Market.[42] The draft directive suggest in article 21 that member states shall ensure that the recipient is not subjected to discriminatory requirements based on his nationality or place of residence.

4.2. Contractual Regulation

The parties of a commercial interaction may as a starting point choose both forum and applicable law (parties autonomy) prior to an actual dispute. A business may benefit from requiring a contract, containing choice of law and forum clauses, with anybody who want to enter the business' website or purchase goods or services.

Most states recognise the parties' autonomy, but may require different standards for recognising such agreements. These requirements may concern how clear the terms have been presented and accepted. It should be noted that there are limitations on the parties' autonomy for certain consumer contracts as described above. Providing misleading information about choice of law or forum in such situations may in itself be unlawful.

39) Se e.g. www.sonyericsson.com, www.levis.com, www.mcdonalds.com

40) It will mainly be product information, offers and contracting ability that businesses should delimit, whereas general information about the business is less likely to give problems.

41) See e.g. www.infosplit.com.

42) Proposal for a Directive of the European Parliament and of the Council on Services in the Internal Market. See http://europa.eu.int/comm/internal_market/en/services/services/docs/2004-proposal_en.pdf.

In a situation where the user is buying goods or services, is it easy to insert relevant clauses in the purchase procedure – to the extent it is legal. The clearer the terms are presented and the clearer the consent is given, the more likely are such clauses to be recognised by foreign states.

As an alternative or supplement to make an agreement on choice of law and forum, the business may post a disclaimer on the website to for example limit the business liability. Disclaimers may not always be recognised, but can help mitigate legal risks.[43]

4.3. Substantive Adjustments

Business may choose to adjust its marketing material in accordance with the law of one or more targeted states and thus reducing the legal risks. Businesses may also choose to adjust the marketing material by observing guidelines of international nature or national guidelines in the targeted states.[44] Guidelines are normally available on the Internet free of charge and are often unlike laws designed for practical implementation.

Guidelines are often less precise than the law itself but can at a relatively low cost provide valuable information on how to mitigate legal risks. Getting precise information about the law is normally an expensive and cumbersome process, which may be preferable for businesses that are more vulnerable to e.g. unfavourable commenting.[45]

4.4. Controlling Litigation Initiative

Cross-border litigation is normally both expensive and cumbersome. This may deter an aggrieved party from suing another party even if the outcome of a case would clearly benefit the aggrieved party.[46] This is especially the case where the subject matter is of insignificant value like in most consumer purchases on the Internet.

---

43) For American case-law se e.g. Bellia, Patricia L, Berman, Paul Schiff and Post, Davis G., Cyberlaw – Problems of Policy and Jurisprudence in the Information Age, Thomson West, 2003, p. 623 ff.

44) See e.g. the 1999 OECD guidelines for Consumer Protection in the Context of Electronic Commerce, www.oecd.org and a number of guides for both consumers and businesses at www.ftc.gov/bcp/menu-internet.htm. See also the 2002 Position Statement of the Nordic Consumer Ombudsmen on E-Commerce and Marketing on the Internet, www.fs.dk/uk/acts/nord_gui.htm.

45) Since there are some similarities in the law of regions, it may be more efficient to only obtain detailed legal information in a limited number of states.

46) See e.g. Cooter, Robert and Ulen, Thomas, Law & Economics, 3rd edition, Addison-Wesley, 2000, p. 336.

In tort the litigation initiative will normally lie with the aggrieved party, whereas the initiative in contract will lie with the party whose contractual rights have not been fulfilled. By making sure that for example a customer pay for his services or goods in advance, the litigation initiative will lie with the purchaser unless the purchaser can seek redress through the payment instrument issuer by rules on charge back.

Online Alternative Dispute Resolution

by Sylvia Kierkegaard

E-commerce is the biggest virtual medium in history. As more and more people are gaining access to computers and Internet connection, many businesses are tapping the vast opportunities that selling online offers. The continuing expansion of e-commerce means greater cross border consumption. A dominant characteristic of the online market is the low entry barriers for new competitors because websites are inexpensive to produce and maintain. Traditional commerce allows buyers to check physically whether the products are suited to their purposes. This lack of immediate interaction is offset by delivery of an array of information in the Internet to assist consumers in their buying decision. The proliferation of information offers opportunities to online buyers for a wide variety of products to choose from at lower cost. However, e-commerce transaction is not fraught without risks and quandary. In a transaction gone awry, buyers have to grapple with a quagmire of issues relating to misleading advertising, defective products, delayed delivery, deception and even fraud!

The electronic marketplace is experiencing a rapid growth of e-commerce usage among consumers and non-business sectors. [1] With the burgeoning e-commerce comes also an aggrandisement of cross-border disputes, especially in the Business–to-Consumer sector (B2C). Consumer disputes are usually characterised by the fact that the goods and services have a low economic value compared to the cost of seeking a settlement. In a B2C transaction, where the value of the disputed product is often low, court litigation for resolving problems may be unsatisfactory due to the cost and delays involved, especially when the dispute is cross-border. The high cost and slow procedure involved in court litigation would discourage online transactions and hinder elec-tronic confidence. Consumers may be reluctant to seek judicial action. Speed in dealing with rogue traders is critical in maintaining confidence. One way to address consumer and business concern is to offer an effective program for consumers and businessmen to resolve their conflict through online alternative/alternate dispute resolution (ADR) mechanisms that might provide timely and low-cost dispute settlement for

---

1) In 1998, the B2B market accounted for a total of 54% e-market revenues measured as retail value at POS. By 2005, the B2C shares of e-commerce will rise to 60% with B2B dropping to 50%. At http://www.supplychaintoday.com.

consumers in cross border disputes. This article will discuss the current developments in cyberspace out-of-court dispute resolution with emphasis on the European Commission's implementation of its ADR schemes. ADR conventions will be analysed to determine whether they can be applicable to online dispute settlements.

Alternative Dispute Resolution

Dispute resolution is the process of resolving disputes between parties and includes litigation, arbitration, mediation, conciliation and other types of negotiation, such as credit card chargeback, escrow arrangements, complaint bulletin boards, and complaint aggregation services. Dispute Resolution is not a new development. Since the middle of the 18th century, there have been formal mechanisms for resolving transborder commercial disagreements; although some scholars claim that its origin can be traced even much earlier, such as its use by warring Greek city states. In Ancient Greece, under Solon, disputes were referred to magistrates and could be appealed to both the *Areopagus*[2] (an assembly of ex-magistrates) and the Assembly. Actually arbitration was one of the earliest forms of dispute resolution practiced by the jurisconsults of the Roman Empire and commercial disputes were referred to the *Praetor Peregrinus.*[3] In the French territory of North-eastern North America, [4] Catholic priests and civil law notaries were used by the local populus as dispute resolution resources.In the US, the Federal government has encouraged commercial arbitration since as early as 1887, when it passed the Interstate Commerce Act.

The term dispute resolution is more commonly used to refer to alternative dispute resolution (ADR), which is an extra-judicial process such as mediation and arbitration. The processes were initially termed " alternative" in the 20th century because they were extra- legal supplements. Mediation and Arbitration are traditional methods of dispute resolution used to settle many types of disputes between individuals, businesses and countries. The parties may agree to their utilization after a controversy has arisen or may require it for future conflicts by including mandatory provisions in a contract highlighted in the terms and conditions agreed to by consumers buying a product or service. In mediation, parties to a dispute reach a voluntary settlement through the assistance of a neutral third party who meets with the

2) Boardman, Griffin and Murray (eds) *Oxford History of the Classical World* (Oxford University Press, Oxford, 1993,pp.31-32.

3) Ibid.

4) The territory included Saint Lawrence River, Mississippi River valleys and Acadia.

disputants, both as a group and on an individual basis, and then makes non-binding suggestions as to how to resolve their controversy. Mediation proceedings are often confidential. The mediator's role is advisory. The mediator may offer suggestions, but resolution of the dispute rests with the parties themselves. If the parties cannot resolve their dispute by mediation, they will often submit it for arbitration, which is a legally binding ruling by a neutral arbitrator chosen either by the parties to the dispute or by an arbitration agency. In commercial matters, since arbitration is based on contract law, the agreement between the parties to submit their dispute to arbitration is legally binding. The arbitrators may be lawyers or experts in a particular field. In arbitration, the parties have control over their agreement and have a wider freedom to choose in which way they want their disputes to be resolved. Arbitration is often used to settle labour disputes.

International Arbitration Conventions and the Model Law

The first major effort to provide an international mechanism to enforce cross-border arbitration awards was the Geneva Convention on the Execution of Foreign Arbitral Awards in 1927. This was invalidated by the New York Convention of 1958 on the Recognition and Enforcement of Foreign Arbitral Awards which has now been ratified by 131 countries. There are 5 other major international conventions on arbitration: the UNCITRAL Model Law on International Commercial Arbitration of 1985, the 1961(Geneva) European Convention on International Convention, the 1965 Washington Convention on the Settlement of Investment Disputes between States and Nationals of Other States, the 1972 Moscow Convention on the Settlement by Arbitration of Civil Law Disputes Resulting from Relations of Economic and Scientific-Technical Cooperation, and the 1975 Inter-American Convention on International Commercial Arbitration. This article will not deal with the last three conventions as they do not cover the constellation of transactions that are formed electronically n the European Union. (EU)

New York Convention of 1958.

The New York Convention of 1958 on the Recognition and Enforcement of Foreign Arbitral Awards [5] is the primary convention for enforcing international arbitration awards. The New York Convention requires member states to recognise and enforce arbitration awards given in other contracting states. The essence of the Convention is that where contracting parties have

---

5) http://www.uncitral.org/english/texts/arbitration/NY-conv.htm.

agreed to decide issues without recourse to law, they will have the opportunity to do so and each contracting state shall recognise the parties' agreement in writing, which shall include an arbitral clause in a contract or an arbitration agreement, signed by the parties or contained in an exchange of letters or telegrams. (Art II) As specified by the Convention, the arbitration agreement is governed by the law chosen by the parties, or in the absence of choice of law, by the law of the country where the award was rendered. (Art. V (1) (a). Arbitral awards include awards made by arbitrators appointed for each case and those made by permanent arbitral bodies to which the parties have submitted. (Art.1) Each Contracting State shall recognize arbitral awards as binding and enforce them in accordance with the rules of procedure of the territory where the award is relied upon and are prohibited from imposing substantially more onerous conditions or higher fees or charges on the recognition or enforcement of arbitral awards than domestic arbitral awards. (Art.III) The party applying for recognition and enforcement of foreign arbitral awards must provide the enforcing state with 1) a duly authenticated original award or a duly certified copy thereof 2) The original agreement or a duly certified copy thereof 3) a duly certified translation of the award or agreement if it is not written in the official language of the Forum state or the country in which the award is relied upon. (Art.IV) Recognition and enforcement of the awards *may be refused* by the Forum State at the request of the party against whom it is invoked provided that the party furnishes proof of the conditions required under Art.V or where the recognition or enforcement of the award is contrary to the public policy of that country. (Art. V (2)) This gives some discretion to the authority which must decide the enforcement. If an application for the setting aside or suspension of the award has been made to a competent authority referred to in Art. V (1) (e),[6] the authority before which the award is sought to be relied upon may, if it considers it proper, adjourn the decision on the enforcement of the award and may also, on the application of the party claiming enforcement of the award, order the other party to give suitable security.(Art.VI)

Although the Convention is the most widely-used mechanism in enforcing arbitration awards, it does not establish the effect that an annulment of the award will have extraterritorially. The public policy exception of Article V (2) has a drawback. It is too general in scope and fails to specify the conditions that may be deemed "public policy." There is a danger that rogue states could refuse recognition and enforcement of awards citing public policy concerns. The Convention's notion of public policy should be interpreted in the narrow sense that "enforcement may be denied only when it would violate

6) Article V 1 *(e):* " The award has not yet become binding, on the parties, or has been set aside or suspended by a competent authority of the country in which, or under the law of which, that award was made".

the state's most basic notions of morality and justice"[7] and" not every infringement of the mandatory provisions of the law of the forum constitutes a violation of public policy."[8]

European Convention on International Commercial Arbitration

The (Geneva) European Convention on International Commercial Arbitration of 1961 was designed to promote the development of European trade by, as far as possible, removing certain difficulties that may impede the organization and operation of international commercial arbitration in relations between physical or legal persons of different European countries. The Convention was ratified in 1961 and entered into force in 1964. It has been ratified by 26 countries.[9] The Convention applies to arbitration agreements concluded for the purpose of settling disputes arising from international trade, but limits its scope to parties "having their habitual place of residence or their place of establishment in the different contracting states." (Art.1.1) Under the European Convention, the term "arbitration agreement" shall mean either an arbitral clause in a contract or an arbitration agreement being signed by the parties, or contained in an exchange of letters, telegrams, or in a communication by teleprinter. (Art.I (2)) Arbitration agreement may deviate from the requirement of a written form in relations between states whose laws do not require that an arbitration agreement be in writing. (Art. I (2)) This provision seems to admit that arbitration agreement can be made electronically provided that evidence of such an agreement can be provided. As regards the appointment of arbitrators, the parties to the agreement are free to designate foreign nationals as arbitrators. (Art.III)They are also free to submit their disputes to a permanent arbitral institution or to an ad *hoc* arbitral procedure. The parties have also the freedom to appoint arbitrators or to establish means for their appointment in the event of an actual dispute, to determine the place of arbitration and to lay down the procedure to be followed by the arbitrators. (Art. IV) The arbitral tribunal has power to rule on its own competence. (Art.V) Another important provision is Art. VII, which authorises the arbitrator to apply the conflict-of-law rules which he deems applicable. He is not bound to apply the choice of law rules of the forum country. Whereas the New York Convention does not obligate the arbitrator to refer to statement of reasons for awards, the European

---

7) Decision of the US Court of Appeals (2nd Cir) of 23 Dec.1972 in *Parsons and Whitmore Overseas Co. Inc. v. RATKA*, cited in Yearbook, vol.1 (1976), p.205.

8) Decision of the Oberlandesgericht of Hamburg of 3 April. 1975 as cited in Yearbook, vol. 2 (1977), p.241.

9) The European Convention is available at: http://www.asser.nl/ica/eur.htm.

Convention requires that the reasons be stated. (Art. VIII) The European Convention explains the procedures available for contesting jurisdiction of the arbitral tribunal and states the procedures available for setting aside an award in Articles V and VI. The courts may also refuse recognition of the arbitration agreement if under the law of their country the dispute is not capable of settlement by arbitration. The Convention also provides for conditions in setting aside the award, (Art.IX) such as incapacity, absence of proper notice, composition of the arbitral authority, the procedure was not in accordance with the agreement of the parties or the provisions of Art. IV, and the award deals with a difference not contemplated by or not falling within the terms of the submission to arbitration, or it contains decisions on matters beyond the scope of the submission to arbitration.

UNCITRAL Model Law on International Commercial Arbitration

The UNCITRAL Model Law [10] has served as a guide for most of the modern arbitration laws in the world. The Model Law is based on the 1958 New York Convention with additional provisions favouring arbitration. It has been enacted into law by a large number of jurisdictions from both developed and developing countries. The model law is limited in scope to international commercial arbitration and takes a wide approach in defining both "international" and "commercial." (Art.1) The most important criterion in defining "international" is stated in Art. 3 (1) (a)," the parties to an arbitration agreement have, at the time of the conclusion of that agreement, their places of business in different States." The term commercial is given a wider interpretation "so *as to cover matters arising from all relationships of a commercial nature, whether contractual or not.* "

Article 3 deals with receipt of written communication and provides that any written communication is deemed to have been received if it is delivered to the addressee personally or if it is delivered at his place of business, habitual residence or mailing address; if none of these can be found after making a reasonable inquiry, a written communication is deemed to have been received if it is sent to the addressee's last-known place of business, habitual residence or mailing address by registered letter or any other means which provides a record of the attempt to deliver it. The communication is deemed to have been received on the day it is so delivered.

The essential feature of the Model Law recognises party autonomy and gives full effect to an agreement of the parties in respect of the composition or the arbitral tribunal and the rules of the procedure (Art.19) However, the freedom of the parties is limited .Otherwise, the party with a weaker

---

10) http://www.jus.uio.no/lm/un.arbitration.model.law.1985/toc.html.

bargaining power might have to accede to the dominant party. The arbitrary tribunal is bound the principle of fairness as provided for in Article 18," *The parties shall be treated with equality and each party shall be given a full opportunity of presenting his case.* "

The Model Law requires that the agreement to arbitrate should be evidenced in writing. "Art. 7(2) states, "An agreement is in writing if it is contained in a document signed by the parties or in an exchange of letters, telex, telegrams or other means of telecommunication which provide a record of the agreement, or in an exchange of statements of claim and defence in which the existence of an agreement is alleged by one party and not denied by another. The reference in a contract to a document containing an arbitration clause constitutes an arbitration agreement provided that the contract is in writing and the reference is such as to make that clause part of the contract." The background note to the Model Law explains the mandatory requirement for the agreement to be in writing: "While oral arbitration agreements are found in practice and are recognized by some national laws, article 7(2) follows the 1958 New York Convention in requiring written form. It widens and clarifies the definition of written form of article II(2) of that Convention by adding "telex or other means of telecommunication which provide a record of the agreement", by covering the submission-type situation of "an exchange of statements of claim and defence in which the existence of an agreement is alleged by one party and not denied by another", and by providing that "the reference in a contract to a document" (e.g. general conditions) "containing an arbitration clause constitutes an arbitration agreement provided that the contract is in writing and the reference is such as to make that clause part of the contract".[11]

Under Art. 8(2), arbitral proceedings may continue while the while the issue of jurisdiction is pending before the court. Chapters IV to VIII deal with choice of arbitration rules, determination of place of arbitra-tion, language of the proceedings, hearings including the taking of evidence, and the recognition and enforcement of awards.

Applicability of international conventions to e-commerce disputes

The New York Convention, UNCITRAL Model Law and European Convention are intended to facilitate and promote international arbitration. However, they focus on traditional means of settling disputes where the agreements and awards must be in written form and some stages of the proceedings require the physical presence of the parties or their duly constituted counsels. The latter would require parties in an on-line dispute to

11) Background to the Model Law, par.19 at http://www.uncitral.org/en-index.htm.

travel to an arbitral tribunal in another country. At the time the Conventions were enacted, the possibility of electronic communication was not envisaged by the participating countries. The requirement of agreements to be in writing could pose a problem because not all countries accept the validity of electronic contracts and electronic signatures. There are also uncertainties connected with electronic signatures that are not authenticated by means of qualified certificates issued by a certification service provider. Contents and form of documents can easily be altered in electronic signatures unless they meet the criteria of integrity, authenticity, confidentiality, and nonrepudiability. The New York Convention requires the agreement to be in writing," contained in exchanges of letters or telegrams "and thus excludes the possibility of similar exchange of information through electronic mails. According to Article IV of the New York Convention, the party applying for recognition and enforcement of foreign arbitral awards must provide the enforcing state with a 1) duly authenticated original award or a duly certified copy thereof 2) The original agreement or a duly certified copy thereof. Arbitral awards in electronic commerce could pose difficulty in enforcement unless the arbitrator has issued a hard copy of the awards in order to comply with the form requirement. In contrast, the Model Law may be construed to encompass agreements resulting from exchange of electronic mails, provided there is a record of the agreement. The European Convention contains similar provisions and allows that in relations between states, any arbitration agreement can be concluded in the form authorized by these laws. In the European Union, electronic contracts and signatures are not denied legal effectiveness. The Model Law provides that any written communication is deemed to have been received on the day it is to be delivered provided there is a record of the attempt to deliver it. [12] This would create problems in e-mail exchanges because the date and time can easily be altered. The Conventions are intended to cover commercial matters, but no distinction is made between B2B and B2C transactions. The absence of separate provisions governing B2B and B2C transaction would diminish its applicability in the internal market. In the European Union, there are specific legislations enacted to protect the consumers. In this context, ADR clauses in consumer contracts could be a breach of Directive 93/13 /EEC on Unfair Contract Terms because in the list of clauses which can be declared unfair are clauses that exclude and hinder the consumer's right to take legal action or exercise any other legal remedy. Existing rules for resolving cross-border disputes are characterised by ambiguities and gaps. They have not been modified to take account of trade in the digital world. The lack of harmony of legal rules for resolution of disputes in transborder e-commerce transaction

12) The time and date of receipt under the Model Law would conflict with Under Article 11 of the E-Commerce Directive, wherein the order and acknowledgement of receipt are deemed to be received when the parties to whom they are addressed are able to access them and not on the date it was delivered.

could be supplemented by the alternative mechanism for extra dispute resolution. With the increase in cross-border transactions, ADR services must be adapted to the realm of cyberspace.

Online Dispute Resolution

The cyberspace environment is characterised by its borderless dimension of interconnections between a vast numbers of computers. Resolving disputes arising from the Internet demands tools which take into primary account the cyberspace characteristics. Courts or traditional out-of-court dispute resolution mechanisms cannot reasonably resolve such conflicts. It makes sense that consumers who buy online and enterprises that trade online should settle their disputes also online. Traditional ADR systems use face-to-face interactions. Due to its impracticability in online transactions, new models for alternative dispute resolution have emerged which use the advantage of on-line technology and are more efficient, more cost effective and more flexible than traditional approaches.

Online Dispute Resolution (ODR) is a resolution process, where parties communicate by electronic means and try to mediate their dispute online or by submitting it to an online arbitral tribunal or cyber court. The parties can communicate by means of emails, chat-rooms, videoconferences and other electronic means. It has the value of flexibility, timeliness and low cost (relative to many court proceedings).Currently, there are no international conventions or model law that specifically deals with online dispute resolution and the existing ODRs are based on the dispute resolution legal frameworks that have already been developed. *ODR Providers* lists 51 companies providing on-line dispute resolution. The most well-known provider in the list is SquareTrade due to its association with eBay. While traditional ADR methods (Complaints Assistance, mediation and arbitration) are still applied where it is more appropriate using network resources, new hybrid systems are emerging characterised by novelty, varying experimentation and little uniformity in approach and methods such as mock juries, automated negotiation, and facilitated negotiation. [13] The following is a brief overview of the major forms of ODR and its current application.

1. Mock Juries is much like a traditional mock jury except that the jurors (or eJurors) participate via the Internet. It was initially conceived as an interface between lawyers who want their cases evaluated by a mock jury. *Wirthlin*

[13] As organisations increasingly offer ODR, more representative models of successful ODR mechanism may arise.

Worlwide [14] provides a PulseLine wherein the participating lawyer can test the persuasive power of his arguments second by second. Graphic feedback shows how jurors will react to his messages, identifying the strengths and weaknesses of the arguments. While mock juries are used to assist lawyers polish their cases for trial, they are also very useful in making settlement decisions. The convenience of online participation allows for a larger panel on each case. Thus the neutral third party is replaced by a number of volunteers (Internet users) acting as if they were an online jury in a civil trial. Each attorney agrees in advance to either a binding or non-binding result. A non-binding result is usually followed by a mediation or settlement conference.

iCourthouse [15] offers a streamlined version of the court system in the real world. Courthouse provides users with access to online adjudication and dispute evaluation and resolution. Summaries of pending cases are listed. An iCourthouse member can see all the evidence and arguments filed in the cases, pick cases to serve on as a juror, ask the parties questions, and give a verdict. Results are enforceable by agreement between the parties.

2. Complaints Assistance provides the parties (mainly for consumers) with tools allowing for effective communication such as forwarding of complaints to respondents and legal advice. The concept of an Internet Ombudsman is now a reality. The Internet Ombudsman[16] is an Austrian-based ODR provider. It was assisted by the EU Commission as a pilot project and was accorded in 2000 the distinguished Austrian State Prize for Public Relations award by the Federal Ministry of the Economy and Labour. The Internet Ombudsman is an adviser on questions concerning e-commerce, shopping on the Internet and has provided assistance to over 600 Internet cases. It also provides a watch list of e-commerce bidders who regularly contravene legal stipulations. It also provides mediation and online arbitration services. Decisions are guided by Austrian consumer law. Mediators and arbitrators are experts in the field of consumer, e-commerce and International trade law. The service is free and provided in both the English and German language. Because of the program's success, Sweden has launched the Swedish Internet Ombudsman, which has a similar concept and function with the Austrian-based complaint assistance. It is a free service for all users and financed by the Government Trade Department, the KK-foundation and the Royal Court.[17]

---

14) http://www.wirthlin.com/pdf/4.12.1_wwlegal.pdf.

15) http://www.i-courthouse.com/main.taf?&redir=0.

16) http://www.ombudsmann.at/tips/index_e.html.

17) Australia has also an Internet Ombudsman.

3. Negotiation is a process usually facilitated by third parties based on the consent of both parties and without binding powers. There are two types of negotiation process in the online world: automated and assisted negotiations.

Automated Negotiation is a form of computer-assisted negotiation in which no third party (other than computer software) is needed. Parties submit to a computer a settlement proposal in the form of a monetary figure. The computer compares them and settles the case for the arithmetic mean of the two figures. It is often based on a system of blind bidding, through which the parties enter successive bids in an attempt to reach agreement, but without knowing what the other party has offered. The process concludes when the bids become sufficiently close to one another and the computer programme can propose a solution.[18] For example the software developed by a company called *SplitTheDifference* makes proposals in behalf of insurers, relying on Algorithms to gauge what discounts the clients might accept in exchange for faster payment. The software is effective in payments that are too small to be handled economically by conventional methods. This software has been used in 20,000 negotiations as of September 12, 2003.[19] *Fujitsu* has also worked for two years on a software program that can run through millions of potential negotiation scenarios in seconds. Instead of just the prices, computers can weigh the relative merits of variables including quantity, delivery time and technical specifications. This would allow consumers to negotiate with the computer by entering preferences in the on-line form, or by allowing computer-to-computer negotiation.[20] The use of the software is based on the theory that "stalemate is unlikely even in the computer face-off because the automated negotiator's power to search for potential solutions is much greater than human minds."[21]

There are currently over 20 providers of automated negotiation. The model is ideal in situations were the issue concerns only monetary settlement and has been applied successfully in insurance disputes. Most uses of automated negotiations have so far been simple: settling insurance claims, selling excess telecommunications capacity etc. Automated negotiation is extremely limited. Most managers are wary about ceding decision-making to a machine. In addition, the bulk of the data is still on paper or is tacit. *WecanSettle.com*, a UK-based company, provides automated negotiation. It

---

18) http://www.olis.oecd.org/.

19) Belson, Ken, Letting the Computers do the Haggling, International Herald Tribune, Sept. 12,2003.

20) Contracts concluded between computers would raise legal issues concerning the validity of the contract such as the legal capacity of the computers to contract and intention.

21) Ibid.

charges only when a settlement has been reached and the fee is based on the settlement. The *WeCanSettle* system enables two negotiating parties to make offers which are called" bids" being the amount at which they are prepared to settle a legal dispute or agree a figure in any other matter.[22] Bids can be made by either party at any time. Whenever a bid is made, the WeCanSettle system compares it with the last bid made by the other side and if the amounts are 20% or less apart, the case is automatically settled at the mid point between the two figures.[23] A settlement reached by the system is binding on both sides. If no settlement is achieved when a bid is made, bidding can continue. If the parties never get close enough to achieve a settlement, neither will ever know what the other party bid.

Assisted/Facilitated Negotiation primarily provides technical assistance (secure site to communicate) and the communication tools for facilitating negotiation. This method of ODR does not use any neutral party to act as mediator nor a computer program to propose a solution. A typical example of assisted negotiation is provided by *SquareTrade* [24], which was founded in 1999 and claims to have resolved disputes in areas ranging from online auctions to traditional home purchases. Square Trade provides an automated consumer-operated ODR service, and backup online mediation services - in affiliation with the hugely successful eBay online marketplace for buyers and sellers throughout the world.[25] During the direct negotiation process, only the two parties are involved. After the parties have agreed to participate in ODR, they discuss their issues through a password-protected Case Page on the SquareTrade website. During the case filing, case response, and direct negotiation stages, there is neither a mediator involved in the case, nor *SquareTrade* personnel who are involved in the parties' discussions, the review of the complaint or in the response information.

4 **Mediation** is the process of dispute resolution based on a neutral third party, who acts as the mediator. The mediator does not have the power to adjudicate. He merely assists the parties to communicate and negotiate

---

22) https://www.wecansettle.com/.

23) The only exception is in the unlikely situation where a claimant is asking for less than defendant offers, when the case settles at the midpoint between the amounts the claimant requests and the amount the defendant offers. When a bid is made the paying party is shown the maximum amount required to be paid based on the bid, and the receiving party is shown the minimum amount.

24) http://www.squaretrade.com.

25) http://www.theclaimroom.com/stop_press/2002feb03.html.

effectively so resolve their conflict. The parties make their own decisions. Mediation is often used in conjunction with Conciliation, which involves a third party or conciliator who assists the parties by helping them establish a positive relationship through communication, clarification of misconceptions and building trust. Online mediation can successfully be deployed in online auction disputes.

In the UK, the first online dispute resolution service is *e-mediator*,[26] which is a project of *Consensus*. The cost is half of the amount charged in face-to-face mediation .*Consensus* contacts the other party to determine whether they are interested in settling the dispute through the *e-mediator*. Each party pays the Mediator's fee,[27] the cost of which is half of the amount charged in face-to-face meditation. The fee structure allows for 6 hours of the mediator's time spent online. E-mail messages are exchanged between the mediator and the party until the mediation is concluded. It uses encrypted e-mail to protect the privacy and ensure confidentiality. Each party checks and responds to his e-mail at least as often as has been agreed in advance. The final deadline for the conclusion of the mediation may be agreed at the outset. This is to ensure that all parties are properly dealing with the process and not causing delay on purpose. The deadline may be extended if everyone agrees. This does not affect the number of hours spent by the mediator, which is a separate issue. The final terms of agreement are binding once they have been set out in electronic writing and agreed by the parties using their digital signatures. If one or more parties choose not to use a digital ID, then the final agreement will be binding when it has been signed by hand by all parties.

ECODIR

The ECODIR (European Consumer Dispute Resolution)[28] is an online dispute regulation supported by the European Commission. It supplements the EEJ Net, which is the European clearing house for national ADR providers. **ECODIR** uses a structured 3-step process of negotiation, mediation and recommendation - all in a private (confidential) and secure online environment. The service is free to both consumers and businesses. The negotiation and mediation phrase, respectively, have a fixed time limit. The ECODIR is restricted to disputes that arose out of an online transaction involving at least one consumer. Disputes related to illicit content are excluded

---

26) http://www.consensusmediation.co.uk/e-mediator.html.

27) $£200 + VAT per party.

28) http://www.ecodir.org/.

from its scope as are issues related to corporal damages, family, taxation and intellectual property. (Art.2 of the ECODIR Resolution Rules).

The process starts with the Negotiation process. (Art. 3) The First party completes the Description and Proposal form available on ECODIR's website, stating his/her version of the facts and one or more proposed solutions to resolve the dispute. If the Second party accepts any of the solutions proposed by the First party, the case is terminated. However, if none of the solutions proposed initially by the Second Party are accepted by the First Party, one of the parties can ask for the appointment of a Mediator or both parties can continue to negotiate. From the creation of the First Party's user account, the parties have eighteen (18) calendar days to negotiate and exchange as many proposals and as much information as they wish. After the eighteen (18) day period, if the parties have not reached a Settlement, a message will be sent to give them the opportunity either to start the Mediation Phase or to terminate the process. If the parties have agreed to participate in the mediation process, then a neutral mediator is appointed to assist the parties. The Mediator's field of expertise, geographic location and language proficiency are taken into consideration in their appointment. (Art.5) The Mediator is prohibited from acting as a representative or counsel of a party in any arbitral or judicial proceedings in respect of a dispute that is the subject of the process. The mediator submits proposed solutions. The dispute is resolved when the parties select one common solution. If the parties did not select a common solution among the solutions proposed by the Mediator within fifteen (15) days from the beginning of the Mediation Phase, the Recommendation Phase is initiated. If the parties do not approve the final recommendation of the Mediator within seven (7) days following the Recommendation, the case is terminated. If both parties accept the final recommendation of the Mediator, the recommendation becomes a Settlement. The Rule also provides that the language of resolution of the dispute is the common language of the parties. By default, the language of resolution of the dispute will be the language of the transaction that gave rise to the dispute. In the case of a valid prior agreement, the Commission Recommendation 98/257/EC on the principles applicable to the bodies responsible for out-of-court settlement of consumer disputes must be applied. A significant element in the ECODIR process is that it is entirely consensual: either party is free to walk away from the process at any stage, or the mediator's recommendation will not be binding on any party unless they have specifically agreed to be bound by it in a separate agreement. The settlement is not legally binding to the consumers.(Art.14) The consumer protection is in accordance with the following EU legislations:

- Under Article 6(1) of the European Convention on Human Rights , a consumer must not be deprived of his legal right of access to the courts.

- The Directive 93/13/EEC of 5 April 1993 on Unfair Terms in Consumer Contracts (O.J. L095, 21/04/1993) considers clauses that exclude and hinder the consumer's right to take legal action or exercise any other legal remedy as an unfair term and Article 17 (1) of the Brussels I Regulation, states that the contractual exclusion of the courts in consumer disputes is void if it takes place before the dispute arises.
- The Council Resolution of 25 May 2000 on a Community-wide network of national bodies for the extra-judicial settlement of consumer disputes (O. J. C 155, 06/06/2000) provides *inter alia*, that any out-of-court resolution of consumer disputes should be based on voluntary participation and should not prejudice any other means for administrative or judicial redress.

Drawbacks of Mediation

Mediation is useful in consumer disputes and allows parties to determine how to solve their conflict. Its drawback lies in its non-binding characteristic and its success hinges on the party's willingness to maintain or establish goodwill with customers. In transactions involving goods of small value, mediation might be too costly for the customer to initiate mediation proceedings. Mediation is also fairly expensive and could take days. This mechanism is more suitable for disputes involving large claims and is not suitable in all consumer disputes. Where the conflict concerns violation of the law, the more appropriate tools would be arbitration where the aggrieved party does not need to conciliate.

5. Arbitration involves a neutral third party, who issues a decision based on the evidence presented by both parties. A semi-legal procedure is adopted. In general, online binding arbitration is based on the New York arbitration rules. However, whether its decision is legally binding or not is still uncertain because the use of electronic signatures does not meet the form requirement of authenticated original or duly certified copy for the enforcement of awards under the NY Convention.

In the context of the online world, two forms of arbitration mechanism have emerged: a binding arbitration and a non-binding arbitration process. The two forms of arbitration mechanism have different scope of application and history, but cover situations that normally arise from cross-border transactions.

Binding Arbitration

The first experiment in online dispute arbitration was conducted in 1996 in America. The case was *Tierney v Email America.*[29] The institution was the *Virtual Magistrate,*[30] which was a joint project of the Cyberspace Law Institute, the American Arbitration Association (AAA), and the National Centre for Automated Information Research. It is a service for resolution of disputes among users of online systems, system operators and persons harmed by the posting of wrongful online messages.

Tierney v Email America involved a disputed message posted on American Online by Email America which offered to sell lists of as many as twenty million email addresses. James Tierney complained against Email alleging that its message was an invasion of privacy, against sound public policy, and deceptive. America Online voluntarily participated in the case. The AOL submission pointed out that its terms of service agreement permit the removal of messages that are harmful or offensive or otherwise in violation of AOL rules. The decision by Virtual Magistrate recommended that the message offering the sale of email addresses be removed by AOL because it violated the AOL service agreement as well as Internet customs. The decision was rendered after four days. In 1996, no statutory safe harbours existed. Today, the Digital Millennium Copyright Act provides a safe harbour for service providers who implement detail procedures for removing material.

In Europe, the first independent online consumer arbitration scheme was first developed by the Chartered Institute of Arbitrators (UK) with Ford Europe and this initiative set the momentum for other organisations to follow. The model was used to develop a scheme with the UK Consumer's Associations Which Web Trader Trustmark Scheme and the European Extra-Judicial Network. The *British Travel Agents* also used the model for developing its online service. A trained and independent arbitrator, who is an expert in the online retailing arena, is appointed by the Chartered Institute. Parties submit documents online and the whole process, which is conducted online, takes a maximum of 3 months. If the complaint is found in favour of the consumer, the cost will be refunded. In this type of situation where the business is located in the UK, the decision would pose minimal problems in enforceability. The main concern, however, would be the enforceability of the award when the parties are spread out in different jurisdictions.

Word&Bond,[31] a UK-based organisation offers i-arbitration. The interactive arbitration system is a consensual legal process. This means that both parties must agree to use it and abide by the *Word&Bond* i-arbitration

29) VM Docket No. 96-0001, 08 May 1996.

30) //www.vmag.org/.

31) www.wordandbond.com/.

rules. It has a trustmark scheme. All traders who display the *Word&Bond* Standard agree to abide by the rules of the *Word&Bond* interactive arbitration system. Complainants will be asked to declare that they are entitled to file the *i-claim* in accordance with the law in the country in which they reside and that they agree to pay the *i-file fee.* The i-file fee is calculated by the system and for claims under £500 is £40, which is lower than the fee required to commence a claim in the courts. If the trader does not display a *Word&Bond* Standard, the complainant may also file an *i-claim* and *Word&Bond* will contact that trader on his behalf. In the unlikely event that *Word&Bond* is unable to process the *i-claim*, it will refund the *i-file* fees less a £10 administration charge.

But what would happen if two competing ODR service providers handled the same dispute? The following case illustrates the pressure that a powerful party can exert to change the outcome of an unfavourable decision in an arbitration proceeding. A privacy-related complaint was filed by a customer against *eBay* with *TrustE* and *BBB Online*, two competing ODR providers, since *eBay* is a member of both *TrustE* and *BBB Online* privacy seal programs. *TrustE* rendered *e-Bay* a favourable decision in contrast with *BBB Online*. *eBay* threatened to withdraw from *BBB Online* unless the latter reverses its decision. *eBay* substituted a new favourable decision.[32] Consumers will lose confidence in arbitration programs if the ADR mechanism is perceived to be biased. The fairness and effectiveness of the arbitration program can only be guaranteed if the arbitrators are independent from the business, have no direct interest in the dispute and posses the skills and knowledge to render fair judgment.[33]

Legal obstacles in B2C Transaction

Online arbitration is a fast method in resolving disputes especially in cases where the decision is solely based on documentary evidences. The proceedings are simplified and there is less formalism in comparison to court proceedings. However, arbitration has its limitations. The arbitration context lacks the right to due process and extensive discovery needed to support one's claims. The fact-finding process in arbitration usually is not equivalent to judicial fact-finding. The record of the arbitration proceedings is not as complete. The usual rules of evidence do not apply and the rights and

---

32) R Gellman, 'Online privacy dispute resolution: BBBOnline' (2000), Privacy Law & Policy Reporter p. 145.

33) There has been proposals to make an accreditation scheme to ensure neutrality of Arbitrators.

procedures common to civil trials, such as discovery, compulsory process, cross-examination, and testimony under oath, are often severely limited or unavailable.[34] Furthermore, damage awards vary widely between trial and arbitration. Unlike courts and juries, which are more likely to adhere to the law, arbitrators are more likely to split the difference.[35] The mean damages awarded by arbitrators from 1993 to 1995 were $ 49,030 compared to $ 530,611 by district courts.[36] Part of the problem is that arbitrators rarely award punitive damages, even though they have the power to do so.[37]

There is no impediment to an arbitration agreement in a B2B transaction. Party autonomy is clearly effective in commercial transac-tions between businesses. Pre-dispute mandatory arbitration agreement is a legally binding agreement in B2B transactions where applicants waive their rights to bring future claims before a court, and instead, requires that those claims be submitted to an arbitrator. This is not the case in B2C transactions. In B2C transaction, the United States and the European Union offer two conflicting approaches to regulation. The US favours self-regulation, while the EU leans towards the use of regulatory mechanism to protect consumers.

A standard clause in a B2C transaction binding the consumer to submit the dispute to arbitration might be in breach of the Directive on Unfair Contract Terms and might not be enforceable in the European Union. In particular, Article 3 of the Directive states that a contractual term which has not been individually negotiated shall be regarded as unfair if it causes an insignificant imbalance in the parties' rights and obligations in the contract to the detriment of the consumer. A contractual term which" excludes or hinder the consumer's right to take legal action or exercise any other legal remedy, particularly by requiring the consumer to take disputes exclusively to arbitration not covered by legal provisions" may be considered unfair under the Directive. The Brussels Regulation puts stringent restrictions on the consumer's ability to waive his right to judicial proceedings in court. According to Article 17 of the Brussels Regulation, an agreement by a consumer to submit to an ADR could only be possible if it is entered into after the dispute has arisen. In contrast, a standard arbitration clause in a B2C

---

34) Alexander v. Gardner-Denver Co., 415 U.S. 36, 57-58 (1974).

35) *Armendariz v. Found. Health Psychcare Servs.*, Inc., 6 P.3d 669, 693 (Cal. 2000) (citing Robert Haig, Corporate Counsel's Guide: Legal Development Report on Cost-Effective Management of Corporate Litigation, 610 PLI/Lit.177, 186-87 (1999)).

36) These figures are based on the AAA employment arbitrations from 1993-95 and 1994 Federal District Court cases.

37) Christine M. Reilly , Achieving Knowing and Voluntary Consent in Pre-Dispute Mandatory Arbitration Agreements at the Contracting Stage of Employment California Law Review: 2002.

transaction is legally recognisable by US Courts, unless the terms are considered "unconscionable."

Resolving online disputes based merely on documentary evidence could pose a conundrum for arbitrators. Because the data transmitted for ODR are legal evidence, the arbitrator must evaluate the following: the data is in fact the data that it claims to be; the author of the messages during the conclusion of the contract and the ODR procedures can be identified; the contents have not been tampered; the program has been received by the consumer; the information stored on an ODR database is protected from unauthorised parties; and that notification to both parties cannot be repudiated.

Recognition and enforcement of awards are also hindered by the current e-mail protocols which are not able to produce receipts. Unless the parties used the advanced electronic signatures based on qualified certificates, it would be entail significant time and effort for arbitrators to determine the integrity and non-repudiability of data.[38] Resolving disputes through arbitration would take longer to be developed, unless technical obstacles are resolved and the solution is given legal recognition.

Non-Binding Arbitration

Non-binding arbitration can be an effective tool in resolving disputes. It could create incentives for the parties to self-enforce the decision. The Internet Corporation for Assigned Names and Numbers (ICANN)[39] is a non-profit organisation established solely for the purpose of managing the domain name systems. When the Internet began to evolve as the most important commercial medium, many companies and individuals saw their personal names or trademarks registered as domain names before they had a chance to register their trademarks as domain names because of the "first come, first served" registry policy. As a result, this has led to increasing conflict as legitimate trademark owners try to protect their rights. Faced with the growing conflict between two conflicting orders (trademark rights derived from national legal order and the Domain Name holders), ICANN established an administrative process for resolving domain name disputes, known as the ICANN Uniform Dispute Resolution Policy (UDRP) .

All registrars in the top level domains (TLD) like .biz, .com, .info, .name, .net, and .org top-level domains follow UDRP .Under the policy, most types of trademark-based domain-name disputes must be resolved by agreement, court action, or arbitration before a registrar will cancel, suspend, or transfer a

---

38) See http://www.hpovua.org/PUBLICATIONS/PROCEEDINGS/ 9_HPOVUAWS/Paper_4_2.pdf.

39) http://www.icann.org/udrp/.

domain name. Disputes alleged to arise from abusive registrations of domain names (cyber squatting) may be addressed by expedited administrative proceedings that the holder of trademark rights initiates by submitting a complaint with an approved dispute-resolution service provider.

All TLD registrars are required to submit to a mandatory online administrative proceeding in the event that a third party (a "complainant") asserts to the applicable Provider, in compliance with the Rules of Procedure, that "i) the registrars domain name is identical or confusingly similar to a trademark or service mark in which the complainant has rights; and (ii) that the registrar has no rights or legitimate interests in respect of the domain name; and (iii) the registrars domain name has been registered and is being used in bad faith."[40] Indications of bad faith include the following circumstances:[41] 1) The domain name has been acquired primarily for the purpose of selling, renting, or otherwise transferring the domain name registration to the complainant who is the owner of the trademark or service mark or to a competitor of that complainant, for valuable consideration in excess of your documented out-of-pocket costs directly related to the domain name; or 2) The domain name has been registered in order to prevent the owner of the trademark or service mark from reflecting the mark in a corresponding domain name, provided that the registrar has engaged in a pattern of such conduct; or 3) The domain name has been registered primarily for the purpose of disrupting the business of a competitor; or 4) The use of the domain name is intentionally intended attract, for commercial gain, Internet users to the web site or other on-line location, by creating a likelihood of confusion with the complainant's mark as to the source, sponsorship, affiliation, or endorsement of his web site or location or of a product or service on the registrar's web site or location. The remedies available to a complainant pursuant to any proceeding before an Administrative Panel is limited to requiring the cancellation of the registrar's domain name or the transfer of his domain name registration to the complainant The mandatory administrative procedure is characterised as non-binding arbitration because it does not prevent the TLD registrar nor the complainant from submitting the dispute to a court of competent jurisdiction for independent resolution before such mandatory administrative proceeding is commenced or after such proceeding is concluded. The UDRP Rules require that all decisions be published on the Internet. To date over 12474 cases on domain name conflicts have been disposed by decision.[42] Because parties can litigate in court while continuing the UDRP proceedings, the non-binding character of the ODR process creates

40) Uniform Domain Name Dispute Resolution Policy, Par.4.

41) Par.4 (b).

42) http://www.icann.org/udrp/proceedings-stat.htm .The figure is valid as of the 10th of September, 2003.

legal uncertainty. Nevertheless, the UDRP has offered a successful mechanism in resolving domain name disputes, enforcing the rights of legitimate trademark holders and returning domain names to the rightful holders while offering a fast service without a need for face to face contact or travel to have the dispute resolved.

6. Trustmark Schemes. The advertising Communities have drafted their own codes of Conduct and standards and then setting up a trustmark schemes which allow advertisers to place an icon or mark certifying that these advertisers adhere to be bound by the Codes of Practice and provisions regulating advertising in the Internet. The guidelines are normally based on the ICC rules concerning advertising. The self-regulatory schemes often include internal complaints. The majority of problems can be expected to be resolved at this pre-dispute. In cross border disputes, the complaint is forwarded to the regulatory body or authority of the country where the business is located.

European Union Initiatives

The ODRs are an integral part of the European Union policy to facilitate access to justice. The European Union has three Directives that touch on the aspects of online dispute resolution: Directive 2002/58/ EC 1997/66/EC concerning the processing of personal data, Directive 1999/93/EC on Electronic Signatures and the Directive 2000/31/ EC on certain legal aspects of information society services. Recital 8 of Directive 2002/58/EC states: "Legal, regulatory and technical provisions adopted by the Member States concerning the protection of personal data, privacy and the legitimate interest of legal persons, in the electronic communication sector, should be harmonised in order to avoid obstacles to the internal market for electronic communication in accordance with Article 14 of the Treaty. Harmonisation should be limited to requirements necessary to guarantee that the promotion and development of new electronic communications services and networks between Member States are not hindered. "The Directive reiterates the basic principle that Member States must, through national legislation, ensure the confidentiality of communications made over a public electronic communications network. They must in particular prohibit listening, tapping and storage of communications by persons other than users without the consent of the users concerned.

The Directive on Electronic Signatures contributes to the legal use and recognition of electronic signatures in the European Union by ensuring that electronic signatures can be used as evidence in legal proceedings in all Member States. (Art.5)

The Directive on E-Commerce encourages out of court dispute settlement. According to Art. 17:" 1.Member States shall ensure that, in the event of disagreement between an information society service provider and the recipient of the service, their legislation does not hamper the use of out-of-court schemes, available under national law, for dispute settlement, including appropriate electronic means. 2. Member States shall encourage bodies responsible for the out of court settlement of, in particular consumer disputes, to operate in a way which provides adequate procedure and guarantees for the parties concerned. 3.Member States shall encourage bodies responsible for out-of-court dispute settlement to inform the Commission of the significant decisions they take regarding information society services and to transmit any other information on the practices ,usages, or customs relating a to electronic commerce."

In 1998 the Commission adopted a "Communication on the out-of-settlement of consumer disputes" with the aim of encouraging and facilitating the settling of consumer conflicts at an earlier stage. It was recognised that consumer disputes are usually characterised by the fact that the goods and services have a low economic value compared to the cost of seeking a settlement. Many consumers do not even try to assert their rights due to the high cost of legal representation and the long delays before a case is judged. To improve consumer's access to justice, the Communication from the Commission of 30 March 1998 on the out of court settlement of consumer disputes advocated three approaches. The first is the simplification of legal procedures; next, the availability of a consumer claim form on the Internet in all European languages to assist the consumers in filing their claims clearly; and the introduction of out of court procedures through Recommendation 98/257/EC. The Recommendation aims to improve access to justice to individual consumers through simple, swift, effective and inexpensive redress channels. The Commission has recognised the need to deploy online systems, which can settle consumer disputes on the Internet swiftly and at low cost.

The scope of Recommendation 98/257 /EC is limited to the settlement of dispute through the active intervention of a third party, which proposes or imposes a solution (arbitration). The Recommen-dation establishes a number of minimum guarantees, applicable to online as well as off-line systems. The minimum guarantees take the form of seven principles with which the out of court bodies should comply : independence, transparency, respect of the adversarial principle, effectiveness, legality, liberty and representation These principle are intended to guarantee that cases will be treated with rigour, fairness and independence with the expected simpler and quicker settlement of their dispute.

Principle of independence. The person appointed must posses the abilities, experience and competence, particularly in the field of law, required to carry out his function. He must be granted a period of office of sufficient duration to ensure the independence of his action and shall not be liable to be relieved of his duties without just cause. During the three years prior to assuming his present function, he must not have worked for this professional association or for the enterprise concerned nominating or remunerating him.

Principle of transparency. These include a provision, in writing or any other suitable form, containing the following: a precise description of the types of dispute which may be referred to the body concerned; the rules governing the referral of the matter to the body; the possible cost of the procedure for the parties, including rules on the award of costs at the end of the procedure; the type of rules serving as the basis for the body's decisions; the decision-making arrangements within the body; and the legal force of the decision taken, whereby it shall be stated clearly whether it is binding on the professional or on both parties. Transparency also includes the publication of the annual report of the decisions taken.

Adversarial principle. The procedure to be followed allows all the parties concerned to present their viewpoint before the competent body and to hear the arguments and facts put forward by the other party, and any experts' statements.

The principle of effectiveness is ensured through measures guaranteeing the following: the consumer has access to the procedure without being obliged to use a legal representative; the procedure is free or of moderate costs; the periods between the referral of a matter and the decision is short; and the competent body is given an active role.

Principle of legality .The decision taken by the body may not result in the consumer being deprived of the protection afforded by the mandatory provisions of the law of the State in whose territory the body is established. All decisions are communicated to the parties concerned as soon as possible, in writing or any other suitable form, stating the grounds on which they are based.

Principle of liberty .The decision taken by the body concerned may be binding on the parties only if they were informed of its binding nature in advance and accepted this. The consumer's recourse to the out-of-court procedure may not be the result of a commitment prior to the materialisation of the dispute.

Principle of representation. The procedure does not deprive the parties of the right to be represented or assisted by a third party at all stages of the procedure.

While the 1998 Recommendation apply to the ADR bodies applying arbitration for settling disputes, the Commission Recommendation of April 4 2001 apply to mediation. The Recommendation sets out four principles that must be respected by third party bodies responsible for out-of-court consumer dispute resolution procedures, which attempt to resolve a dispute by bringing the parties together to convince them to find a solution by common consent.

1) Impartiality should be guaranteed by ensuring that those responsible for the procedure are appointed for a fixed term and have no perceived or actual conflict of interest with either party information about their impartiality and competence must be provided to both parties.

2) The principle of transparency is guaranteed by making available the following information: the contact details, functioning and availability of the procedure; how the procedure will operate, the types of disputes that can be dealt by it; the rules governing any preliminary requirements and other procedural rules, notably those concerning the operation of the procedure and the languages in which the procedure will be conducted; the cost to be borne by the parties; the timetable applicable to the procedure; any substantive rules that may be applicable; the role of the procedure in bringing about the resolution of a dispute; and the status of any agreed solution for resolving the dispute. Any agreed solution for resolving the dispute by the parties should be recorded on a durable medium and should clearly state the terms and the grounds on which it is based. The record should be made available to both parties and information on the performance of the procedure should be made publicly available.

3) The principle of effectiveness implies that: the procedure should easily be accessible and available to both parties, for instance by electronic means, irrespective of where the parties are situated; the procedure should be either free of charge to consumers or any necessary costs should be both proportionate to the amount in dispute and moderate; the parties should have access to the procedure without being obliged to use a legal representative; once a dispute has been submitted it should be dealt with in the shortest possible time; and that the body responsible for the procedure should periodically review its progress to ensure the parties' dispute is being dealt with expeditiously and appropriately.

4) The principle of fairness should be guaranteed by the following: the parties should be informed of their right to refuse to participate or to withdraw from the procedure at any time and access the legal system or other out-of-court redress mechanisms at any stage; both parties should be able to freely and easily submit any arguments, information or evidence relevant to their case on a confidential basis to the procedure unless agreement has been given

by the parties to pass such information to the other party; both parties should be encouraged to fully cooperate with the procedure, in particular by providing any information necessary for a fair resolution of the dispute; prior to the parties agreeing to a suggested solution for resolving the dispute, they should be allowed reasonable period of time to consider this solution; and the consumer should be informed in clear und understandable language, before agreeing to a suggested solution, that he has the freedom to agree or disagree to the suggested solution, a right to seek independent advice before making the decision, and that the use of the procedure does not preclude the option of referring his dispute to another out-of-court dispute resolution mechanism, in particular within the scope of Recommendation 98/257/EC, or of seeking legal redress through his own judicial system.

EEJ-Net

In order to further strengthen consumer's access to justice, the European Commission has established the Network for Out-of-Court Settlement of Consumer Disputes (EEJ-Net).[43] Each Member State designates a central contact point (clearing house) to act as a point of contact for consumers wishing to settle a dispute out of court in another Member State. The role of the network is to allow the consumer to approach the single contact point in his country to gather information concerning the possibilities of ADR mechanisms, to facilitate cross-border complaints by providing practical assistance such as translating complaint forms, facilitate the lodging of complaints using the appropriate standard ADR forms and follow up resolution of complaints and action taken involving ADR within the network. Taken together, these contact points make up an "extra-judicial network" intended to make it easier to settle cross-border consumer disputes.

FIN-NET

The EU is facilitating access to justice through the creation of an information system which is maintained and updated by a network of competent authorities. The European Commission has launched on 1 February 2001 an out-of-court complaints network for financial services to help businesses and consumers resolve disputes in the Internal Market fast and efficiently by avoiding, where possible, lengthy and expensive legal action. This network,

---

43) http://www.eejnet.org/.

called FIN-NET (Consumer Complaints Network for Financial Services) ,[44] has been designed particularly to facilitate the out-of-court resolution of consumer disputes when the service provider is established in an EU Member State other than that where the consumer lives. The network brings together more than 35 different national schemes that either cover financial services in particular (e.g. banking and insurance ombudsmen schemes) or handle consumer disputes in general (e.g. consumer complaint boards). Both online and off-line services are covered. The FIN-NET framework is designed to allow the complainant to contact his national ADR scheme even when the complaint is against a foreign financial firm. The FIN-NET in the home country will help the consumer identify the relevant complaint scheme and transfers it to the relevant scheme in the service provider's country. This will allow the complainant to file the complaint in the language of the contract, or the language the customer has normally used in dealing with the financial institution.

SOLVIT

The SOLVIT [45]scheme covers cross-border disputes with public administrations and is complementary to B2C problems covered by EEJ-NET and FIN-Net. It aims to help citizens and businesses in matters related to misapplication of Internal Market rules by public administrations in another Member State. It builds on an existing network of national Co-ordination Centres, to resolve such problems as efficiently as possible without the need for legal action. Other problems faced by citizens and businesses that SOLVIT could deal with include: voting rights, car registration, border controls, market access of goods and services, public procurement, taxation, establishment of a company, setting up as self-employed, etc. The system is free of charge. It operates through a network of SOLVIT Centres based in the national administration of each Member State. The local SOLVIT Centre enters the case in an online database system, which automatically forwards the case to the SOLVIT Centre where the problem has occurred (also called the Lead SOLVIT Centre). The Lead SOLVIT Centre confirms within one week whether or not it will take on the case. The target deadline for finding a solution to the problem is 10 weeks. The two SOLVIT Centres will liaise with each other during the period of investigation. Proposed solutions are non-binding on the applicant. If no solution is reached, more formal proceedings can still be initiated.

---

44) http://finnet.jrc.it/doc/en-FINNET-GUIDE.doc.
45) http://europa.eu.int/comm/internal_market/solvit/index_en.htm.

Legal Problems /Barriers

Given their speed, efficiency and degree of privacy, arbitration and mediation alternatives to traditional dispute resolution means have gained important ground in recent years. Nevertheless, the wide use of ODR faces many hurdles and should not be viewed as a panacea for consumers. This was the finding of *Consumers International*, which carried out in 2001, the most up-to-date research on ODR for B2C transactions. Thirty ODR service providers offering 30 different distinct ODR services were analysed using the following eight criteria: independence/ impartiality, affordability, transparency, effectiveness, availability for use by consumers, due process, legality and oversight. The criteria are based on the following description:

- Independence. ODR is neither credible nor effective unless it is conducted by individuals who are truly independent and impartial with respect to the disputing parties.
- Impartiality. All dispute resolution personnel should be free of any real or reasonably perceived bias, should have adequate training in the form of dispute resolution they practice, and should be required to adhere to a code of conduct which includes rules to avoid conflicts of interest.
- Transparency. Information on all aspects of its service must be readily available
- Availability. The ODR service should be available geographically for use by consumers and businessmen. It should also, optimally, cover the full spectrum of B2C disputes.
- Affordability. The service should, optimally, be free to the consumer. If there is a user fee charged to the consumer, such fee should be low relative to the amount in dispute, and should be refundable to the consumer in the event that the consumer prevails in whole or in part.
- Effectiveness. The ODR service, to be useful, should be well publicised (visible) such that interested consumers and businesses can become aware of it when the need for ODR arises. ODR systems should be made available to disputants in a timely fashion and should resolve disputes quickly. Where offered internationally, the ODR provider should address and seek appropriate solutions to the possibility of significant language or cultural differences between disputants. Different kinds of disputes call for different approaches to dispute resolution. Scaleability also requires that the procedural formality and complexity of the process be proportionate to the type of dispute and amount in dispute. The ODR provider

should take measures to ensure that any confidential communications in the context of ODR are appropriately secure from unauthorised access, and to authenticate the identity of the parties in the process of online communications.

- Due process. ODR providers should provide both parties with a reasonable opportunity to make their case, and to hear and respond to the opposing party's arguments.
- Legality. Participation in ODR should be a truly voluntary option for consumers.
- Oversight. Some kind of international oversight is, if not essential, at least highly desirable so as to ensure compliance of these criteria by both by the ODR provider and the trader.

Using the above criteria to analyse the ODR services, the result of the *Consumer International's* research contains grim news for consumers. [46] It reveals that the vast majority of ODR providers are private business ventures and are funded by users' fees. The most available ODR mechanisms are arbitration and mediation. The following summarises the result of the research:

- None of the services we reviewed satisfy fully the criteria for effective online dispute resolution between business and consumers in the global marketplace
- Few ODR services help consumers to deal with uncooperative merchants, and those few provide limited assistance.
- Most ODR services are, as a practical matter, available only to speakers of English.
- Businesses enjoy a wider range of ODR services than consumers
- Most of the ODR services available to consumers are disproportionately costly
- Few ODR service providers give adequate assurance of their impartiality
- Most ODR services offer inadequate information on their governing structure and ODR officials
- Most service providers give poor information on the results of their ODRs
- Most ODR services fail to provide adequate incentives for compliance with ODR results.

The report concluded that consumers at present cannot and should not trust that alternative dispute resolution systems available online can offer adequate redress.

46) http://www.consumersinternational.org/document_store/Doc35.pdf.

Conclusion

The global nature of e-commerce means that international approaches to the provision of dispute resolution facilities will be important. The unfamiliarity with the different regulatory frameworks for ADR in different countries deters consumer confidence. Given the special nature of e-commerce and legal issues that would arise with the volume of cross-border transactions, there is indeed a need for a globally accepted international standard and existing code of conducts to govern online out of court dispute settlement and ameliorate existing problematic situation in cyberspace.

The determination of the rules and laws to which the settlement could be achieved could be based on current globally accepted rules , codes or legal frameworks, in the form of a Convention and based on the principles of transparency, access, affordability, flexibility, impartiality, effectivity, due process and enforceability. Such a convention must address the issue of jurisdiction and the rules governing the recognition and effects of electronic signatures as a form requirement and in evidentiary rules.

If a new convention or amendments to the existing international conventions would entail a lengthy period before being ratified, supplementary or new rules could instead be added to the UNCITRAL Model Law as a guideline for countries. The Model Law is intended to provide national legislators with a set of basic rules that would remove a number of existing impediments to the encouragement and growth of electronic commerce. Although it is not a treaty or convention, it has been enacted in whole or in part or used as the basis for legislation in some countries. Such a convention would present a daunting challenge for the design of a consumer dispute resolution system. International conventions dealing with arbitration need to amend existing rules to conduct the online arbitration. Most of the modifications should be concentrated on communication rules such as security risk and authentication in transferring information over the Internet.

In the absence of harmonised rules at international level, the European Union which has taken a lead initiating ADR schemes to assist consumers in cross border disputes, could transform Recommendation 1998 into a Directive, make the principles mandatory for all ODR services operating in Europe, encourage a European level cross-border self-regulatory norms, promote the national Internet Ombudsman scheme which has been proven to be very effective, and implement a framework for the implementation of the award in an arbitration agreement.

A reliable system that would allow consumers to identify companies pledged to a set of common standards of online commerce and effective dispute resolution must be developed in order to underpin consumer confidence in e-commerce. The creation of an office for an EU Internet

Ombudsman is also worth implementing. The EU Internet Ombudsman should be tasked with providing concrete assistance and on-line advice similar to the task by the Austrian Internet Ombudsman, such as providing a watch list of e-commerce bidders who regularly contravene legal stipulations.

The establishment of an EU cyber court offers an effective alternative forum to resolve disputes in cyberspace. In the UK, the *Court Service* has a money claim online scheme which allows creditors to make claims up to £100,000 over the Internet. If the claim is not defended, the matter could be settled without the claimants having to set foot in court. However, defended claims will still have to be dealt with physically in court. The pilot project, which began in December 2001 and ends in January 2004, handles around 25,000 online cases each year. In 2000, 1.6m claims were made and only 36,000 debt cases went to trial.[47]

It is also possible to envisage a levelled hierarchical approach to resolving consumer complaint. It can be a three-step process, which seeks to resolve a dispute initially though an alternative dispute prevention where complaint resolution mechanisms can be organised internally by the business concerned to find solution to consumer complaints before they become a dispute. For example, America Online's ("AOL") Certified Merchant Guarantee is a self-described "dispute avoidance" program by which AOL guarantees consumer satisfaction if a dispute arises with any AOL-certified merchant. If an online shopper is dissatisfied with a purchase "for any reason," the consumer notifies the vendor of the issue. However, if the complaint is not resolved by the merchant, then AOL Customer Service Help Desk will step in to resolve the outstanding issue. When provided in an easy to use and accessible way, most of the complaints can be resolved before resorting to the next step. If amicable agreement is not reached between the supplier and the consumer, disputes could be elevated to negotiations facilitated by third parties and if needed, the parties enter into formal proceedings for resolving disputes that involve 3rd party decision makers, such as arbitration.[48] Legal aid should be granted in cases where disputes are settled via extra-judicial procedures and the entire proceedings must be resolved within a maximum time-frame. Finally, consumers must be informed about their redress rights. Dispute Resolution is useless unless consumers are made aware of its availability and where to find it. They must be educated to know that they can file complaints with consumer organisations and public bodies.

These proposals are only a small beginning in increasing trust and minimising transaction risks. As cyberspace continues to grow, compatible dispute resolution processes, a common code of conduct, a d international trustmark that consumers will recognise regardless of their country of origin

47) http://news.bbc.co.uk/1/hi/programmes/working_lunch/1836237.stm.

are essential for businesses and must be developed in order to expand and encourage ODR.

Finally, consumers must be informed about their redress rights. Dispute Resolution is useless unless consumers are made aware of its availability and where to find it. They must be educated to know that they can file complaints with consumer organisations and public bodies.

These proposals are only a small beginning in increasing trust and minimising transaction risks. As cyberspace continues to grow, compatible dispute resolution processes, a common code of conduct, a d international trustmark that consumers will recognise regardless of their country of origin are essential for businesses and must be developed in order to expand and encourage ODR.

Bibliography

Belson, Ken, Letting the Computers do the Haggling, International Herald Tribune, Sept. 12, 2003

Boardman, Griffin and Murray (Eds) Oxford History of the Classical World, Oxford University Press, Oxford, 1993.

Commission Recommendation of April 4, 2001 and Commission Recommendation 98/ 257

Consumers International. Disputes in Cyberspace at http://www.consumersinternational.org/document_store/Doc35.pdf

Gelmann, R. 'Online privacy dispute resolution: BBBOnline' (2000), Privacy Law & Policy Reporter

Geneva Convention on International Commercial Arbitration at : http://www.asser.nl/ica/eur.htm

K. Boudaoud1, M. Gagnebin1, J. Harms1 and T. Schultz, Online Dispute Resolution Systems as Web Services, University of Geneva Faculty of Law. May be viewed at : http://www.hpovua.org

Kuner, Christopher, Legal Obstacles to ADR in European Business to Consumer Electronic Commerce at http://www.kuner.com/

International Chamber of Commerce Summary Report of Business to Consumer and Business to Business Dispute Resolution Inventory Project, at http://www.iccwbo.org

NY Convention on Recognition and Enforcement of Foreign Arbitral Awards

Pravir Chawdhry and Marc Wilikens, Consumer Protection and Redress in e-Payments: Issues, Policies and Technologies, *IPSC*, Joint Research Centre. May be viewed at :http://www.jrc.es/pages/iptsreport/vol63/english/ICT5E636.htm

Reilly, Christine, Achieving, Knowing and Voluntary Consent in Pre-Dispute Mandatory Arbitration Agreements, California Law Review, 2002.

Resolving E-Commerce Disputes On-Line, OECD Directorate for Science, Information and Technology.
R Gellman, 'Online privacy dispute resolution: BBBOnline' (2000) ,Privacy Law & Policy Reporter
Yearbook, vol.1 (1976)

Others:

European Convention:http:/www.asser.nl/ica/eur.htm; http://www.intersting-people.org ; http://www.icann.org/udrp/
http://www.uncitral.org/english/texts/arbitration/NY-conv.htm;http://www.ftc.gov/bcp/altdisresolution/transcripts.htm
http://ww.consumersinternational.org/document_store/Doc35.pdf;
http:// europa.eu.int/comm/internal_market/solvit/index_en.htm
https://www.wecansettle.com/ ; http://www.claimroom.com;
http://www.consensusmediation.co.uk/e-mediator.html
http://www.eejnet.org/ ; http://finnet.jrc.it/doc/en-FINNET-GUIDE.doc ;
http:// www.ecodir.org ; http:/www.vmag.org ; www.wordandbond.com;
http://www.jus.uio.no/lm/un.arbitration.model.law.1985/toc.html;
http://europa.eu.int/scadplus/
http://www.wirthlin.com/pdf/4.12.1_wwlegal.pdf ; http://www.i-courthouse.com ; http:// www.squaretrade.com ;
http://www.ombudsmann.at/tips/index_e.html ; http://www.olis.oecd.org/ ;
http://www.resolvemydispute.com/

Electronic agents: Spies, lies and villains in the online world?

by Emily M. Weitzenböck[1]

1. Introduction

In the last few years, there has been an increased interest in electronic agents not just in fields such as computer science, philosophy and the social sciences but also in law. There is growing legal discourse on the legal issues and challenges arising from the use and operation of electronic agents in the electronic marketplace.[2]

This paper will focus on autonomous, mobile software agents. Autonomy is an important characteristic of electronic agents and, in effect, means that such electronic agents operate without the direct intervention of human beings and have some kind of control over their actions and internal states.[3] Agents may also be mobile, in the sense that they can move to and from different locations on the Internet. They can communicate with other agents and interact with their environment.

Electronic agents may have a variety of functions. There are, for example, *search agents* which look for and gather information for their users, *filtering agents* which sift through the incredible amount of information available on the Internet and *broker agents* that mediate between online sellers and buyers.

---

1) LL.M. (Southampton), LL.D. (Malta); Emily is currently a doctoral research fellow at the Norwegian Research Center for Computers & Law (NRCCL), Faculty of Law, University of Oslo. She is an advocate and a member of the Bar in Malta. Contact details: emily.weitzenboeck@jus.uio.no; http://folk.uio.no/emilyw.

2) To mention but a few examples, projects funded by the European Commission such as ECLIP II (Electronic Commerce Legal Issues Platform – IST-1999-12278), ALIVE (Advanced Legal Issues in Virtual Enterprises – IST-2000-25459) and ALFEBIITE (A Logical Framework for Ethical Behaviour between Infohabitants in the Information Trading Economy of the Universal Information Ecosystem, IST-1999-10298) have focused on selected legal issues related to electronic agents, and conference workshops such as those on The Law and Electronic Agents (LEA 2002 and LEA 2003 - http://www.cirfid.unibo.it/~agsw/lea02/index.html, http://www.cirfid.unibo.it/~agsw/lea03/ (last visited 5.1.2004)) have also discussed a broad range of legal issues.

3) M.J. Wooldridge & N.R Jennings, "Intelligent Agents: Theory and Practice", Knowledge Engineering Review, Vol 10, No. 2, June 1995, pp. 115-152, Cambridge University Press, 1996.

Electronic agents may possess a combination of these and other functions.

The scenarios examined in this paper deal with electronic agents that gather or obtain data (which may include personal data) from other electronic agents or from another person's computer system. The paper will not seek to examine further the reason for such actions, for example, in order to spread a virus or to commit fraud, blackmail or another crime, as these acts are typically already addressed and proscribed by many national computer misuse legislation.

The aim of this paper is not to paint a scenario of doom and gloom but to highlight some of the threats that may arise because of the increased use of intelligent agent technology, and to focus on some recent legislative responses in Europe to such threats.[4] Specifically, this paper will look at recent legislative developments in three areas: privacy and data protection, cybercrime and unfair competition.

2. Privacy

One of the main threats of electronic agents today is to personal privacy.[5] Agents can visit websites, select and collect certain data on individuals and deposit such data in databases. Where the collection is done in such a way as to enable the identification of individuals ("data subjects"), then such data would be deemed to be personal data in terms of most current data protection legislation, not least of which the European Union's ("EU") Data Protection Directive, triggering the application of such legislation.[6] A profile may be built from keeping track of an individual's behaviour and used by companies to target certain products or services to that individual. Where, as is likely to be often the case, the surveillance is covert, fears of the development of an Orwellian society abound.

---

4) Put more precisely, as regards privacy and data protection and unfair competition, the paper will look at recent developments in the European Union; whereas with regards to cybercrime reference will be made to an international instrument.

5) For an extended discussion of threats to privacy by electronic agents under the Data Protection Directive, see L.A. Bygrave, "Electronic Agents and Privacy: A Cyberspace Odyssey", 2001, *IJILT*, Vol.9, No. 3, pp. 275-294.

6) The Data Protection Directive defines personal data as "any information relating to an identified or identifiable natural person ("data subject"); an identifiable person is one who can be identified, directly or indirectly, in particular by reference to an identification number or to one or more factors specific to his physical, physiological, mental, economic, cultural or social identity". See Article 2(a) of Directive 95/46/EC of the European Parliament and of the Council of 24 October 1995 on the protection of individuals with regards to the processing of personal data and on the free movement of such data, OJ L 281, 23/11/1995, pp. 0031-0050.

2.1. Agent surveillance

As mentioned above, agents may be mobile and may communicate with agents of other users and interact with their environment. It is possible that an electronic agent enters the terminal of a user without the knowledge of the user in order to gain access to information stored there. The Directive on privacy and electronic communications[7] acknowledges in its recitals that:

> "so-called spyware, web bugs, hidden identifiers and other similar devices can enter the user's terminal without their knowledge in order to gain access to information, to store hidden information or to trace the activities of the user and may seriously intrude upon the privacy of these users".[8]

An electronic agent would fall within the general term "other similar devices". The use of such devices

> "to store information or to gain access to information stored in the terminal equipment of a ... user is only allowed on condition that the ... user concerned is provided with clear and comprehensive information in accordance with Directive 95/46/EC [the Data Protection Directive], *inter alia* about the purposes of the processing, and is offered the right to refuse such processing by the data controller."[9]

Thus, any covert intrusion by electronic agents whereby they gain access to information stored on the terminal equipment of the user either by directly accessing the terminal of the user or by interacting with spyware or other similar hidden devices on the user's terminal is prohibited.

Electronic agents may, thus, interact with cookies or with spyware residing in an individual's hardware. Spyware is software that has a tracking facility residing surreptitiously in an individual's computer, keeping tabs on the online activity of that individual and transmitting such data to the software provider. Such spyware may either be published as "freeware", "adware"[10] or packaged

---

7) Directive 2002/58/EC of the European Parliament and of the Council of 12 July 2002 concerning the processing of personal data and the protection of privacy in the electronic communications sector (Directive on privacy and electronic communications), OJ L 201, 31/7/2002, pp. 0037-0047.

8) Recital 24, Directive on privacy and electronic communications, *op. cit.* fn. 7.

9) Article 5(3), Directive on privacy and electronic communications, *op. cit.* fn. 7.

10) Adware is typically freeware which has advertisements embedded in the programme and which show up when the user opens the programme. Most adware authors provide the free version with ads and a registered version whereby the ads are disabled. Thus, it is the user who decides whether to use the freeware with ads or to licence a registered version. See further on this, *Spyware* at http://simplythebest.net/info/spyware.html (last visited

with a licensed software but, obviously, without the user being aware of its existence. Needless to say, the use of such electronic agents that interact with spyware or hidden identifiers without the knowledge of the user would be in breach of Article 5(3) of the Directive on privacy and electronic communications as discussed above. However, the Directive empowers Member States to allow the use of such covert devices where this

> "constitutes a necessary, appropriate and proportionate measure within a democratic society to safeguard national security (i.e. State security), defence, public security, and the prevention, investigation, detection and prosecution of criminal offences or of unauthorised use of the electronic communication system".[11]

It is perhaps worth pointing out that the Directive proscribes the act of gaining access to stored information on the user's terminal: it is thus irrelevant and not necessary, for this provision to come into effect, to also prove that such information has also been copied, transmitted or stored elsewhere, for example, in the data controller's network.

This Directive cross-refers to and applies the information duties that data controllers have towards data subjects under the Data Protection Directive, i.e. Articles 10 and 11. The data subject must therefore, besides details of the purposes for the processing, also be provided with other information, such as the identity of the controller and any representative of his/her, the recipients or categories of recipients of the data, and the existence of the data subject's right to access and to have rectified the data concerning him/her.

As abovementioned, the user must also be provided with the right to refuse such processing. Thus, what the Directive requires is not that the user consents[12] to the processing of his/her data, but that the user does not refuse such processing.

The *raison d'être* of this provision is a recognition that the terminal equipment of users of electronic communication networks and any information stored on such equipment are part of the private sphere of the users requiring protection under the European Convention for the Protection of Human Rights and Fundamental Freedoms. The Directive on privacy and electronic communications applies to users who are natural persons using a publicly

---

16.12.2003).

11) Article 15(1), Directive on privacy and electronic communications, *op. cit.* fn. 7.

12) In the Directive on privacy and electronic communications, "consent" has the same meaning as that found in Article 2(h) of the Data Protection Directive, i.e. "'the data subject's consent' shall mean any freely given specific and informed indication of his wishes by which the data subject signifies his agreement to personal data relating to him being processed". See Article 2(f), Directive on privacy and electronic communications, *op. cit.* fn. 7.

available electronic communications service for private or business purposes, without necessarily having subscibed to that service.[13]

The Directive recognised that devices such as cookies can be a legitimate and useful tool and the recitals cite as examples the use of cookies to analyse the effectiveness of website design and advertising and in verifying the identity of users engaged in online transactions. In such cases, the use of a device such as a cookie is allowed provided that the two contitions mentioned earlier in this paper are complied with: that the user (i) is provided with clear and precise information in accordance with the Data Protection Directive, and (ii) is given the option to refuse to have a cookie stored on his/her equipment.[14]

2.2. Surveillance or interception of communication of data

It should also be mentioned that the surveillence or interception of communications and the related traffic data by electronic agents would fall within the prohibition in Article 5(1) of the Directive on privacy and electronic communications. This Article exhorts EU Member States to "prohibit listening, tapping, storage or other kinds of interception or surveillance of communications and the related traffic data by persons other than users without the consent of the users concerned, except when legally authorised to do so" to safeguard national security (i.e. State security), defence, public security, and the prevention, investigation, detection and prosecution of criminal offences or of unauthorised use of the electronic communication system. Thus, collecting click-through data and other web browsing information can constitute a violation of this provision where this is without the consent of the user. However, any legally authorised recording of communications and related traffic data carried out in the course of lawful business practice for the purpose of providing evidence of a commercial transaction or of any other business communication is allowed.[15]

---

13) In fact, this is the definition of "user" in Article 2 (a) of the Directive on privacy and electronic communications, *op. cit.* fn. 7.

14) See Recital 25, Directive on privacy and electronic communications, *op. cit.* fn. 7.

15) Article 5(2), Directive on privacy and electronic communications, *op. cit.* fn. 7.

3. Cybercrime

The scenarios described in this paper such as obtaining access to data and surveillance may also be proscribed under the Convention on Cybercrime,[16] when this Convention enters into force and is implemented into the law of the states which ratified it.[17] Two articles of this Convention are of particular relevance in this context – Article 2 on illegal access and Article 3 on illegal interception.

3.1. Illegal access

The access to the whole or any part of a computer system without right and when committed intentionally is proscribed by the first part of Article 2. Two questions may immediately be raised. What constitutes "without right" in this context, and how is intentionality to be understood when the access is sought and obtained by an intelligent agent acting autonomously, i.e. without the knowledge or direction by the person who activated the agent?

3.1.1. Access without right

Where the owner or other rightholder of the computer system or part of it has authorised access (e.g. to test the security of the system), this is not an infringement of Article 2. The Explanatory Report to the Convention also provides that there is no criminalisation for accessing a computer system that permits free and open access by the public, as such access is "with right".[18]

Sometimes, the application of certain technical tools such as cookies or bots to locate and retrieve information may result in an access under Article 2. The Explanatory Report provides that the application of such devices is not *per se* "without right":

> "The application of standard tools provided for in the commonly applied communication protocols and programs, is not in itself "without right", in particular where the rightholder of the accessed system can be considered to have accepted its application, e.g. in the case of "cookies" by not rejecting the initial instalment or not removing it."[19]

---

16) Convention on Cybercrime, signed at Budapest, 23.11.2001, Council of Europe ETS No. 185.

17) To date, the Convention on Cybercrime has not yet entered into force. By end December 2003, it has been ratified by Albania, Croatia, Estonia and Hungary. It requires ratification by one other state to enter into force.

18) Explanatory Report to the Convention on Cybercrime, para. 47.

19) Explanatory Report to the Convention on Cybercrime, para. 48.

This illustrates the broad scope of the abovementioned first sentence of Article 2. The drafters of the Convention recognised this and allowed Parties to the Convention to take a narrower approach by attaching certain qualifying elements to the access proscribed in the first sentence of Article 2. In fact, Article 2 further provides that a state implementing this provision

> "may require that the offence be committed by infringing security measures, with the intent of obtaining computer data or other dishonest intent, or in relation to a computer system that is connected to another computer system."

Thus, where an Internet user deploys an electronic agent to breach another user's security measures such as a firewall, or by using an illegally obtained password, the access would be illegal in terms of Article 2.

The access must be of "the whole or any part of a computer system". What happens if the electronic agent of company X obtained data from the electronic agent of user Y? Is the electronic agent of Y to be deemed as "part of [the] computer system" of Y? The term "computer system" is defined as:

> "any device or a group of inter-connected or related devices, one or more of which, pursuant to a program, performs automatic processing of data".

Furthermore, the Explanatory Report explains that:

> "A computer system under the Convention is a device consisting of hardware and software developed for automatic processing of digital data. It may include input, output and storage facilities. It may stand alone or be connected in a network with other similar devices. ..."[20]

Let us illustrate the above example further. Imagine the electronic agent of Y was a software agent licensed by Y and intitated by him from his computer system to identify, select and buy a weekly cinema ticket for Y. The agent interacts with other software in Y's computer system (e.g. a data file which contains Y's bank details, Y's calendar or personal digital assistent). It is submitted that such a software agent should be deemed to be part of the computer system of Y. However, what if the data was intercepted while the electronic agent – a mobile agent - of Y had migrated to another platform to search for the best priced ticket? Doubts could be raised whether the agent could still be deemed to be part of Y's computer system and hence, whether Article 2 would be applicable. It is submitted that, in any case, such behaviour would fall within Article 3 of the Convention, dealing with unlawful interception of data.[21]

---

20) Explanatory Report to the Convention on Cybercrime, para. 23.

21) See section 3.2 below.

3.1.2. The question of intention

Though one might be able to prove the existence of the material elements (*actus reus*) of the offence in the first sentence of Article 2, that is:

(i) the access to the whole or part of a computer system
(ii) without right,

for the offence to subsist, one must also prove the existence of the intentional element (*mens rea*), i.e. that the access is "committed intentionally".

The difficulty that might arise is how the prosecution in a criminal case – where the standard of evidence required in most countries is proof beyond reasonable doubt[22] - may ascribe the actions of an autonomous intelligent agent to the person who initiated it (the user). It is submitted that this is a question of fact and depends on the circumstances of each particular case. It would depend on factors, for example, such as: whether the user had himself designed and written the software agent, whether the user had initiated the agent (i.e. supplied it with its terms of reference – what it should or perhaps even should not do), the type of electronic agent software deployed to carry out a particular task and its suitability thereto (e.g the reputation of such types of software agents), etc. In other words, as often happens in criminal matters, the actions or omissions of the user very often reflect and can be used to infer his/her state of mind (intention).

3.2. Unlawful interception of data

Article 3 of the Convention outlaws:

> "when committed intentionally, the interception without right, made by technical means, of non-public transmissions of computer data to, from or within a computer system, including electromagnetic emissions from a computer system carrying such computer data."

It is clear from the Explanatory Report that the term "technical means" includes "the use of software" and hence, it is submitted, also interception by software agents.[23] The requirement of using technical means was meant by the drafters as a restrictive qualification to avoid over-criminalisation.

3.3. The importance of a causal link with the user: the "Trojan horse" defence

Electronic agents can operate as a kind of "Trojan horse" on another

---

22) This is in contrast to the standard often required in civil suits which usually requires a balance of probabilities.

23) Explanatory Report to the Convention on Cybercrime, para. 53.

person's computer system. A mobile agent can move to another person's computer and carry out certain operations from that computer, without the knowledge or consent of that computer's user or owner, an act that is likely to be proscribed by most national laws on hacking and by Article 2 of the Convention on Cybercrime. In the UK, the "Trojan" defence – that one's computer has been taken over for the commission of a crime by someone else who has hacked into the computer - has been successfully used in two cases where the owner of a computer was charged with a computer crime (respectively, hacking into another computer system and possession of child porn).

What was of particular interest in the former of these cases,[24] dealing with a severe denial-of-service attack on the port of Houston in Texas, is that this defence was successful even though prosecution experts could find no evidence that the accused's computer had been broken into. Moreover, both the defence and prosecution acknowledged that the attack came from the defendant's computer. The danger, as Dave Morrell, a computer consultant for the Houston pilots who worked with the FBI after the attack, explained, is that this defence "sets a precedent now in the [English] judicial system where a hacker can just claim somebody took over his computer, the program vanished, and he's free and clear".[25] It is perhaps not inconceivable that a similar defence would be attempted by the owner of a deviant electronic agent whose acts could amount to a criminal offence, i.e. that the agent was hijacked by another agent. In today's complex computer network architecture, it may be difficult to prove a causal connection between an electronic agent which has acted deviantly and the person (including such person's electronic agent) who controls or took over control of the agent. However, the danger of using a defence such as the "Trojan horse" defence in situations where there is no evidence that a computer system or part of it has been

---

24) Mr. Aaron Caffrey was accused of crashing systems at the port of Houston in Texas by hacking into its computer system, and faced one charge at Southwark Crown Court in the UK of unauthorised modification of computer material. The port's computer system was bombarded with thousands of electronic messages, freezing its web service which contained vital data for shipping, mooring companies and support firms responsible for helping ships navigate in and out of harbour. Mr Caffrey admitted being a member of a group called Allied Haxor Elite and hacking into computers for friends to test their security, but he insisted he was not responsible for the attack on the port of Houston. Both the defence and prosecution acknowledged that the attack came from his computer. The jury believed the defendant's argument that his computer had been taken over by a hacker using a Trojan horse program. A forensic examination of Mr Caffrey's computer had found no trace of a hidden program with the instructions for the attack. See further on this "Questions cloud cyber crime cases", BBC News, 17 October 2003, http://www.bbc.co.uk/go/pr/fr/-/2/hi/technology/3202116.stm (last visited 15.12.2003).

25) E. Mills Abreu, "Hackers get novel defense: The computer did it", *Computerworld*, 28 October 2003, http://www.computerworld.com/printthis/2003/0,4814,86600,00.html (last visited 16.12.2003).

taken over by a hacker, can considerably water down the effectiveness of criminal sanctions such as those in the Convention on Cybercrime discussed above.

4. Unfair commercial practices

4.1. Aggressive commercial practices

Among the abilities of intelligent agents is that of targeting a service or a product that fits the specific needs of a customer at the opportune time, i.e. when the customer is likely to need such service/product. Such agents can be a very effective marketing and sales help to the seller, and also of assistance to prospective buyers in identifying the right product and the right seller or service provider for their needs. There have, for example, been cases in some countries where parents of newly born babies have been sent samples of baby food or brochures of baby-related products such as prams, nappies, etc. Such type of behaviour by companies is usually considered acceptable as long as it is reasonable and not abusive. The proposed Unfair Commercial Practices Directive[26] prohibits what it calls "aggressive commercial practices", that is a commercial practice:

> "where by harassment, coercion or undue influence, it significantly impairs or is likely to significantly impair the average consumer's freedom of choice or conduct with regard to the product and thereby causes him or is likely to cause him to take a transactional decision that he would not have taken otherwise."

"Undue influence" is further defined in the Proposal as:

> "exploiting a position of power to apply pressure, without using physical force, in a way which significantly limits the consumer's ability to make an informed decision."

Among the factors to be used to determine whether a commercial practice uses harassement, coercion or undue influence are *inter alia* its timing, nature or persistence,[27] the use of threatening or abusive language or behaviour,[28] and the use by the trader of any specific misfortune or circumstance of such gravity as to

---

26) Proposal for a Directive of the European Parliament and of the Council concerning unfair business-to-consumer practices in the Internal Market and amending directives 84/450/EEC, 97/7/EC and 98/27/EC (the Unfair Commercial Practices Directive), 18.6.2003, COM (2003) 356 final.

27) Article 9(a), Proposal for an Unfair Commercial Practices Directive, op. cit. n. 26.

28) Article 9(b), Proposal for an Unfair Commercial Practices Directive, op. cit. n. 26.

impair the consumer's judgment, of which the trader is aware, to influence the consumer's decision with regard to the product.[29] For example, the targeting of consumers who have recently suffered a bereavement or serious illness in their family in order to sell a product which bears a direct relationship with the misfortune is considered by the Proposal to be an aggressive commercial practice and hence outlawed.[30] The Proposal, in an Annex, contains a blacklist of commercial practices which are considered in all circumstances to be unfair.

The aim of the Proposal is to strike a balance between business needs (e.g. to increase profit, to expand) and the protection of consumers (e.g. protection from exploitation, from making a decision he/she would not have otherwise made).

4.2. Unfair practices

Commercial search agents are often used by consumers to help them search for, identify and purchase goods or products from online retailers. It is not inconceivable that a search agent of this kind would have a bias towards certain websites. Though such a search agent may operate autonomously, i.e. without the direct intervention or control of a human being, it does not mean that behind the scenes, there could not be an agreement(s) between some companies advertising their products or services on the Internet and the company controlling the search agent's functions. It has, until now, not been clear whether such "defects of neutrality" are proscribed at an EU level since there is no Community legislation on unfair competition in force as yet.[31] The question arises whether this would be proscribed by the recent proposal for a Directive on unfair commercial practices, if and when this Directive is passed. It should be mentioned that the proposal applies only to business-to-consumer transactions and not to business-to-business transactions.

The proposed Directive defines the conditions which determine whether a commercial practice is *un*fair. It does not impose any positive obligations which a trader has to comply with to show he is trading fairly. The proposal contains a general prohibition of unfair commercial practices and also provides two key types of unfair commercial practices – those which are misleading and those which are aggressive. Misleading commercial practices can be either misleading actions or misleading omissions.

The general prohibition of unfair commercial practices establishes three

29) Article 9(c), Proposal for an Unfair Commercial Practices Directive, op. cit. n. 26.

30) Annex 1, paragraph (4) of the list of aggressive commercial practices, Proposal for an Unfair Commercial Practices Directive, op. cit. n. 26.

31) For further discussion of this, see S. Feliu, "Intelligent agents and consumer protection", IJILT, Vol. 9, No. 3, 235-248, in particular at pp. 243-244.

conditions for determining whether a practice is unfair, all three of which have to be proven in order for the practice to be judged unfair:[32]

- the practice must be contrary to the requirements of professional diligence
- the practice must materially distort or be likely to materially distort the consumer's economic behaviour
- the benchmark consumer to be considered is the "average consumer", i.e. a consumer who is reasonably well informed and reasonably observant and circumspect.

It is submitted that the provision of a biased software agent by a trader is not, *per se*, enough to constitute an unfair commercial practice. The consumer might, for example, reasonably expect a search agent provided on a particular website to have a certain bias towards the products or services of the group of companies of which that website company is known to form part. Such a practice cannot be said to be "contrary to the requirements of professional diligence" which is defined in Article 2 (j) as "the measure of special skill and care exercised by a trader commensurate with the requirements of normal market practice towards consumers in his field of activity in the internal market". However, if the search agent is touted as a neutral agent by the website owner, when in fact it is not, then this could be deemed to be against the requirements of professional diligence.

It is also submitted that the licensing of a search agent software acquired by a consumer principally for its search functions/qualities but which, in fact, does not have neutral search functions, is likely to be deemed to be a misleading omission in terms of Article 7 of the Proposed Directive which considers misleading a commercial practice:

> "which, in its factual context, taking account of all its features and circumstances, omits material information that the average consumer needs, according to the context, to take an informed transactional decision and thereby causes or is likely to cause the average consumer to take a transactional decision that he would not have taken otherwise."[33]

Article 7(2) also regards as a misleading omission the situation

> "when a trader hides or provides in an unclear, unintelligible, ambiguous or untimely manner such material information or fails to identify the commercial intent of the commercial practice."

A transactional decision includes a decision about whether to buy and from

32) Article 5(2), Proposal for an Unfair Commercial Practices Directive, op. cit. n. 26. See also the explanatory memorandum to the proposal, para. 51.

33) Article 7(1), Unfair Commercial Practices Directive, op. cit. n. 26.

which supplier.[34] In this specific example, it is reasonable to assume that the consumer would not have licensed that particular software agent had he/she known that that electronic agent had a defect of neutrality.

What about the provision of a software agent which contains spyware that sends information about customers to the seller who provided the agent? Besides being in breach of the Directive on privacy and electronic communications as explained above,[35] it is submitted that this would also be considered a misleading action and, hence, an unfair practice by the proposed Directive on unfair commercial practices. Article 6 prohibits a commercial practice that "causes or is likely to cause the average consumer to take a transactional decision that he would not have taken otherwise because it deceives or is likely to deceive him in relation to the main characteristics of the product, such as its ... risks, ... composition, accessories, ... or the results to be expected from its use." Had the consumer been aware of the existence of the hidden spying features in the software agent, he/she might not have acquired or accepted such software in the first place.

The Proposal is thus a step in the right direction in that it addresses a number of threats to consumer transactions, including those made online and which may involve the use of electronic agents. It now remains to be seen whether and, to what extent, the proposed Directive on unfair commercial practices is adopted.

5. Concluding remarks

Autonomous software agents have often been hailed as revolutionary tools, assistants or helpers for actors in the electronic marketplace such as buyers, sellers and service providers. In this paper, an attempt has been made to highlight some of the threats arising from the use of such agents and to discuss some recent developments in Europe in three fields of law, viz. privacy and data protection, cybercrime and unfair competition. As discussed in this paper, these recently enacted or proposed pieces of legislation address many of the threats arising from the use of agents in the electronic marketplace. However, the indiscriminate use of certain defences, such as the "Trojan horse" defence in situations where no evidence of hacking is found, can water down the effect of such laws. Moreover, one should also recognise that the state-of-the-art of agent technology and the marketplaces in which such agents operate is still in its infancy and it is likely that more challenging legal questions will be raised when more sophisticated autonomous agents are available.

---

34) Explanatory Memorandum to the Proposal for an Unfair Commercial Practices Directive, para. 55.

35) See section 2 above.

Competition Law Issues

by Jens Fejø

1.

If we let memory pass over the history and development of electronic commerce, over computers, programmes and over other tools used for that purpose, and when remembering the companies involved in the development of this highly modern area of business – one could easily get the impression that this field is not normally of interest for competition law people here thinking of competition law in the sence of antitrust law not unfair competition law. One might even possibly get the idea that the fast development within the electronic commerce and computer industry has the consequence that this area of business is not at all suitet for competition law regulation.

One other reasons for such an impression of no interest for competition regulation has its background in the very fact that antitrust law – competition law – to a large extend is concerned with the phenomenon of choice. If the consumers do not have the possibility of choosing, and if this is a result of the behaviour of the market participants – then it is the concern of competition law. But with electronic commerce there are lots of choices, new products, many interested companies, new companies on the market, many offers of honest legal information managements, etc., etc.

Yet, another reason for thinking competition law not to be necessary within this field might be the very fact that the legislation on e-commerce itself is so well build up that it will be able to avoid all the risks of having no choice. The strict requirements that are put on the professional market participants (the suppliers) – such as the requirements of giving information to the consumers in accordance for instance with the Distance contracts Directive or the Directive on the Distance Marketing of Consumer Financial Services – may be assessed as a solid protection against abusing the consumers.

2.

Competition law, however, comes into play for instance if a company has a position on the market that it is so overwhelmingly strong that the company is able – in one way or another – to exclude its competors from selling goods to the strong company´s customers. In such situation with a strong market postition it may be found that there is a situation of abuse of a dominant market postition which for instance is prohibeted by the EC Treaty Article 82 and on national level prohibited under national competition legislation in the soon to be 25 EU member states. Since here the consumers – because of the behaviour of that market dominating company – is excluded from the choice of buying products from the competitors of the strong company. And the competitors are retained from selling to that market.

Furthermore competition law is regulating agreements restricting competition and competition law is about merger control.

So a central question is whether the fast developing e-commerce and computer business can fall under the competition law.

3.

Despite my introductory remarks – let me me point to some areas, among several, where competition law may be relevant and of interest to issues and companies linked to e-commerce.

4.

One should start by noticing that what in competition law is called "the relevant market" might bring some unclear elements into the picture when talking about electronic commerce, computers and programs. Since even though many of these phenomena may point to the situation where the playing field may be seen as the totality of the internet and all the possibilities lying within the internet – the fact is that very often the consumers or the intermediaries don´t have the choice in practical life of using all those possibilities which the internet is providing. Instead they will often be limited by the behaviour of one or another market acting company to be more narrow. Relevant market is not – as many companies think themselves the place where they sell their products or services – but the place where the buyers have a choice for buying in the real life and that may – even on the internet – be much more limited than seen from the point of view of the selling companies.

5.

Let me also stress the "tying arrangement"-problem. Here the requirement from the side of a dominating company of buying additional products or services of another kind than what has initially been bought – for instance financial services together with buying a machine or other commodity – will constitute an illegal abuse if the company is in a dominant market position. This will do it impossible for other suppliers/competing suppliers of the tied product to deliver to the customers of the dominating company. Also tying out for instance some sorts of financial solution such as payment before delivering of the goods might be an anti-competitive way of behaviour.

6.

One should also recall that the merger between independent companies into one larger company may have very detrimental effects on some markets and it is very clear from the case law in relation to the EU merger control regulation from 1989 that especially within the modern telecom- and IT-industry severe situations have seen the daylight.

7.

Let me turn to another area where competition rules are of relevance when talking of IT. I here think of the ways in which computer programs and additional elements are sold. It is perfectly all right that a producer of a compuer program when he offers that program to his customers at the same time decides to offer additional services or additional programs. If the customers don´t like the additional services or additional goods they can just turn to other suppliers of the main product. But the situation is different when the supplier is in a market dominating position – meaning for instance that there are not other suppliers that can offer competing products or services.

One recent example here in Europe of that problem has been heavily discussed in relation to the Microsoft case.

8.

We all know from the newspapers or elsewhere that Microsoft has been involved in a very big case under American antitrust legislation accused of violating that legislation by putting its explorer on the machine together with its main steering program. This has been said to be a bundling practise that violate the Sherman Act. As for what we know the agreement that Microsoft has entered into in this relation with the American antitrust authorities is now under scrutiny by an American court and what the eventual outcome of this will be we will have to wait for.

But there have also within the European Area been several competition law issues in relation to Microsoft that have been looked upon with great interest.

Most recently the European Commission has held hearings in the Microsoft-case where the American company has been under suspicion for making tying and also being suspected for lack of interoperability. By these ways of behaviour the European Commission has drawn the conclusion – that so far has only been a preliminary conclusion – that Microsoft has abused its dominant position on the EU-market. Thus Microsoft seems to be charged with the accusation that it ties its "Media Player" into Windows which runs may be 90 % of desktop computers. This is said to weaken competition by stiffeling product innovation and ultimately reducing consumer choice. And the Commission wants Microsoft to disclose more software code to competitors in the market for low-end servers so they can make products that work as well with Windows as Microsoft´s own products.

9.

This Microsoft-case must give rise to various considerations linked to electronic commerce. One might start by looking at the fact that the interests of the consumers might go hand in hand with Microsoft´s interests. Thus it could be argued that the possible damage on the market of Microsoft´s behaviour might be reduced by the mere fact that Microsoft is giving the market what the market wants. The inclusion of Microsoft´s new features in its operating system – originally the browser, later on the inclusion of the internet search tool will come – might thus be so beneficial to the consumers that it could be difficult to be convinced that this would constitute an abuse. It has on top of this been announced that Microsoft is close to entering the music market as well.Let me also think at a situation that is not covered by the present case but very interesting. If, as is apparently the case with Microsoft, a company has a market dominating position, but this strong position is the result of heavy investments in research and development, hereby making it able to make new and valuable investments, for instance if the company has invented software that will increase the power of its machines, but this company decides that it will not apply this newly invented software but instead go on producing and selling its machines with the well known software, is this form of behaviour then to be assessed as an abuse of a dominant position that can be reacted against on the basis of EU-competition law? The reason for not applying the new software might be that the calculation has lead to the result that the invention would be so attractive that the models being sold for the time being would no longer be attractive and for that reason could not be sold. Is this an illegal restriction of competition? Some competition lawyers would react to this with an affirmative answer. Others would be more reluctant to assess this way of behaviour as a refusal to deal that would violate the prohibition to abuse a dominant market position. So far, the European Commission has not intervened against situations just described, but the argument has been aired that it should do so. Usually, however, we se that those who argue that we here have a competition law case are not lawyers but industrial economists and they are not always quite reliable in relation to precise competition law issues. On this point is to say that a well functioning market is a vital thing to have but another thing is to recognize that to establish such market through intervention and use of remedies that are not foreseen in the legislation should often not be acceptable. To put up a requirement to put the newest and best technology on the market might be a violation of some human rights protection principles such as the protection of property right for example.

The European Microsoft case will most likely be decided in Spring 2004 and we must therefor wait the outcome until then.

10.

Before ending my presentation a few words on restrictive agreements should be said. Allow me to draw your attention to for instance the Directive on Distance Contracts. Here article 4 provides that the consumer shall be provided in good time before the conclusion of the distance contract with i.a. information of ... "b) the main characteristics of the goods or services, c) the price of the goods or services including all taxes ". Is this kind of information identical with consumer protection? Yes, of couse. But at the same time it raises the question of a competition law matter. Since hereby the legislation has decided that prices and content of the goods are open to the consumer. That is naturally a good thing for the buyer. But if this information is likewise available to competing suppliers the information may turn out to be anticompetitive. Since this way the competitor may ajust his own price or product quality to that of the first supplier and hereby have a relatively safe place where he can operate. On the other hand if – and that is a duty in accordance with the Directive – the second and the third suppliers are likewise forced by the directive to disclose their prices and conditions then it can – under certain circumstances only, I admit that – turn out to be the basis for a classic cartel between the suppliers. And here established through this piece of legislation that has been shaped to protect the consumers. I must on the other hand admit that this is the consequence of legislation (here the Directive) and it cannot be challenged directly by competition law. But an interesting thing in connection with electronic commerce here sees the daylight. Since when private companies or associations of private companies establish rules of "fair trade" or of "reasonable trade conditions" or of "consumer protection rules" this very easy turns out to be a substitution for legislation. And here we are on dangerous ground. Such "fair trade" arrangements have several times in the history of the European Union – before e-trade was started – been striken down by the Commission for having violated Article 81 – the provision prohibiting anticompetitive agreements or concerted practices among enterprices or associations of enterprices. Depending of the content of such private arrangements they are not well suited for being accepted in a competition law context. The learning in this respect has been that it is for the legislator to decide the amount of protection against unfair business behaviour not for associations of compeeting companies. Generally speeking it is not acceptable that a new set of rules of which the core elements are restrictions of competition among themselves are invented by the business itself.

11.

My concluding remarks will be a reflection based on history. Today we see many very strong companies being active within the IT-world. But the companies that exist today have predecessors. Thus for instance IBM that decades ago had an extreamely strong position on the market or markets is today as we know still strong, respectable and powerful but there are totally new companies that have fought their way through to power including market power. So if antitrust legislation is not doing the work other forces might work in the same direction in a developing world. E-commerce is an interesting area of business but in relation to competition law it has not yes shown its final position.

Copenhagen
Business School
HANDELSHØJSKOLEN

PROGRAMME

for the Law Department of Copenhagen Business School's
international research conference on

EU Electronic Commerce Law

Hotel Hvide Hus, Køge, Denmark - 27 and 28 November 2003

Conference Website:

www.e-commerce-law.cbs.dk

Thursday 27 November 2003

0900 – 1000 *Breakfast*

1000 – 1015 **WELCOME AND INTRODUCTION**
Jan Trzaskowski & Søren Sandfeld Jakobsen, Copenhagen Business School

1015 – 1115 **MEGATRENDS IN ELECTRONIC COMMERCE**
Technology, Head of Solution Engineering, Henrik Haagensen, Nokia Denmark A/S
Economics, Professor Jan Damsgaard, Department of Informatics, Copenhagen Business School
Law, Professor, dr.jur. Ruth Nielsen, Copenhagen Business School

1115 – 1205 **RESEARCH WORKSHOP**
Regulating E-Commerce on New Media in the Information Society, *Søren Sandfeld Jakobsen, Copenhagen Business School*
Can Information Database Protection Balance the Interests of Businesses and Information Consumers?, *Robin Elizabeth Herr*

1205 – 1315 *Lunch*

1315 – 1415 **MARKETING LAW AND SELF-REGULATION**
CHAIR: **Dr. Emily M. Weitzenböck, University of Oslo**

Harmonization of Marketing Law in EU, Jennifer Long, Health and Consumer Protection DG, European Commission
Self-Regulation – Status and future, Professor Jan J. C. Kabel, Amsterdam University

1415 – 1440 **RESEARCH WORKSHOP**
E-Commerce Taxation Policies in the EU and the US, *Ana Penn, St. Thomas University, School of Law, Miami, FL*

1440 – 1500 *Break and Networking*

1500 – 1600 **CONTRACT AND INFORMATION REQUIREMENTS**
CHAIR: **Professor, Dr. Peter Mankowski, Hamburg University**

Information Requirements, Professor Geraint Howells, University of Sheffield
Convergence Challenges, Dr. Hans Christoph Grigoleit, LL.M., University of Munich

1600 – 1625 **RESEARCH WORKSHOP**
Information Requirements, *Annette Nordhausen, University of Sheffield*

1625 – 1640 **CONCLUSION**

1830 – 1900 *Welcome Drink*
1900 – 2200 *Dinner*
2200 – ? *Music and Dance*

Friday 28 November 2003

0800 – 0900	*Breakfast*
0900 – 0915	**INTRODUCTION**
0915 – 1015	**ELECTRONIC SIGNATURES** ***CHAIR:* Professor Geraint Howells, University of Sheffield** ***Purpose and Possibilities***, Professor Jos Dumotier, Leuven University ***Implementation Status and Challenges***, Professor Cecilia Magnusson Sjöberg, Stockholm University
1015 – 1040	**RESEARCH WORKSHOP** ***Principles of European Contract Law and Formation of Contracts in the Information Society,*** *Katarina Kryczka, Utrecht University*
1040 – 1100	*Break and Networking*
1100 – 1200	**INTERNATIONAL ELECTRONIC COMMERCE** ***CHAIR:* Dr. Hans Christoph Grigoleit, LL.M., University of Munich** ***Jurisdiction and Enforcement in the Information Society***, Professor, Dr. Peter Mankowski, Hamburg University
1200 – 1225	**RESEARCH WORKSHOP** **Cross-Border Law Enforcement in the Information Society**, Jan Trzaskowski, Copenhagen Business School
1225 – 1325	*Lunch*
1325 – 1350	**RESEARCH WORKSHOP** ***On-Line Arbitrary Dispute Resolution***, *Sylvia Kierkegaard, Århus Business School*
1350 – 1450	**INTERNET MARKET PLACES** ***CHAIR:* Professor, dr.jur. Ruth Nielsen, Copenhagen Business School** ***Intelligent Agents***, Dr. Emily M. Weitzenböck, University of Oslo ***Competition Law Issues***, Professor, dr.jur. Jens Fejø, Copenhagen Business School
1450 – 1500	**CONCLUSION**